THE PCT HIKER'S HANDBOOK

Innovative Techniques
and Trail Tested Instruction
For the Long Distance Backpacker

By Ray Jardine

Illustrations by Jenny Jardine

First printing 1992

Although the author and publisher have exhaustively researched all sources to ensure the accuracy and completeness of the information contained in this book, we assume no responsibility for errors, inaccuracies, omissions, or any inconsistency herein. Any slights of people or organizations are unintentional.

OF DANGERS THERE ARE MANY
ON THIS TRAIL TO THE NORTH.

No book can make the wilderness a safe place, especially to the person who ventures into it bereft of judgement. Although we feel the principles set forth in this book will make for a safer (not necessarily a safe) journey afoot, we can assume no responsibilities. The reader is advised to exercise the utmost prudence.

Printed on recycled paper

Published by AdventureLore Press
Box 804, LaPine, OR 97739

Library of Congress Catalogue Card Number: 92-71251

ISBN 0-9632359-0-7

THIS BOOK IS DEDICATED

To Jenny:

    Intrepid companion in ten years of adventuring,
and steadfast co-worker in preparing the manuscript
for this book.

To all our friends:

    who have lent their encouragement.

And to you, the readers:

    May you cast your visions afar,
        Load your backpacks lightly,
        Leave your cars a thousand miles behind;
    And may this book send you powerhiking
        into the Twenty-First Century.

For ye shall go out with joy, and be led forth with
       peace;
the mountains and the hills shall break forth
       before you into singing,
and all the trees of the field shall clap their
       hands.
                     —Isaiah 55:12

ACKNOWLEDGEMENTS

A special thanks:

> To Jeffrey Schaffer, principal author and cartographer of the
> Pacific Crest Trail guidebooks, Volumes 1 & 2 (Wilderness Press),
> who very capably reviewed the manuscript and offered a great deal
> of insightful and constructive criticism.

> To Karl Diederich, who supplied a quantity of material resulting
> from his 1991 through-hike of the PCT, and who also apprised
> much of the initial writing, and supplied many excellent comments.

> To Sue Lockwood and Gordon Smith, who examined the material
> and provided a number of entirely beneficial suggestions.

Thanks also to members of our family of distance hikers, who lent their
encouragement. These include:

> Mike Anderson; Jerry Hogerheide and his daughter Eve; Walt
> Chance; Nick Gilmow and Simon Farmer (of Great Britain);
> Jerome Richard and Roman Pfeiffer; Joris Naiman and Lesya
> Struz, Ken and Laura Wild; Andre Siegenthaler; Alice Gmeur;
> Paul Shapcott (Bristol zookeeper); Willem Vermeulen (of The
> Netherlands); Alan Thomas; Bernie Krull and Mark Orr; Sandra
> Johnson; Jen Schemm and Francie Parker; Paul Lenzo; Ed Talone,
> Rob Lauchner, and Doc Hank Horak; Mark and Cindy Rutledge;
> Katie Geiser, Donna Bebout and Colleen Cooke; John Stevenson,
> and Ruth Waterfield.

Our gratitude to these people who lent special help.

> Milt Kenney: (PO Box 95, Castella, CA 96017) philanthropist and
> "Mayor" of the PCT; Ed and Paz Colberg; Charlie and Tracie
> Knarr; Fred Sudds; Bernice Macmillan; and Patrick Krasnoff.

And finally, our love and a special mention to our parents, who helped us
in many ways:

> Raymond and Elda Jo Jardine
> Ken and Sandy Maurer

TABLE OF CONTENTS

PREFACE

Nature has given the opportunity of happiness to all,
knew they but how to use it.
—Claudian

THE PACIFIC CREST

The Pacific Crest is a spine not unlike the Continental Divide. It extends the length of California, Oregon and Washington, and generally parallels the Pacific coast, although at a considerable distance. Remarkably, much of its high deserts, forests, and lofty mountain ranges remains undeveloped. Great expanses are in a condition that the early Indians, explorers, and pioneers might still recognize today.

THE PACIFIC CREST TRAIL

The PCT winds nearly 2,700 miles along these marvelous crest provinces, from the Mexican to the Canadian borders. Some 30 years in the making, at a cost of millions of dollars and incalculable hours of volunteer labor, it is a walkway of unprecedented diversity and genuine awe. As such, Congress has granted it the status of National Scenic Trail. But to hikers seeking extended withdrawals from the cities, it is the *magnum opus*.

Indeed, for those looking for an exemplary, well defined, yet convenient wilderness experience, the PCT might be the last place they need look. Nearly anywhere along its length they can hike for days in the wilds, arrive at a resupply station and collect a load of mailed provisions, then set off onto another stretch of backcountry trail. And they can do this time and again while making way along the trail's length.

And yet we celebrate not the trail, but the wild places it passes through. The trail is merely a means to enjoy the end. It is also a long, winding invitation to shed the ennui; a beckoner of souls that would come sojourn in its higher regions, if only for a few glorious months.

THE ADVENTURE AFOOT

Indeed, a through-hike of the PCT is a perfect example of the long-distance backpacker's dream. First and foremost it is an escape of structured, citified living, a temporary withdrawal from our fellow metronauts. It is a return to nature; a journey in search of what parts of ourselves might lie in the deserts, forests, and mountains.

Trail life can be a time of rising early, of traipsing wet footed through meadow grasses, and then later of feeling the luxurious warmth of the morning sun. It can be a time of ambling through quiet, hallowed forests, and perhaps in the same day, of laboring to gain a high vantage; and finally in conquest, to feel the supremacy of the mountaineer. Expansive, hard won views are one of the PCT's exemplary features; many are the times when the distance-hiker can gaze far back at a prominent landmark that a few days previously had stood far ahead.

A REJUVENATION OF SELF

Trail life is also a time for shedding lethargy; of loosing weight perhaps, and of growing stronger and healthier. It is a time of gaining better control of ourselves, and of extending our capacities for personal growth. It can be a time of meeting kindred spirits: of relating with other distance-hikers, whose aspirations and experiences generally parallel our own. It is also a chance to discover innumerable out of the way places, inaccessible to mechanized travelers, and in fact unknown to most people. And in the process, it might be a time of engendering a kinship with our ancient predecessors who must have known these same places well.

Trail time affords opportunities to encounter wildlife. It is a chance to witness etherial displays of light, as the colors of each day fade into the shadows of eventide. It is an opportunity to breathe fresh air and drink pure water, to savor a well deserved and spicy batch of spaghetti at the end of a long day, to spread the bedroll and fall fairly into a heap, to view with grateful heart the star studded skies, note the changing phase of the moon, and then at last to fall into a sleep that was never better slept.

Distance-hikers rely almost entirely on their own resources. They alone decide the course of the day's events. And they are subject to little if any commercialism, politics, crime or demoralizing current events.

For the restless buccaneers, the endless trail lures ever onward. Granted, the way is garnished with toil and fatigue, but they are the right kinds of toil and fatigue. And of course there are the usual adversities of snowpack, mosquitos and so forth. But adversities only strengthen those hikers who learn to deal with them. So indeed, the journey is a test of abilities: of mental and physical strength and stamina—truly a test of selves.

Succinctly, a through-hike of the PCT is a metaphor of life itself: its hardship and toil, its vivacity and rewards. But far more than that, it can be a supremely enriching experience. In fact, it can be an adventure unparalleled in all of one's life.

THE HANDBOOK

The PCT Hiker's Handbook is a compendium of trail tested information and instruction addressing all the aspects of planning, preparing for, and of hiking the PCT. It is also an instructive in the art and skills of long-distance powerhiking, whatever trails the reader's feet are eager to tread.

Most of the material contained herein is original. This is not a dry textbook of imagined facts, but an assemblage of knowledge gained firsthand through actual practice. In many instances the underpinnings of much of this knowledge are related ancedotally.

The *Handbook's* main focus is on the though-hike: the long and distinguished journey afoot, border to border, in a single season. Granted, most people who hike the PCT do so in segments, spending a day, a weekend, or a few weeks on the trail. Still, these folks should find a great deal of useful information in *The Handbook*, even though it is not designed specifically to enhance their short jaunts. For after all, those techniques that prove worthy to through-hikers should also be of great benefit to the weekend hikers.

SMELLING THE FLOWERS

For many hikers, the notion of distance hiking according to a schedule seems the antithesis of the wilderness experience. Through-hikers are often accused of not seeing anything along the way, as if to infer that they hike with their eyes closed. Nothing could be farther from the truth. In fact, the high-mileage backpackers adhering to the principles in the *Handbook* walk no faster than most day hikers. And generally they stop and rest every hour or so, which is not always the case among the more exuberant weekend warriors out smelling the flowers. In the final analysis, at least some of the apparent resentment might stem from a lack of long-term vitality. Yet the vast majority of day-hikers could acquire the prowess needed for border-to-border hiking. The *Handbook* teaches how this is best accomplished.

THE NEED

Along the same lines, the *Handbook* finds much of its need in the ignominious drop-out rate among aspiring PCT through-hikers. Historically, of those who began at the Mexican border each season, only fifteen or twenty percent managed to walk even the first hundred miles. How disappointing, that after hiking only a week or two, the majority of aspiring distance hikers abandoned their determination and relinquished their intents to continue. Yet imagine the irony—they quit their hikes generally for the same reasons every year. Collectively, these reasons had little or nothing to do with bundled enthusiasm, hours of preparation, (although not necessarily of the most effective kind) physical strength (as opposed to meticulously apportioned stamina), high-tech equipment, or with a deep-felt love of nature. Instead, the reasons had everything to do with...

HAPLESS HIKER

*We find after years of struggle
that we do not take a trip;
a trip takes us.*
—John Steinbeck

Hapless Hiker is a fictitious character. He doesn't exist and never did. However, the mistakes he makes along the way are actual, for with only minor variations they are generally the same ones made every year by scores of real hikers. For emphasis, I have italicized them.

Hapless decides to hike the Pacific Crest Trail. He begins preparations by *bragging to friends*, telling them that *as an experienced backpacker he is going to cruise the trail*. He emphasizes his intent to start late in the mornings and stop early in the afternoons. The secret of backpacking, he asserts, is to take things easy, and not to get too physical. *This hike is going to be a vacation.*

Hapless spends most of his evenings reading about backpacking gear, and poring through equipment catalogues. He has visited every outdoor store in the area, and has also driven to larger cities and perused the stores there. He does not consider himself a gear fanatic, despite his extensive backpacking-equipment inventory. Show him virtually any piece of gear, though, and he can probably tell you not only its brand and model, but its relevant specs. Hapless is proud of his backpacking-equipment knowledge, and *considers this a tremendous advantage*, failing to realize that his knowledge is gleaned from advertising rather than from experience. In actuality, Hapless' wealth of knowledge is only an enormous agglomeration of promotional material.

Ultimately unable to resolve bewilderment on several equipment issues, Hapless contacts a number of experienced PCT hikers, asking for recommendations and advice. Unfortunately, none agree on any one subject. But they do provide reams of advice, the majority of which reflects certain problems each person had experienced. For example, one fellow lost one of his fondest possessions: his pocket knife. That knife had been with him always, and he all but doubted his ability to survive in the wilds without it. Emphatically, he recommends that Hapless carry a spare knife. Two would be even better. After all is said and done, it seems that just about everyone helps to increase Hapless' packweight.

Hapless has it all, and every item in his hiking inventory represents hours of meticulous research and forethought. Moreover, every piece of his gear is of the best (and heaviest) construction. *He feels well prepared.* Granted, his pack is very heavy, but turning the prospects of adversity to temporary advantage, Hapless only *boasts about his prodigious load all the more.*

A few hikers recommended starting the hike in mid April, but figuring he'd better get a head start, Hapless *departs from the Mexican Border two weeks earlier than that.*

The first day begins with exuberance, but very soon the fact becomes apparent that his 95 pound load is too heavy. The weight requires that he rest every 15 or 20 minutes. *He compensates, in part, by carrying very little water.* The day is *"desperately"* hot, and in many places the trail is overgrown in *"frustrating"* brush. Hiking ten miles the first day nearly brings an early demise to the adventure. And it certainly makes him *glad that he had not squandered his precious energy by training for the hike.* Nevertheless, he stops early, according to plan. Removing those *heavy, stiff boots* feels heavenly. Feeling far less thirsty than he had during the day, (and therefore not rehydrating his body adequately) he gormandizes on several packages of lightweight, *freeze dried food* (which lacks the nutrients his body so desperately needs at the moment).

After a multi day struggle, Hapless is on the flanks of Mt. Laguna. There, *to his astonishment* he encounters early-season snow: deep, trackless and pervasive. Incredulous, he begins trudging ahead to the knees.

We join Hapless at the end of his first week on the "trail" at the Mt. Laguna Post Office. He is writing in the register a rather indignant commentary pertaining to the decided lack of a trail. "I'm wallowing in 3 feet of snow!" he exclaims. Readily admitting the futility of slogging another 20 miles through the snow while descending the mountain, Hapless *manages a ride* northward with a passing and sympathetic motorist. (And it is here that his journey's continuity, his intent to walk all the way to Canada, is irrevocably breached.)

Several hours and another ride later he lands at the torrid outpost of Banner. Here he feels the obligation to hike southward up the canyon to rejoin the trail; however, *he is extremely reluctant to waste energy by hiking in the wrong direction.* After all, he <u>is</u> trying to reach Canada. And besides, the trail's "inefficient" routing *seems an insult to Hapless's intelligence.* But more importantly *he is reluctant to address two of the trail's most extensive waterless stretches*, in succession. And failing to see the humor in walking along the busy highway directly across the San Felipe desert, he decides the matter by *stretching forth the golden thumb.* Presto, he is delivered once again from his troubles by automobile, and later is deposited near the trail at the far end of the desert.

After trudging another day and a half, Hapless stumbles sore footed into the small community of Warner Springs. Collecting his first resupply parcel (he should have resupplied at Mt. Laguna), he retires into the shade to consider his plight. His body is deeply fatigued, and extremely uncomfortable for lack of bathing. His clothes stink. His feet are blistered and the tape is not helping. Things are not as he had dreamed. His vision has given way to imaginings. And aside from the appalling dangers, the journey is beginning to seem inconvenient. This time he points the golden thumb toward civilization.

INTRODUCTION

Go forth under the open sky,
and list to Nature's teachings.
—William Cullen Bryant

Each hiking endeavor, whether completed or ended prematurely, represents a success in terms of experience gained. But how that experience is then treated psychologically will have great bearing on the outcome of the succeeding adventures. Hapless Hiker will have lots of time to think about this. His choices are essentially two: he can conjure myriad and convincing excuses with which to justify himself to his friends and relatives, or he can accept his mistakes and consider the experiences as those of enlightenment and the potential for personal growth.

THE AVALANCHE OF ADVERSITY

Imagine a titanic avalanche bursting stalwart timbers, mowing them asunder and sweeping them down a slope. And imagine the flexible aspens and willows simply bending to the incredible pressures, then springing back upright. These flexible shoots teach us something about withstanding the awesome powers of nature. Those hikers who venture unyielding into the wilds are likely to meet with attendant obstacles every step of the opprobrious way. And as likely as not, these individuals will eventually retreat, if not sooner then later. But those who recognize the need to bend and flex to Nature's dictates are likely to find themselves far more in harmony with the natural world.

Even so, nature is generally not as overbearing as Hapless Hiker had imagined. For one thing, we are stressed less by situations than by our views of them. This is because our minds tend to treat imagined possibilities as though they were real; and our central nervous systems have no way of distinguishing the differences. Also, much of our fatigue is borne of anxiety. And in turn, fatigue can make an obstacle far more foreboding. Oftentimes a good rest will reduce what seems a monumental obstruction to manageable proportions. A positive mind-set will greatly increase the chances of success.
They are able because they think they are able.
—Virgil

For another thing, Hapless was exhausting himself with his colossal backpack, heavy boots, deepening dehydration and utter lack of nutrition. And he discouraged himself by casting aspersions on the scapegoats of water unavailability, and trail overbrush and routing. Rather than taking the obstacles as personal affronts, he could have **channeled his consciousness**

around them. And rather than demanding that reality change to suit his whims, he could have adjusted his interpretations of reality. For example, deep snow is an indication, not of some cosmic injustice, nor of abnormal conditions to the ruination of his inviolate itinerary, but simply that he had begun the hike too early in that particular season.

Rather than accept reality, Hapless attempted to change it to suit himself. And when it wouldn't, he grew frustrated. This was particularly true regarding the weight of his pack. We hikers are not pack mules, no matter how we try to emulate them. The magnum size backpack is often an expression of machismo, and a desperate crusade for security. In actuality, the heavier our packs, the less will be our security and our backpacking enjoyment.

The Pacific Crest Trail, and most other long, winding paths, recognize no distinction between hikers young and old, fit and flabby, Type-A and carefree. They care not whether folks pass through in groups, pairs or singles; in gear high-tech or Army surplus. And they have been known to grant passage to the handicapped person of particular grit. The only traits they insist upon, and this at times emphatically, are a wee amount of perseverance and a substantial willingness to shed those misconceptions that do not align with reality.

Jenny and I gained much of this insight not only by watching other hikers, and attempting to analyze their mistakes, but by making a treasure trove of mistakes of our own devices.

In 1987 we hiked from the Mexican to the Canadian border. Despite a background reasonably aglut with camping and hiking adventures, the on-going nature of that tri-state quest made me feel almost as though I had begun anew. And during the ensuing four years, that enlightenment had apparently coalesced; for the more I pondered the meaning of our PCT hike, the more I began identifying some of the mistakes we had made. But despite the negative, I became increasingly aware of how the quest had enriched our lives.

In retrospect, like Hapless we had set off from Campo with heads brim full of curious delusions and impeding antipathies. Despite a moiling pre-hike anxiety, I had underestimated the trail's difficulties. More significantly, I had neglected to consider my aptitude for coping with what eventually seemed the trail's sometimes staggering idiosyncracies. Yet here was the herculean obstruction: The need had not occurred to me to release my ironclad misconceptions of the trail, of the wilderness experience at large, and some of those of myself within. But watching fellow hikers dropping out, and threatening to do so myself a few times, eventually I had to admit that an unwillingness to change, to grow, is the PCT distance-hiker's only insuperable.

Another through-hiker, on reaching the Canadian border, had written:

I began this journey with many hopes and many fears. Glittering expectations blinded me as I crossed my trailheads. What I wanted to find and what I found never matched, yet the final experience has granted me profound illumination.

Knowledge gained and not used soon evanesces. So to apply what Jenny and I had learned while pursuing another extended journey afoot, we decided to hike the PCT again, in 1991. But this time we determined to address the pilgrimage in an entirely different vein, one well tempered by our previous struggles with trail reality. Rather than sally forth into the perilous wilds bent upon conquering every adversity, while generally clawing our way tooth and nail toward Canada, (as humorously it seemed we had done the first time) this time we determined to proceed as fledglings. Humbled and ultimately molded by the rigors of our first hike, my intent was now to throw open the doors of my mind to nature's profusion of teachings. Manning Park—the goal, I determined, could take care of itself.

Consequently, nearly each day of this second pilgrimage proved one of enlightenment. And indeed, the more we yielded to the lessons encountered, and experimented with various ways to mold ourselves around them, the more nature's truths began weaving themselves into a tapestry of a heightened wilderness consciousness. As a result, we found ourselves moving ahead more in harmony with the natural cadence. And purely as a byproduct, the miles began reeling past as never before.

After reaching Monument 78 we returned home and I began writing this *Handbook.* I imagined that some of what we had learned might help ameliorate the drop-out rate among well intentioned PCT aspirants. And for those who persevere, I hoped the material would make their adventures safer, less arduous, and more enjoyable.

It seems to me that the requisite personal growth must begin long before the hike's outset. With the proper mind set, adequate nutrition and pre-hike training, Hapless's dilemmas need not apply to the aspiring PCT hiker. The disabling misconceptions can well be ameliorated at the start if the proper instruction and encouragement is given.

And that is what *The Handbook* is all about.

A trail-side lake

Hiking along the crest of the Northern Sierra.

Toward Glacier Peak

Approaching the summit of Mt. Baden Powell

Umbrellas in action

The author near Snoqualmie Pass

Jenny climbing Mather Pass in early season

GOALS

Audentes fortuna juvat
(Fortune favors the bold)

It was my dream that made it good, my dream that made me go,
to lands of dread and death disprised of man,
But oh I've known a glory that their hearts will never know,
when I picked that first big nugget from my pan.
It's still my dream, my dauntless dream, that drives me forth once more,
to seek and starve and suffer in the vast,
That heaps my heart with eager hope; that glimmers on before,
My dream that will uplift me to the last.
—Robert Service

We live with the new and the old: the new technology—launching us into the future, and the old tenements of clay—inherited from our primordial ancestors and designed to insure the survival of the species. The new measures change in hours and days; the old, in millennia. The new strives to create and live in a sophisticated society, but the old was designed to function in the natural world, where physical exertion and exposure to the elements were commonplace.

Technology has largely freed us from the pressures of survival. We buy our food (loaded with chemicals, or in some cases that is the chemicals). We journey near and far while seated (in cars that have plunged us into debt). Having essentially removed ourselves from the elements, we harbor the notion that progress is to be measured in how far we have bulldozed nature away from us. Physical challenges are rarely imposed on us.

So we must contrive them.

We must invent goals that shun luxuries and comforts; for even once gained, those same luxuries and comforts only debase us, mentally, physically and emotionally. Instead, our goals must necessitate sweat-induced labor and discomfort, and they must reintroduce us to uncertainty and risk.

Why? Because we are subject to a disordering of life: an all pervading cosmogonic force acting on us the way gravity would act on a rock lying tenuously upon a steep hillside. The rock's only future would be to skid slowly downward, as it is nudged by storms, earthquakes or erosion. Citified living debases the primordial aspects genetically programmed into us, and which if addressed, would sharpen our lives. But high civilization saps the lives out of us, however acclaimed, well clothed, automobiled, housed, and entertained.

In his book *Personal Best*, George Sheehan draws a compelling likeness between alcoholics and runners; (or perhaps backpackers, mountain climbers, ocean voyagers, et al) in that people in each group seem to be possessed with an innate urge to strive against what evils would consume their lives. The ruinous agent the alcoholic battles is of course liquor, and that which the athlete or adventurer dreads is languor. As A. Conan Doyle, writer of the Sherlock Holmes adventures, wrote in one of his dialogues, "My life is spent in one long effort to escape from the commonplaces of existence."

Yes, the goals are to be contrived. Of themselves, they do not exist. What exists, though, are dreams. But a dream is like electricity with no wire: ineffective despite its great potential. All of us have dreams, but not all of us act on them and turn them into goals. Instead, most people await the right opportunities. Generally, though, even if the right opportunities were to happen along, they might only ensnare us into the will of the people who created them. When we embrace an opportunity, it might turn around and embrace us.

Personal goals, on the other hand, beckon us ahead of our own volition. This is because they are self forged.

A goal is like a fine painting, which begins as a blank canvas. Before the first stroke of the brush the painting is empty, meaningless, uncommunicative. When complete, the art is obvious to all, even though not all understand it.

Dispersed campfire coals extinguish themselves. But scooped together they might ignite the kindling to produce a heartening blaze. And so it is with dreams. Scoop them carefully but purposefully together, and they might engender a blaze of resolve and purpose. And scoop together the disparate but glowing fragments of our lives: the innate talents, abilities and courage within us all, and we become more capable. When we define a goal, however contrived, and when we begin moving toward accomplishing it, we begin shedding any stagnation. And perhaps then we will begin to metamorphose from crawling grubs into creatures of flight.

Indeed, there is a longing in us all to escape the increasing crowding together, the world foul with pollution and crime, and the people who might prey upon us. To set off on the PCT is to escape these mundane commonplaces of life. Granted, the way is not without toil, certain privations, and the occasional danger, but these pale in light of the ineffable rewards to be gained.

Each season, as aspiring distance hikers arrive at the Mexican Border they are willfully turning their backs on what might seem their life's lack of definitions. Shouldering their backpacks, they are commencing a glorious and unbounded summer afoot. And in making the long pilgrimage they are fending off, or at least resisting, the inexorable and permeating lethargy. They are attempting to live life, if not at its fullest, then at least at vastly elevated levels. During their long summers of hardship and toil, and of inexpressible joys, they will be awakening their senses. Their lives are likely to be taking on sharpened meanings. In the process they will be gaining better understandings of their strengths and weaknesses, and of their natural surroundings—the biosphere that sustains all life. And in surmounting the many problems along the way they will be gaining self confidence. Thus equipped, they needn't compare themselves with their contemporaries at home, in order to interpret their self images.

TRAINING
Making light of toil

Success to the strongest,
who are always, at last,
the wisest and best.
—Emerson

As a disclaimer perhaps, the writer of one popular PCT book recommends against hiking the entire trail in a single season, because, among other reasons, "the human body was not meant to carry heavy packs continuously over a rugged 2,600-mile distance."

ARE WE SO INEPT?

Indeed, the spurious belief in humankind's physical ineptitude is rife in today's mechanized societies. But when we consider the hunting and gathering lifestyles of our primogenitors we might begin to believe otherwise. These people must have been accustomed to running, walking, and carrying heavy loads over great distances. And genetically, we have inherited those bodies. So it is probably still true today that regular and vigorous exercise stimulates health and vitality.

It is only within the past few hundred years that civilized humankind has become immobile. In the distant future we might adapt to interminable slouching in recliners and office chairs. But meanwhile our incessant vegetating will probably continue to result not only in atrophy and advanced aging, but also in the usual host of acquired diseases. Clearly, the slothful existence we have come to accept is neither normal nor healthful.

To set out on an extended backpacking journey is to turn one's back on today's accepted standards, physically deleterious that many of them are, and to begin a restorative journey back in time. However, embarking on a multi thousand mile hiking adventure with an idle-atrophied body, or with one that had not toughened to begin with, would be a monumental indiscretion. True, our bodies are probably capable of adapting to prolonged and strenuous exertion. But we can acquire the necessary strengths only gradually, over the course of many months. And this strengthening is best accomplished **prior** to the trek's beginning.

Summarizing the considerations found in the section on distance-hiking injuries, page 103: Stress injuries occur, but I maintain that they are largely the result of:

- ☒ Disregarding the pre-hike physical conditioning.
- ☒ Hiking while severely dehydrated.

⊠ Wearing heavy boots containing steel shanks.
⊠ Neglecting the hourly calf stretching exercises.

THE MORE WE TRAIN, THE EASIER IT BECOMES

Training is simply a matter of shouldering the backpack, walking out the doorway, and hiking for a few hours; this, once every two or three days. If you live in the city and imagine that you lack a suitable training area, consider that wherever you can walk, you can also train.

The conditioning is best begun several months prior to the actual hike. Each week, the prospective hikers would add a few pounds to their training backpacks, and they would hike a little farther.

It is a common misconception that the training becomes progressively tougher from day one. In truth, as we condition our bodies we become more capable. So even though we carry heavier loads for longer distances with the passing of each week, we might not *feel* the increases. And the net result is this: Setting off from the Mexican Border, the well-trained aspirants might hike 20 miles the first day. The un-trained ones might hike only half that. And in theory, *both groups feel that they have exerted themselves equally.* But the main benefit comes not at the end of the first day, but at the beginning of the second. The well-conditioned hikers are far more likely to arise in excellent condition despite the previous day's exertions. The out-of-shape hikers will arise probably feeling muscle sore and much less energetic than previously. And of course the well trained PCT hikers will enjoy greater chances of vitality and success in the ensuing weeks. And in all probability they will go away from the summer's extended trek in even better health.

One of the most important features of the pre-hike training regimen is the one or two day rest periods between each training foray. The out-of-shape person setting out from Campo, and using the actual journey as the conditioning regimen, is not afforded these indescribable luxuries. But those who had begun training well ahead of time are likely to be fully capable of hiking vigorously nearly every day.

OVERCONFIDENCE

Winter is a time for aspiring PCT hikers to formulate plans and to begin preparations. But it can also be a time of making critical errors.

One mistake is to confuse experience with strength, failing to realize that strength unused might have long since atrophied. Along that same line, another is to believe that being accustomed to carrying a heavy pack during the occasional weekend trip will assure the strength and stamina required to carry it day after day, two and a half thousand rugged miles. Another is to realize that you might not be in peak physical fitness, but like Hapless Hiker, to rationalize the matter by imagining that you will proceed slowly at first, taking it easy for the first week or so, and thus allowing your body to condition while on the trail. The prodigious hike, you might imagine, will *be* your training. The fallacies in this logic are that the body takes months to attune and toughen, not days or weeks; and that the conditioning **must** begin gently. And finally, some hikers suffer the ultimate delusion: that, almost magically, once they begin the hike, the quest's etherial attributes will buoy them along the yellow brick road to the Canadian Border.

We have all read narratives written by out-of-shape hikers struggling in the natural world. And if these teach anything, it is that nature makes no special provisions. Also, they teach that the hiker who misjudges his or her physical conditioning, in comparison to the rigors of distance backpacking, might be in for disappointment and possibly an injury.

But this synopsis needn't apply to you.

TRAINING TOO DIFFICULT?

Those who don't enjoy pre-hike training are unlikely to enjoy the distance hiking. Put differently, those who find the training too troublesome are ideal candidates for PCT drop out.

Indeed, the training regimen will command a considerable amount of your time. And unlike the actual hike, the training hikes generally lack adventure. So whenever the routine becomes lackluster, try dragging the vision to the forefront of your mind.

One of the keys to the successful training regimen is to make it fun. Personally, I enjoy the training hikes immensely. The routine induces me out of the house, and to spend considerably more time in the woods than I otherwise would. Always there are pressing items on my agenda, but once I have escaped them, my priorities invariably shift. And I find that the exercise, fresh air, and the increased circulation stimulate vitality and productiveness.

Another key is in learning patience and persistence. Training has nothing to do with instant gratification; hence its wide lack of appeal. So we need to concentrate on slowing down, relaxing, and extending the workouts by exercising not only our legs and backs, but our patience. Also, the training regimen is a good chance to practice dealing with the occasional lethargic mood.

TRAINING REDUCES TREKKING TIME

For every three hours you spend training, you might lessen your distance hike by about an hour. For example, should you arrive at Campo out of condition, you might do best with a 6 month itinerary. Spend 3 months training beforehand, hiking several hundred miles in the process, while burning the midnight oil at ridding your packweight of every needless ounce, and your chances of hiking the trail in 5 months are excellent. Train for 6 months, and you might cruise the trail in 4 months. I cannot say that the faster through-hike is the more enjoyable one; but we have all heard and read stories of out of shape hikers lumbering along in enormous discomfort. Mileage, then, is merely a by-product of a fit hiker's *vivre*.

HOW TO BEGIN

Consider taping onto the wall a homemade chart such as this one:

WEEKLY PRE-HIKE TRAINING SCHEDULE

	Miles hiked	Weight carried	sit-ups	squats	calf raises	Stretch-ing
Mon						
Tue						
Wed						
Thu						
Fri						
Sat						
Sun						

Divide into thirds the number of months you can allot to training. For the first third, you might train every third day. For the remaining months, you might train every second day. Then a week before the actual hike you would cease training.

GRADUALLY INCREASE PACKWEIGHT

Hiking exerts the muscles of the legs and back: muscle groups used to a lesser extent in everyday living. But the act of carrying a backpack also exercises the groups supporting the shoulder girdle. These are muscles that most stay-at-homes don't even know they have. So training with a gradually heavier pack is essential. During the initial two weeks of the hiking-training program you would not carry a pack. Thereafter you would carry a lightweight pack, and every second week you would increase its weight a few pounds. Near the end of the training regimen you would carry whatever load you deem realistic. My target load is 50 pounds.

TRAIN ON UNEVEN GROUND

Walking on city-flat surfaces strengthens the fore and aft muscles, tendons, and ligaments of the ankles and feet; but it does little for the lateral ones. These debilitated lateral parcels are largely responsible for the weekend hiker's need for stiff boots, which provide more ankle support. So your training is best done on uneven, irregular ground. Make those ankles rock and roll.

It matters little whether you train in the snowbound mountains, in the broiling desert, or in any type of intervening terrain. Whatever your homeland climate and topography, it will surely occur in great quantities along the PCT. If the earth in your vicinity is fairly level, though, you might do well to spend some of your training time climbing and descending flights of steps, or their equivalent.

STRENGTHENING THE QUADRICEPS

Hiking-training does not sufficiently strengthen the thigh muscles. Even a well conditioned hiker can set out from Campo unaware of a markedly weak set of quadriceps. The following two exercises are important in helping the heavily burdened hiker to step one legged and repeatedly out of snowpack post holes and moats, to surmount steep terrain, and to climb over wind-felled timber blocking the way.

The barbell squat, when performed correctly, is considered a safe and effective thigh strengthening exercise. The technique is to stand erect, hold a barbell across your shoulders and behind your head, and squat down. As a beginner, use a broom handle with no added weight. Or simply hold a few jugs of water. As you squat, keep your chin up and your spine as erect as possible. And do not squat below the comfort level. Any knee pain indicates that you are squatting too low to begin with.

The foot lift is practiced while seated. Place the leg to be exercised over the chair's arm rest, so that the foot hangs free. Loop a small weight, suspended by a short length of rope or webbing, over the foot. Then slowly unbend, and bend the knee (raising the leg as far as it will go, and then lowering it). Exercise gently, and use very little weight to begin with. If your knee makes grating noises, use the weight statically, rather than lifting it up and down.

STRETCHING

No training regimen is complete without a twice-daily stretching ritual. And while engaged in the actual journey, stretching out your calves should comprise an important part of every wakeful hour. See the following chapter for the specifics.

WESTON THE PEDESTRIAN

In 1909, Edward "Weston the Pedestrian" walked 4,500 miles across the country in 105 days. He was 71. The following year he repeated the journey in the opposite direction, remarkably in 76 days. One of the most accomplished walkers of his era, Weston believed that walking was as healthful and natural as sleeping. Throughout most of his life he walked 12 to 15 miles every day of the week except Sundays. He didn't consider his daily walking as training for his long walks, but merely as an integral part of his life.

STRETCHING

Oiling the machinery

If you blow upon this wheel,
even though it be only a breath,
you will set it turning.
—Unknown

We live our lives without articulating our joints to their full extent. This might be one reason why, later in life our bodies stiffen painfully.

A peek into a weight lifting gym might reveal the sight of machismos lifting huge weights while attempting to impress any incredulous onlookers. But ironically, bodybuilding competitions are not won by the person lifting the most weight. The same apparent contradiction applies to stretching. The intent is not to demonstrate one's suppleness by stressfully laying the torso flat against the legs.

In the introductory pages of his excellent *Yoga 28 day Exercise Book*, Richard Hittleman writes "[Stretching] requires a minimum of effort to attain maximum results." That summarizes the principles. Any negative after-effects from stretching, such as pain or stiffness, serve to remind us of the need to moderate the disciplines.

Muscles can be stretched only when they are relaxed. If taut muscles are forced to elongate they might tear, or they might gradually shrink. The latter is one of the body's methods of guarding, or protecting itself against abuse. The most difficult part of the stretching regimen is in allowing the muscles to relax. A muscle group is not relaxed until it fairly sags. Only then can it be stretched effectively and safely. Even so, it must not be over stretched. When you feel the tension, back off somewhat and hold for 20 or 30 heartbeats.

Another caveat: The stretching exercises should not work the joints rigorously away from the axes in which they are daily being used. This is because out-of-axes stretching might weaken the stabilizing ligaments. To mention but one specific, backpackers should refrain from practicing the lotus position.

THE CALF STRETCH

Distance backpacking places extraordinary demands on the hiker's calf muscles. In an attempt to guard against the perhaps unaccustomed exertion, these muscles might relinquish much of their elasticity. In fact, they might become so stiffened that continued and vigorous hiking might actually cause tears in them.

The novice approach to calf-stretching is to attempt the exercises while using the target muscles to support the body. This is an invitation to disaster. Instead, the body should first be placed deliberately out of balance. This shunts the balancing mechanisms that subconsciously interfere with the attempt to relax the target muscles.

The best calf-hamstring stretching exercise for our purposes is what I term the cross-legged calf stretch. During the journey, the distance hiker would do well to practice it at least once an hour while hiking. It is performed by standing facing a tree, rock, or embankment—the feet positioned a yard or more from it. Knees straight, the hiker leans into the object, bracing the hands against it as though doing a push up. One leg is stretched at a time. The other is crossed in front of the first, supporting it at the knee. The second leg helps the stretching leg to relax, by preventing it from buckling. The foot of the leg being stretched is kept flat on the ground. And its ankle is not allowed to pronate, to roll inward, which would place great strain on its ligaments. In order to prevent pronation, the hiker would stand with the inner edge of the foot on a small rock or stick.

Relaxing the muscles to be stretched requires a great deal of practice. After the first gentle stretching, lift the leg in question and let the foot hang limp, as though it were a rag mop. Here the aggressive hiker might feel an increasing surge of pain; a throbbing caused by the blood vessels dilating and the blood pooling into the lower leg. This happens because the muscles giving shape to the veins are now being asked to relax. The vaso pain is a sure indication of the need to give much more attention to the stretching exercises, and to keep them gentle. When the dangling calf has relaxed as much as it's going to, the hiker places its foot back down, shifts body weight onto it, crosses the other leg in front of it once again for knee support, and relaxes and stretches again, but gently.

For the second phase of the leg stretching exercise, it helps a great deal if the terrain is inclined. This provides more favorable leverage. The terrain will usually be sloped appropriately; if not, the hiker might keep walking until coming to some trailside object that would make for a small platform. Leaning forward against a tree, one foot back and flat on the ground, the hiker brings the second foot forward and places it on the sloped ground or on the platform. Without placing body weight on the forward foot, the hiker rocks it up onto the ball, and flexes the toes gently back. Then the foot is rolled gently, pivoting it on the toes. This bends the toes in every direction, and helps loosen the ankle. Then the leg is relaxed, and its weight is allowed to flex the ankle. That position is held for 20 heart-beats. The forward calf should be feeling a nice stretch. The rear leg is being used for support. The procedure is then repeated with the legs reversed.

STRETCHING AN INJURY

The distance hiker who overlooks the regular stretching exercises is subjecting him or herself to considerable risk of incurring a stress injury. However, once the injury occurs, stretching would be potentially hazardous unless done with the utmost gentleness.

TIGHT CALVED HIKING

As you hike, the slope's steepness, the terrain's ruggedness, and the backpack's weight will affect how tight your calves become. But more importantly, so will your walking style. If you lift your heels off the ground prematurely with each step, and if you shove off too hard with the toes, then your overworked calves might become inordinately tight. These supplementary motions tend to enlarge the calves; however, some of the effort is wasted. The most efficient hiking styles minimize pogo sticking, which squanders forward effort.

Laurence Morehouse originated the technique of cruising. His intent was to minimize the person's head bobbing needlessly up and down. Practice it by bending the knees very slightly, while imagining that you are carrying a jug of water atop your head.

Also, critique your tracks. Craters at the toes indicate you might be pushing off too hard. When walking on soft sand or crusty snow, the toe push will retard forward motion enormously, and the distance hiker would practice instead lifting the toes at the end of the stride rather than shoving ahead with them. Walking on normal terrain, though, a certain amount of toe push is beneficial. Only the individual can discover the balance; and this can be achieved only with a great deal of conscious effort. And once again, the optimal techniques vary with the terrain.

HIKING WITH THE BRAKES ON

Another factor that contributes to inefficient hiking style is unnecessarily tensing muscles that are not being used. With each stride, the leg's forward muscles flex as they draw the leg quickly forward. Then they must relax to allow the aft muscles to haul the leg back. If the forward muscles fail to relax fast enough, they resist the aft muscles. This inadvertent braking action holds true with a multitude of opposing muscle groups in the lower body and appendages. To reduce the tendency, the hiker might practice tensing and relaxing all the muscles of the body while hiking. The technique is to hike stiff like a robot, then loose as a noodle, and then increase the tension until achieving the bare minimum of stiffness required to carry on. Once again, this is an ongoing and conscious endeavor.

INTERLUDES

While hiking, we can exercise our necks frequently by looking far around to both sides. This will also enhance our awareness. To break a monotonous rhythm, we might turn around and walk several steps backward. And we might do this often. Also, we might occasionally hook our thumbs behind the backpack's shoulder straps, at chest height. This relieves our shoulders and helps ventilate the lungs by allowing the chest cavities to expand. Also, it helps reduce any swelling in our hands and fingers.

THE PYRAMID

of Hiking Style

Men go abroad to admire the heights of mountains,
the mighty billows of the sea,
the long courses of rivers,
the vast compass of the stars,
...and yet they pass themselves by.
—St. Augustine

Assuming you have begun your pre-hike training and stretching exercises, it's time to consider your hiking style. This can affect your summer's adventures almost as much as your degree of physical fitness.

Imagine a pyramid of style: distinguished by its massive base of indolence and its lofty apex of efficiency. We choose our position on the pyramid during the journey's planning stages; and we can adjust it during the journey.

A DESCENT

Let's start midway on the pyramid's flanks, and begin a descent. In the ensuing scenarios we are planning for an 8 day trek between resupply stations. Intent on taking our time and enjoying life, we allow ourselves a little more food, a thick paperback, and perhaps even a harmonica. But because the extra gear won't fit into our already overly crammed pack, we might as well buy a bigger (and therefore heavier) pack.

While carrying this new and heavier pack loaded with the extra belongings, we will travel a little slower. But we will compensate by allowing ourselves longer rests, and by sleeping-in whenever we feel like it. After all, we are in no hurry. So we need to plan on taking an extra day to reach the distant way point.

In order to accommodate the additional day, though, we will need to lay in more food and fuel. The new pack affords plenty of space for these items, which, unfortunately, will increase our load once again. Not to worry; the pack was advertised to carry loads in comfort; and because we will be carrying more food, we can plan for more variety. So let's include another cooking implement.

The heavier pack lessens the distance we are able to cover every day, and far more importantly, it degrades our enjoyment of the experience. And besides increasing our chances of enduring feet and leg problems, it will increase our fatigue, all day and every day.

But originally the plan was to take life easy; this hike is supposed to be enjoyable. So let's divide the segment by hiking out to a distant resupply station midway along its length. That will allow us to lighten our load somewhat. The resupply is a nine mile hike, each way, and then a long hitchhike from the trailhead. So we will add two days; one for going to and from our main route, and one for relaxing and enjoying city life.

Adding those two days to the nine, the journey has lengthened to eleven days. But during each of the two segments we need carry only 5½ days of food and fuel. So we have plenty of room for accoutrements. Might as well bring along a backpacker's chair and a couple of extra lenses for the SLR.

As we descend the pyramid, step at a time, the duration of our journey lengthens and our *overall* load increases. We have attempted to lessen our daily packweight by dividing the hiking section, resupplying at an intervening and trail-distant station. In theory we are lightening our packs somewhat, but in truth we are only carrying even more weight over the tri-state distance. We are, in short, descending the pyramid of hiking style.

AN ASCENT

Now let's return to the starting point, midway on the pyramid's flanks, and begin an ascent.

Again, we are planning to hike the original distance in 8 days, and we hope to do so while enjoying the traveling. But this time we are going to tighten the reins.

> *The day shall not be up so soon as I,*
> *To try the fair adventure of tomorrow.*
> —William Shakespeare

Hiking 17 miles a day at 3 miles an hour will require that we hike 5.7 hours each day, not including the rest stops. Surely we can hike more than 5.7 hours a day! Let's get going an hour earlier. Disciplining ourselves into hiking 6.7 hours each day, and allowing 8 hours of sleep each night, still we have a whopping 9.3 hours for resting and relaxing every day. And if we travel at the same 3 mph, our daily average will expand to 20 miles. That one hour makes a tremendous difference.

At 20 miles a day we could travel the total distance in 6.8 days instead of 8. Subtracting the 1.2 days from our itinerary, we can remove that day's food and fuel from our pack.

Now, because our load is less ponderous, we will hike, not faster, but with less fatigue. The lessened packweight will virtually offset the extra daily hour of hiking! Covering the 20 miles per day while carrying a lighter pack, we will arrive in camp no more fatigued than had we hiked 17 miles a day while carrying the heavier pack. The esprit will therefore win us extra mileage, with little if any additional effort. And that is precisely the kind of trade-off we are looking for.

The distance hiker who grasps the foregoing principle is well on his or her way on the ascent of the pyramid. Now let's consider a few more techniques, albeit of lesser consequences.

Let's send home a few items we haven't used in weeks. If sometime we need them, then so what? We will make do without them. Meanwhile, we won't be lugging them unprofitably every hour and every step of the way.

So let's send home the spare fleece sweater; the rain pants; two pairs of the most worn (and dirtiest) socks; the down booties; four pads of the moleskin; the cotton t-shirt emblazoned with the nifty art and used only in camp; the 2 spare tent stakes; the carabiner dangling affectatiously off the back of the pack; the salt and pepper shaker (keeping a little salt in a small plastic bag); the candle lantern (keeping half of one of the candles for emergency fire-starting); and the electronic pedometer.

That makes a surprisingly large pile of non-essentials. Ridding ourselves of it lessens the pack's mass and increases its maneuverability. Greater maneuverability translates into easier hiking over rugged terrain. And because we will be carrying less weight, we will move ahead with less strain, meaning that we will be not as prone to injury. And finally, as the greatest bonus of all we will be traveling more enjoyably.

The box we sent home lightens our load maybe 5 pounds. Subtracting the 5 pounds from the original 50, we have lessened our load by 10%. Transposing that ahead; we are going to hike maybe an additional half-mile each day, *while exerting no additional effort.*

Because we will be hiking the half-mile farther each day, we can cover the distance to the next resupply station in less time.

Once again, we are not compromising the hike's enjoyment. On the contrary: the aesthetics of the journey will increase, as we travel less encumbered. And please note that we are not striving to increase our hiking speed. **Speed is not the issue.** To hike fast is to court an injury.

Nevertheless, having readjusted our overall itinerary, we will need to remove, say, a lunch from the pack.

Because the pack load is lighter and smaller still, we can reduce the hiking time further again.

Now let's consider the following. Because we have radically improved our hiking style, we might be in a position to skip the resupply at station B, which is at a considerable distance from the trail. Instead, we could hike another 2.5 days, in this example, to station C. Our packs will be relatively light as we bypass station B, meaning that those final 2.5 days will be quick and easy. This tactic will save us many hours of hiking out to station B. The disadvantage is that we are adding back the weight of 2.5 days' supplies to our packs. But because station B is at a considerable distance from the trail, skipping it will more than compensate for the weight gain.

Summarily: those in the first scenario hiked to resupply station B in 11 days. Those in the second, hiked to station C in just over 9 days. And the hikers in both groups exerted themselves comparably.

FORGING BEYOND

Having led the way up the pyramid, I've demonstrated the principles. The remaining ascent is left to your creativity and inventiveness. As you climb in the footsteps of those who have ventured ahead, and perhaps as you forge beyond, you might find your horizons expanding more than you could have imagined.

PACK WEIGHT

On a long journey even a straw weighs heavy.
—Spanish proverb

THE ENORMOUS PACK LOAD

Humankind spent thousands of years clawing out of the wilderness and establishing select kernels of civilization. And only within the last few generations have we begun returning. Yet our present culture has become so ingrained that when we go backpacking we tend to lug along as many impediments as possible. The usual intent is to reduce the hazards and insure the comforts. But the astute distance hiker recognizes that the innumerable appurtenances are neither essential, nor do they contribute to safety or well being. On the contrary, by their mass they create an aura of general intolerability. And they retard the hiking progress as well.

We have all seen hikers lumbering along, each carrying a 75 or 80 pound backpack. Are we to take these hikers as experienced and serious? Or merely as uninformed?

It is a common misconception among prospective distance hikers that months of trail life will require considerably more gear than does the usual weekend hikes. Another fallacy is to imagine that their bodies will gradually accustom to the weights.

Initially, a 75 pound pack feels merely heavy, including when training with it at home. After the first 50 miles of actual PCT hiking, though, that pack will begin to seem more like an unwieldy, ponderous burden. And 100 miles along the trail, such a burden will have become a genuine insult to the hiker's flagging body. And it will remain an insult throughout the long hike. Never will the hiker accustom to it, and always will the act of taking it off bring immense relief. And besides making the hiker miserable, every day on the trail that load will deprive him or her copiously of mileage and enjoyment.

Overweight backpacks not only sap strength, they tax the feet and ankles. They increase the hikers' risk of injury, and they effectively steepen the hills and magnify the distances. And continuing ahead with them will become an ever-increasing effort.

Regardless of how they try, backpackers cannot make asses of themselves. Regrettably perhaps, we humans are wrought with limited capacities, particularly regarding hauling loads over long distances. In fact, studies have shown that doubling the load far more than doubles the effort required to haul it. The progression is geometric.

Hikers carry heavy packs generally for these reasons:

✓ They are trying to be prepared for any and all unforeseen occurrences, falsely imagining that great quantities of equipment will provide for safer journeys. (Generally, the more experienced and self-confident a person becomes in the wilds, the less gear will be carried.)

✓ They have largely succumbed to the mental programming exerted by commercialism.

✓ They are attempting to impress others.

✓ They have perhaps acquired inefficient techniques from people and organizations they respect, such as from their parents, the Boy or Girl Scouts, or from the Military.

In actual fact, the longer the hike, the less gear it requires. When Jenny and I set out from Campo in 1991, our water bottles were empty but we carried a 3 day supply of food and all the gear needed for the first month of the hike, including cold-weather gear for the mountains. Our packs weighed 22 pounds apiece. The Check Lists chapter (page 267) specifies the gear we used that summer.

OMNE IGNOTUM PRO MAGNIFICO
[everything unknown is (taken as) grand]

Most people over-equip themselves for a long hike. This error generally stems from a lack of knowledge regarding human abilities, adaptabilities, and the environment.

For example, in attempting to accommodate the average reader, as opposed to the though-hiker, the PCT guide books (Wilderness Press; see page 277) describe terrain largely free of snow. Aspiring through-hikers realize that this terrain is much different when snowbound during early season, yet they often dramatize the extent of those differences. For example they might venture into the Sierra carrying far more stove fuel than needed, against the possibility that every water source might be frozen or buried in snow, and that they will have to melt snow to produce their water for drinking and cooking. They might carry also full-length climbing ropes, crampons, snowshoes, expedition tents, and heavy mountain boots—as though they were setting off to climb Annapurna.

USING FORESIGHT

Most sailplanes lack engines and propellers. To the novice this might seem such a major shortcoming as to obviate the functions and safety of the aircraft. What the novice might fail to realize is that by flying unburdened of the attendant weight and aerodynamic drag of engine and propeller, the sailplane can soar with an efficiency and splendor unattainable by conventional aircraft. How is it done? Not by using the brute force of gasoline power, which is noisy and expensive, but instead by using natural lift in the form of invisible thermals of upwelling drafts, which is silent and cost free. By tuning in to the forces of the natural environment and using them to best advantage, the glider pilot might soar for hours unshackled of the false notions of motorized humanity.

It can be much the same with backpackers. By forsaking the clumsy equipment, and using nature to best advantage, we too might soar high above those who trudge heavily burdened.

For example, during our PCT excursions Jenny and I were not equipped to camp on snow, mainly as we did not carry thick sleeping pads as bedding insulation. I believe that the weight and bulk of these pads undermines their advantages of warmth and so-called "comfort." In springtime the snow exists only at the higher elevations. Even so, the alpine landscape features occasional patches of bare ground, depending on the time of year, altitude and the direction of slope. So against what might be expected, while traversing the hundreds of miles of snowbound High Sierra during the early season we camped on bare ground each night.

Like glider pilots, we tuned into the environment, and sought those aspects that would work for us, rather than to bumble ahead and accept those that would not. Does that mean we camped in the valleys? No. Often, in the late evenings and all through the nights, alpine air flows katabatically down the drainages like invisible rivers, and the frigid air pools in the valleys. A fatal error sometimes made by lost hikers is to descend to the valley floors, thinking the nights will be warmer there. Nevertheless, even at altitude, it is extremely rare for the springtime ambient temperature to drop below 20°F. However, in high winds, if Jenny and I can't find shelter behind a landform or a patch of foxtail pines, we might readily abandon our camp-high regimen, and seek protection on the lower flanks.

Another factor in our favor is our policy of stealth camping, the description of which begins on page 177. We refrain from sleeping in designated campsites, where hundreds of predecessors have scraped away not only the pine cones and sticks, but also the forest litter and duff, and where both people and steel-shod beasts have compacted the soil. At pristine, virgin tent sites of our own discoveries, the natural forest litter and duff provide the perfect bedding, insulation, and drainage.

So in effect, rather than groping ahead wherever the trail leads and encamping in places recommended by guide books or rangers, we rely on our own attentiveness and foresight.

Thus, the type of gear needed depends largely on how we react to nature's variables. If the skies are foreboding, we keep an eye for possible sheltering features of the terrain and forests. As we travel the high crests we watch for escape routes that would lead us safely down, in the event of a storm. And the act of formulating contingencies is a conscious endeavor.

SHARING GEAR WITH A PARTNER

Those who hike with a partner might be able to reduce their loads considerably by sharing some of the gear. Obviously, which items can be shared depends on the nature of the partnership, on how tolerable each person is to encroachment of personal space, and to what extent each partner is willing to depend on the other.

Even the closest alliances might separate, whether intentionally or not. For some reason, partners that habitually venture ahead or lag behind are often prone to selecting the wrong fork in the trail and loosing the way. With this in mind, each person in a group would do well to maintain a certain autonomy by carrying various items essential for safety and well being. At the minimum, these would include a sealed packet of matches, money or traveler's checks, identification, food, a relevant map, and some type of shelter. If your partner carries the tent, then you would do well to carry the desserts.

REDUCING PACK WEIGHT

Typically, hikers cut the handle off a ½ ounce toothbrush, trim the margins off a few maps, toss out a few aspirin, and with sense of accomplishment they call the job done. This is incorrect thinking. When reducing gear weights we would do better to concentrate first in the more productive areas.

Weight carving begins in the dreaming and planning stages. As you peruse the shops and equipment catalogues, resist the temptation to indulge in superfluous gear. This results in a one to one weight reduction. Obviating a piece of equipment reduces its weight by 100%.

The second phase takes place at the store. Buying a 4½ pound backpack rather than a 9½ pound one saves a whopping 5 pounds in one fell swoop. Using a 4 pound tent rather than a 6 pound one saves another 2 pounds. Of course, one must remain aware of the compromise between weight and function. But function is often defined subjectively. And incidentally, one might be wise to take a kitchen scale to the store and to personally weigh the intended gear. Rarely are the published specs accurate.

The third phase entails selecting the lightest and most useful in the usual profusion of small items, such as the compass, knife, and so on.

The forth stage takes place in the field. It is the mailing home or ahead of any and all gear that has proven even vaguely unnecessary. Except for emergency goods, the possibility of an item someday proving necessary is inadequate justification for carrying it. If you are not using it, consider ridding your pack of it.

Incidentally, small items and bags that are bright in color might reduce the chances of your loosing them. It is impractical to leave things lying haphazardly about, at a rest stop or at camp. After using an item, make a habit of stowing it in its proper bag or pouch. And when setting off from camp or a rest stop, walk a few paces then turn around and inspect the area for anything you might have left behind.

THE TABULATION

We tend to take much of our equipment for granted. Whether or not it has proven worthy, we usually believe in it. And the marketer's hype burnishes our minds and only further saps our objectivity. Thus, during the planning stages, the prospective hiker would do well to weigh every piece of intended gear, and to tabulate the items and their weights in ounces and tenths of an ounce. Refer to the examples beginning on page 267. Seeing your gear in letters and numbers, black and white, might be to see it in an entirely different vein. And in all likelihood this exercise might bring to light a number of flagrant items.

And finally, remember the distance hiker's trail-worn adage: Don't set off from a resupply carrying spare change; spend it on snacks.

CLOTHING

Five wardrobes

While we are in it we bring it life.
When we have gone it no longer exists,
it fades into anonymity.
–Daphne Du Maurier

Before amassing your PCT wardrobe, consider that the rigors of trail life are extremely hard on clothing. For this reason, less expensive garments might be more practical. In fact, most of them you can make yourself, as described on page 194.

The Crest trekker needs clothing of five types. These are:

★ Lightweight, full length clothing to shield against the intense solar radiation encountered in the desert climes. These garments must ventilate well.

★ Medium weight clothes to be worn most of the time. Short pants are preferable with most hikers, but in some sections of the trail long pants would offer more protection for the legs against the inevitable bushwhacking (Lycra™ (DuPont) works well). Also, full-length Lycra pants offer protection from ticks.

★ Loose-fitting, lightweight, and highly breathable nylon shells that would thwart the onslaught of mosquitoes. The mosquito pants can also shield the legs from the wind.

★ A waterproof-breathable parka, for use during inclement weather.

★ A set of warmer clothing to don in the evening, and perhaps to use as ground insulation during the night.

Without exception, every garment should possess the ability to dry quickly. All would be of 100% synthetics, with one exception: the wool-blend socks. Even as much as one percent cotton in any garment is unacceptable. However, you might carry two items of cotton: a small hand towel, and a bandanna cut in half. One half might be used to clean the eye glasses, if any; and the other might be used as a dish towel.

The garments not being worn at the time are best stowed in a waterproof clothing bag, as described on page 197.

The parkas, jackets, sweaters and heavyweight shirts need to be fully opening. For the person hiking strenuously, maximum ventilation is of the utmost importance. The more skin exposed to the air, the more efficient. The full length front openings also permit the heavier garments to be worn backward, the advantages of which are described on page 167.

During warm weather, lightweight shirts of polyester might be ideal. These dry marvelously fast, and even after spending days compressed in the confines of the packs they are likely to emerge acceptably wrinkle free. This is an important consideration on resupply days.

In cool weather, one might wear a shirt made of a wicking fabric. These dry fairly readily, yet because they are thicker than polyester, they are considerably warmer. While wearing two wicking shirts inside a waterproof-breathable parka, and one pair of wicking pants inside a lightweight pair of mosquito-wind pants, one might be suitably equipped to trek through even the coldest early season weather in the High Sierra—as long as one keeps moving briskly, consumes an adequate supply of usable calories, and avoids exhaustion by making camp early.

When hiking briskly in hot or cold weather, the hiker will usually perspire freely, despite an attempt to regulate the outer insulation to suit the conditions. So during an extended trek, hiking in wet, or at least in noticeably damp clothing is an unavoidable fact of life. Yet wet clothing can subject the wearer to considerable risk. Hikers who suffer hypothermia often do so from wearing damp clothing. And it is an oversight to assume that danger occurs only at higher altitudes and in extremely cold and windy conditions. Hypothermia poses but minimal danger to the person exercising vigorously, especially when travelling uphill. At these times the well-fed body generates ample metabolical heat to discourage the malady's onset. But it is while resting during cold weather that one becomes immediately susceptible.

When the evening camp is reached, the prudent hiker will immediately divest him or herself of all working clothing, and don dry garments. After pitching the tent, the damp garments might then be hung under the awning. The matter is discussed at length beginning on page 162.

SHORTS

When the weather is fine and the bugs are largely absent, hikers might wear shorts (or perhaps skirts for the women). Unlike long pants, these garments don't pull at the knees with each step, resisting the motion slightly.

The type of shorts that work best depends on the person's body type. Thighs that rub together with each step are prone to a painful rash. And the problem is vastly compounded when the skin begins to sweat, as this increases the friction. In this case, the legs of short pants are likely to offer scant protection against chafe because they might climb, leaving the exposed thighs rubbing against each other. In this instance, Lycra shorts are superior. Properly fit, they cling to the thighs, and refuse to climb.

As an aside, if buying Lycra pants, consider avoiding those that feature reflective patches or stripes. These might ruin a number of your photographs as the light from the camera's flash bounces back and over-exposes the emulsion.

SOCKS

For hiking the PCT I recommend three weights of socks: ultra lightweight synthetic socks for hiking during warm weather, medium weight wool-blend socks for hiking during cool and wet weather, and heavier weight wool-blend socks suitable for use only in snowy conditions.

In warm climes the hiker might need 3 or 4 pairs of ultra thin socks of synthetic material. Usually, these can be purchased inexpensively at variety stores.

Wool has certain miraculous qualities in keeping feet warm when wet. (Refer to Footwear, page 63.) But the material is poorly resistant to abrasion. Thin socks of 100% wool might wear out very quickly. During our most recent PCT hike I included a few pairs of lightweight 100% wool socks in a few resupplies. On the trail, their average life span was 10 hours, after which time they began sprouting holes, which grew larger by the hour. This demonstrates the need to compromise our wool socks with a blend of more durable synthetics; preferably with more wool than synthetic.

We would do best to wear our socks for no more than one-third of a day before laundering them. The longer worn, the more they become sweat-mixed-with-dirt hardened and abrasive. And also, geometrically the more difficult they are to launder. The socks can be laundered in the tub filled with water, and without using soap. At those resupply stations that feature laundry facilities, we would avoid laundering wool-blend socks in hot water and detergent, which dissolves the natural oils. Instead, we might use cold water and Woolite™, or the equivalent, packed with our resupplies ahead of time.

Each pair of wool blend socks lasts me about two weeks of use, after which time they begin "fossilizing" into what resembles a pair of undersized mukluks.

COLORS

Because the activity of backpacking can generate tremendous metabolical heat, hikers must dress as lightly as the conditions permit, and perhaps in light colors. The darker the clothing, the more it will absorb the sun's radiation; but also, the less it will radiate body-heat. Dark colored fabrics seem to attract flying and biting insects far more than light colored ones do. Also, ticks are more easily discerned upon light colored clothing. Most ticks in southern California seem to be a light brown color; which might therefore be a poor color choice for use when hiking in that area.

EQUIPMENT
The basics versus the technojunk

The first step is the only one that costs

EXAMINING NEW GEAR

As an experienced backpacker, no doubt you own a fair amount of equipment. Yet you might feel that the border-to-border PCT trek will require more specialized gear; gear that is efficient, lightweight and durable. So you might pore through stacks of backpacking equipment catalogs, and visit the local shops to examine and try on loaded backpacks, compare sleeping bags, and to crawl into tents.

SALES PRESSURE

Enter the sales clerks. By the nature of their jobs they must appear energetic and knowledgeable. And indeed their expertise generally meets the needs of the vast majority of hikers. But as an aspiring distance hiker your requirements are unique. Many clerks are very capable. But some lack the appropriate knowledge, and might compensate with overbearing tactics. Relying on your own experience, combined with the parameters given in this *Handbook*, you are more likely to know what qualities you are looking for in your equipment. And you should be able to recognize any off-the-mark advice that might lead you astray. So be alert to any sales pressure, and use your own judgement.

THE DELUGE OF HYPE

You might find the variety of paraphernalia on the market dazzling, yet the more you study and compare, the more you might feel inundated by an avalanche of hype. Much of that gear, when examined closely, might seem inappropriately designed.

Another problem you might encounter is in holding up various manufacturer's claims to reality, and seeing the light of day come flooding through. Fierce competition engenders the practice of tagging equipment with advertising superlatives. These are often exaggerated and in some cases, misleading.

Here, we might do well to back off, take a deep breath, and remember that whatever equipment we select, it is only a means to enjoy the end. Never in the history of the PCT has a gear fanatic hiked the full distance. Most drop out of the game early as a result of their stoves sputtering, their packs leaking, or their $600 sleeping bags loosing loft.

Life is a matter of compromise; especially on the trail. So after you select those compromises and purchase the major items, you might wish to modify them, in some cases extensively. For many people, taking a knife to a newly purchased and expensive piece of equipment is not easy. But the ensuing chapters provide the necessary guidance.

SHUN BOLD LOGOS

The *Handbook* recommends against purchasing gear emblazoned with bold logos or name brands. Swiss Army and Victorinox knives would seem to exemplify the small, tasteful design logos that readily identify the pieces, but that don't taint the wilderness with their obtrusiveness. Advertising is out of place in the backcountry, be it on billboards, tents or water bottles. When we enter the sanctuary of the primeval regions, ours should be the freedom from the distractions of commercialism.

Increasingly, manufacturers are using bold logos to identify their products from among the myriad and often remarkably similar items of their competitors. This is because the features of their products, alone, are generally insufficient to draw attention to themselves. So the marketing staff attempts to compensate by using bold logos in their advertising. And generally, the more they advertise their bold logos the greater are their sales.

To a certain extent, the consumer is being duped. And I imagine that should the trend continue, then one day the photos in the outdoor magazines and books might be spangled with logo-advertising. Like race car drivers, backpackers might have emblems festooning their clothing, banners decorating their hats, and huge symbols embellishing their equipment.

Most backpacking stores feature merchandise emblazoned with bold logos. Conscientious buyers might note any offending items and the companies that manufactured them, and then tactfully protest to the manager. If enough people were to object, then the purchasing agents might turn their attention to other suppliers.

Edward Abbey suggested the benefits of sawing billboards down, but I favor attacking the problem at its root. Curtailing the demand might be our best method of affecting the supply.

THE BACKPACK

As the state of the art "advances," each year, the market sprouts backpacks that are more complicated, gaudy, weighty, unwieldy, and of course more expensive. The competition might be to our advantage only insofar that it encourages improvement. But which is being improved, the products or the marketing strategies? In point of fact, some of the contrivances nailed to packs these days are so singular that they patronize even the most stolid customer. Many of these devices fail to address the needs of the distance hiker, and they usually add weight in the process. Perusing today's fodder, we find expensive internal-frame packs weighing 7 to 9 pounds! And the pack weights specified might be as much as two pounds under the *actual* weights; such are the "variations in manufacture."

The distance hiker is trying to carve fractions of an ounce from the gear, and the pack manufacturers are adding them back in pounds.

QUALITIES BEST WALKED AWAY FROM

Before we examine ways of modifying the backpack, let's discuss what qualities are best. Better yet, let's first begin with a few qualities that might best be walked away from.

A hiker I once met complained bitterly that the shoulder strap had torn off his new backpack. No wonder: he was carrying a 75 pound load. Nevertheless, his pack was one of those designed such that the shoulder straps attach to the external frame with grommets and cotter pins. This arrangement usually holds together, but sometimes it does not.

Planning ahead, then, consider that as you set out from Kennedy Meadows and into the High Sierra, your load will probably be very heavy. And the dealer who guaranteed your backpack, whatever its type and construction, and who promised to repair it free of charge, will probably be thousands of miles distant. Oftentimes when a backpack comes apart, the owner will hitchhike out to civilization, make the appropriate phone call to heaven, as it were, order the replacement part, then wait for days-complaining (and of course resting and feasting) all the while. How convenient. In truth, if the pack fails, the accountability is most likely the hiker's. The manufacturer who supplied the arguably inferior equipment was merely responding to the demand for cheaply-made gear. The marketing staff writing the glossy but possibly prevaricating hype was only working for paychecks. And the people writing favorable magazine reviews, and their publishers, might have been acting under influence. So the reality of the situation is that the consumer is responsible for recognizing hype, for considering any advice from salespeople, and finally for exercising personal judgement when deciding to buy the product. Therefore, it might also be in the distance-hiker-consumer's best interests to improvise the repairs, when and where any problems occur. If a strap rips off, it can be tied or stitched back on. If a bag rips, it can be sewn or taped back together. If a frame breaks, it can be repaired temporarily by taping and lashing.

CUT AND WHACK

If there is one modern creation so innovative that it literally takes our breath away, it is the sternum strap. This strap constricts us where most of us need it the least, especially when breathing laboriously. I recommend pruning it.

Ditto the compression straps. Prune all but the ones on the sides, which might serve as clotheslines. To fashion a clothesline, remove the compression-strap buckle, cut the straps just long enough so that they overlap one inch where the buckle was (while the pack is fully loaded). Pin the straps in position against each-other, then sew them together.

Prune all plastic lashing pads. After referring to my chapter on honing a knife to a razor's edge, page 203, insert the blade beneath the lashing pad and carefully slice the stitching. Use the gizmos for little frisbees.

SHOULDER STRAP ADJUSTMENTS

Most of the more expensive backpacks feature complicated (heavier and vulnerable) arrangements for adjusting the upper shoulder strap attachments. If we can find a suitable pack lacking in this feature, but which fits to begin with, then so much the better. In most cases, we can achieve adequate adjustment by cinching or loosening the lifter straps. These effectively raise or lower the pack strap attachment points, and I think they were a considerable innovation. Once you have adjusted the lifters just right, (sometimes a long and fiddly process) you can leave them be. While hiking, I adjust mine only once every several weeks, as the high-technology buckles gradually slip.

COMPARTMENTS

Many internal-frame packs are compartmentalized horizontally. They feature a partition between the main loading area and the lower sleeping bag compartment. In theory the shelf allows stowing the heavier food above the sleeping bag. And the zippered, external access allows the sleeping bag to be removed, leaving the stores in place. The configuration affords good weight distribution, and permits transporting the heavy food items centrally in the pack. But beware: the arrangement is also well known for destroying expensive sleeping bags. The fabric shelf does not protect the sleeping bag from being squashed by the load above. In time, the load of provisions pressing down upon the compressed fill will **radically** diminish its loft. Judging practicality more important than convenience, I recommend surgically removing the shelf, and then placing most of the heavy food items into the cavernous hold. The load might not carry quite as well, but as the journey progresses into autumn, the hiker is likely to sleep much warmer. And the vulnerable access zipper(s) can rest in peace.

On top of the sleeping bag and as close to your spine as possible, stow any remaining items, such as water bottles, breakfast, and that magnum-size coulter pine cone you've been lugging the past few days as a present for Mum. But try to avoid packing heavy items above where the shoulder straps attach to the pack. Otherwise your pack might ride with less stability.

THE INFERNAL FRAME

An external or internal frame pack with its belt cinched tightly about the waist restricts the natural motions of the hiker's torso. As we walk, our pelvis moves in three ways: It swivels as though we are dancing the "twist," opposite the arms as they swing to and fro. It see-saws, one side up, the other down, then visa versa. And it shuttles side to side as our body weight shifts from one leg to the other. The motions of our shoulder girdle are similar to those of our pelvis, but in opposite phase. Our spine connects the two, and accommodates the opposition by bending and twisting. A backpack with its hip belt cinched is not so accommodating. Instead, it acts as a brace, counteracting the opposing motions. By inhibiting the natural mechanics of walking, the frame degrades our speed and saps our energy. Furthermore, by restraining our spine, which was designed for suppleness in absorbing the shocks of walking, the frame might increase our susceptibility to stress injuries.

VERTEBRAL ARTICULATION

The internal-frame pack allows greater vertebral articulation because in most cases (but not all) its frames are not connected. Again in most cases, the intervening material acts somewhat as a joint. Even so, the waist belt restrains the natural motion of the pelvis. If your internal-frame pack features hip belt stabilizing (read pelvis immobilizing) straps, consider pruning them.

Even then, unless your pack is loaded with more than 30 pounds or so, consider buckling its hip belt only rarely. You might walk more efficiently without the restraint.

DISTRESSINGLY COMFORTABLE

Claims that backpacks provide "load carrying comfort" are ubiquitous these days. Folks, when packs begin carrying heavy loads in comfort, cows might begin jumping over the moon. Ponderous loads and comfort don't mix, especially after the first several hundred miles. A well-designed pack does not make a 60 pound load feel like a 40 pound one; for no pack imbues its contents with gossamer qualities. Succinctly, a packload is a packload is a packload. Even had it's engineers designed the pack with mercurial computers generating reams of data, constructed it with newly discovered and exotic materials, outfitted it with every imaginable accoutrement, and embellished it with LED flashing sequins—a heavily loaded pack is an odious burden, an insult to the human musculoskeletal system. Ask anyone who's carried one 2½ thousand miles.

DONNING THE PACK

When your pack is of reasonable weight, here is a good method of shouldering it: Grasp it by its haul loop and by one strap, hoist it to bended knee and support it momentarily there. Then heft the pack to shoulder height and quickly turn your back into it, inserting an arm between the pack and a shoulder strap. The pack would now be hanging from your shoulder. As you walk away with it, insert the opposite *elbow* into the other strap loop and shoulder that strap. Finish bringing the arm through at your convenience.

Another method is to place the pack upright on a rock or log, sit before it, harness the straps, then stand up. However, this tends to limit your resting places to those that feature naturally situated objects.

If you are hiking with a partner, and if each of you are carrying a heavy pack, you might routinely help one-another shoulder your loads. Remember that our spinal disks are even more susceptible to injury if we allow ourselves to become dehydrated.

HIGH DUPERY

If you ever imagined that much of today's high tech is mostly hype, consider that even a $500.00 backpack pack requires a separate rain cover, and that even so, the sleeping bag and clothing will have to be carried in waterproof stowbags (see Sewing, page 194), or perhaps in plastic trash-bags. And consider also that after surmounting a hard-won mountain pass, you might stand triumphantly on its wind lashed crest as your pack's myriad and brightly colored adjusting straps flog you with a vengeance.

THE TENT

Many of today's backpacking tents are modern marvels. Even though they are comparatively light in weight, (3 to 4½ pounds) they offer remarkably good shelter against insects, rain, wind and cold—in that order of consequence.

However, most of them suffer two shortcomings: lack of ventilation, and doorways shaped to admit rain.

LACK OF VENTILATION

Many tents provide less than adequate ventilation. While sleeping we lose several pints of moisture through respiration and insensible perspiration. And warm air from our bodies rises, carrying the effusion of moisture with it. The tent's ceiling acts like a hot-air balloon, trapping the buoyant, warm and moist air. On a calm night, the ventilation gap between the fly and ground is essentially useless. Largely confined, much of the entrapped moisture then pervades our sleeping bags and clothing. And most of the remainder condenses on the fly's inner surface.

DOORWAYS SHAPED TO ADMIT RAIN

In trying to reduce the troublesome humidity, you might wish to increase the tent's ventilation by leaving its doorway open. Yet this is rarely possible during inclement weather. As you study prospective tents, consider the various configurations that would permit the rain to fall straightway into their open doorways. And imagine that you've spent days inside such a tent during a storm, and that its paucity of ventilation has ultimately *forced* you to open the door. In this scenario, rain streams down the tent-fly walls and pours into the open doorway, and in despair you zip the fly closed.

CONDENSATION

Along the PCT, condensation will form on the inside of most tent flies, most mornings. So before setting off early we will often be packing a wet fly. We will wad it with its driest part (if any) facing out, and stow it in the top of our pack, ready to withdraw at the first or second rest stop. If none of the fly is dry, and the day is without rain, we might wrap the wet fly in our pack cover. Depending on the weather, we will also avail ourselves the opportunities to air the sleeping bags each morning. Even if they are of synthetic fill, venting the absorbed moisture will reduce their added weight. And occasionally we will be seen hiking along while airing our sleeping bags draped round us like emperor's robes.

During my tenure as a professional wilderness instructor, we did not use tents. Instead, we slept beneath rectangular sheets of clear polyethylene. There were certain advantages and a few disadvantages to using these. Obviously the shelters were inexpensive. And being open to all sides, they permitted the best possible ventilation. So our gear remained much drier than had we been living in tents. However, the ventilation was also an advantage to the mosquitos. We tied lengths of alpine cord to the corners with sheet-bend knots, which adamantly resist ripping out. When the rain slanted down we simply lowered the tarps. One time we spent two weeks traveling the Continental Divide. There, powerful winds called for a little ingenuity in pitching the frail plastic tarps. We laid out our beds, set our packs between them, then covered the lot with a tarp. Then we placed smooth rocks all around the tarp's circumference, creating the ultimate in streamlined housing. To enter the structures, we used the standard spelunking techniques of squirming and crawling. And no matter how tightly we had rocked the tarp's perimeter, the gale-force wind provided adequate ventilation.

ALTERATIONS

During an uncommonly heavy deluge, (7 inches in 24 hours according to one source) Jenny and I were forced out of the Three Sisters Wilderness mainly because our tent's rain fly was not cut generously enough around its perimeter. Dollops of rain falling into puddles rebounded underneath the fly. They wet the tent, and eventually soaked our clothing and sleeping bag. This problem we later rectified by sewing a short weather skirt to the fly. The weather skirt allows the fly to be staked out during periods of heavy rain, rather than being affixed to the pole ends. This reduces the problem of splashing water entering the tent, and it increases ventilation markedly. We also sewed a lightweight awning over the doorway, so that the fly's doorway could remain open during rainy weather. See Sewing, page 194. When we want to maximize the tent's ventilation we fold the awning back and secure it to the aft tent pegs. We also strung a pair of permanent clotheslines inside the tent, running the length of its ceiling.

SEAM SEALING

After you buy a tent or other "waterproof" garment that is not factory seam sealed, you become an unpaid employee of the company charged with the tedious and time consuming job of sealing the seams.

Incredibly, most commercial seam sealing compounds harden and begin flaking uselessly away within a few weeks after application, especially if exposed to strong sunlight. This is not an encouraging sight, viewing the results of your ten hours work and ten dollars of compound chipping away freely of its own accord. And speaking from experience, the act of removing the nefarious compound in order to begin the task anew is even more discouraging.

I've tried most compounds on the market, and have found only two of them to be effective:

* AquaSeal(R) Repair Adhesive and Sealant *for Neoprene*, from the McNett Corp, Bellingham, WA. Curiously, a number of sealing products bear the name AquaSeal, yet they are quite different. The only one I've found that works is the above.

* SealCoat™ from Chouinard (Black Diamond) in Ventura, CA.

While applying the sealing compound, stretch the seam in tension, as though trying halfheartedly to pull it apart. This exposes more of the stitching. Apply the compound *sparingly*, rub it in using a match stick, then wipe away any excess. Work only for 10 or 15 minute intervals, allowing your respiratory system to recover and the compound's solvents to evaporate. Seal both sides of the seams. Twenty four hours later apply a second coat. Again, stretch the seams and apply the sealant sparingly. But this time do not wipe away the excess. Forty eight hours afterwards rub talc into the seams. This will prevent them from adhering together when the garment or tent is compressed within its bag.

In camp, you can improvise a seam sealing repair using a dab of lip balm, peanut butter, or etc.

TENT STAKES

Tents that are not free standing are generally lighter than their free standing counterparts. However, they usually require much more substantial stakes. In most cases these stakes must be purchased separately. Thus, the weight of these stakes must be added to that of the tent. Consequently, what is gained might be lost.

A free-standing tent is generally more aerodynamic than its non-free standing counterpart. Thus, it might place less strain on its stakes. And because of its design configuration, it generally requires minimal staking. Some hikers find this a tremendous advantage, particularly on pumice or sandy soil where the arrangement lessens puttering about camp.

For free-standing tents, and along the PCT, the skewer type stakes generally work well. These are made of hardened aluminum 2024 (T6) rod, 3/16 inch diameter, and bent nearly into a ring at their tops.

Regardless of your tent's genre, I recommend permanently fitting 3½-foot lengths of parachute cord to the tent fly, one at each of its stake loops. In ground so loose that the stakes won't hold, you can lead the guy lines out to bushes, limbs, rocks, or to sticks weighted down with rocks or buried laterally in the dirt.

TENT RECOMMENDATIONS

The *Handbook* does not recommend specific tents because the choices are myriad, and with the passing of each year, improved tents are bound to appear on the marketplace. The hiker needing a single-person tent could choose one weighing 3 pounds or less. Add another pound of tent for a second person. And remember that the domicile need not be commodious. The smaller it is, generally the stronger and warmer. Also though, the smaller the tent, the less ventilation it usually provides for, and the more condensation it might foster. In the long term, for example, waterproof-breathable bivy bags are said to be sweat sacks.

GROUND SHEET

The function of the ground sheet is to protect the waterproof tent floor against abrasion, dirt and pitch. I recommend the All-weather Sportsman's Blanket, manufactured by Metallized Products. It is a four-layer sandwich comprising plastic film, aluminum, fiber scrim, and plastic film. One side is a reflective silver color, and the other a ripstop-like plastic, which comes in various colors. Rescue orange might be a good choice, in case you need to assist with a rescue. But we would avoid airing the ground sheet in the open, orange side up. An aviator might misconstrue such an act as a plea for help.

At home, spread the ground sheet, pitch the tent on it, then draw a line on the ground sheet, close around the tent's perimeter. Cut away the sheet's extraneous material outside the tent floor's footprint. Otherwise, this might collect the water running off the fly, and channel it beneath the tent.

In short order, pine needles will probably riddle the ground sheet in pin holes. But these don't seem to lessen the sheet's performance. If so motivated you might repair any larger holes or tears using duct tape, which you could use also to mend mosquito netting, the tent fly, and waterproof bags.

THE SLEEPING BAG

Sleeping bags filled with goose down, synthetic techno-wonderfill, kapok, or crumpled newspapers would all offer comparable insulation for a given thickness. Regardless of the type of fill material, the warmth of a sleeping bag depends almost entirely on its loft. I use the word "almost," because design indiscretions such as sewn-through seams can reduce the bag's effective loft. However, despite various claims there is no way yet known to *increase* the effective loft.

The matter is discussed further in the "Cold!" chapter, page 162. Summarily, low density insulating materials act by creating minute pockets of stagnant air. It is the air that insulates, not the materials. The materials themselves neither conduct nor insulate appreciably. If the air is compartmentalized into volumes of 1/16" across or less, it will provide the insulation we require.

THE TEMPERATURE RATING FORMULA

By measuring the sleeping bag's approximate half-loft we can readily determine the bag's temperature rating. The Jardine formula is

$$TR = 100 - (40 * L)$$

TR is the temperature rating in degrees Fahrenheit. L is the sleeping bag's half-loft: it is its thickness, in inches, covering the sleeping person. The half-loft is multiplied by 40, then the result is subtracted from 100.

While ensconced within your sleeping bag, poke a measuring ruler from the outside, vertically downward until it contacts your body. How far the fill material compressed is a measure of it's thickness, or half-loft.

Suppose your bag is 2 inches thick above your body. Plugging that into the formula gives, TR = 100 - (40 * 2"). Multiplying: TR = 100 - 80. Thus, regardless of what it is made of, a bag featuring an upper-layer thickness of 2" would provide adequate insulation in 20°F weather. Again I qualify this: any sewn-through seams or other design oversights will reduce its temperature rating. And of course, each individual hiker *reacts* differently to night-time temperatures.

To leave the face and neck exposed might be to degrade the temperature rating of an otherwise effective sleeping bag. I recommend that during cold weather the hiker wear a skullcap of wicking fabric pulled down over the face. The cap is detailed on page 196.

TEMPERATURE RATING REQUIREMENTS

For those hiking the PCT, I recommend using a sleeping bag rated from 10°F to 20°F. However, one must note how a bag's temperature rating decreases *radically* as the bag's loft diminishes throughout its life span, however abbreviated. Again, the half-loft of this ideal bag is 2" or slightly more. The full loft, (the bag's thickness from the ground) would be 4" if the bag were filled equally top and bottom. But many sleeping bags of synthetic fill contain less loft beneath than above. The theory is that the ground pad compensates. Notwithstanding, reducing bottom thickness affords tremendous advantages to the manufacturer, who thinks in terms of mitigating production costs, increasing profits, and advertising lesser weight (and supposedly more efficient) bags for a given temperature rating.

LOFT DEGRADATION

Reduction of loft is a major consideration with sleeping bags. The first time you ram pack your new sleeping bag into its stuff-sack it loses perhaps 8% of its loft. Forever. Those imprudent enough to use a compression stuff sack can bid an additional 10% goodby. That 18% loss is the damage incurred during the first occasion. Add another 3% for each subsequent hyper compression.

Distance hikers must be extremely careful to preserve the loft in their sleeping bags. Otherwise they might eventually sleep cold, especially near the end of their journeys in the North Cascades, during the first brushes with early winter. For best results, use the largest stuff sack practicable, refrain from stowing heavy gear or provisions on top of the bag, and resist the temptation to use the stowed sleeping bag as a bench.

THE SLEEPING BAG USED AS A BLANKET

Many years ago I used a mummy-style bag. In it, a few hours after falling asleep I would typically awake with overheated feet, and an urge to claw out of the bag. I solved the problem by placing a water jug in the foot of my bag each night. As my feet began radiating excess heat, the water absorbed it. Thus, in the morning I would awake with comfortable feet and with a bottle of water not frozen.

Then one day I discovered the advantages of opening the bag and draping it over myself like a blanket. After sleeping like this for awhile I came to realize that I had been trying to adapt to sleeping in far too much insulation. I suffered the misconception that the confines of the sleeping bag were mandatory and to a certain extent my body had adjusted to the oven-like environment.

Sleeping underneath the open bag necessitated lying on the ground pad. At first this seemed unpleasant, but then I came to realize that it was merely unfamiliar.

With the passing of years I began noticing that as the ground pad lost much its loft in the course of a summer, I slept no colder. Perhaps I was unconsciously adapting by selecting campsites that featured natural ground insulation. During Jenny's and my PCT hike of 1987 we began the trip with a torso sized pad of 3/8" ensolite. By the end of the summer the pad had become flat as a crêpe. Still, we slept as warmly as ever.

As an aside, I would like to dispel the notion that we had toughened ourselves to the cold. Nothing could be farther from the truth. The rigors of distance hiking deplete a person's reserves, and one of the first qualities degraded is body warmth. Many times on our long hikes we would encounter day-hikers far from the trailhead and lightly dressed in short sleeves and short pants, where in contrast we were dressed in long shirts, pants and parkas!

Sleeping beneath an open bag has advantages for couples. A man and wife sleeping together need carry only one sleeping bag. When Jenny and I first began experimenting with the technique, we fabricated a couplet sheet that zipped to the sleeping bag and acted as its lower layer. The disadvantages with this system were many, and after making several prototypes we finally discovered that we could do better by dispensing with the couplet. The only adjustment necessary was a bit of mental reprogramming. The knack is in learning to roll over without dragging the sleeping-bag blanket off the other person, or knocking it off yourself. One learns to roll over a little more gracefully. And if a draft is felt somewhere, the edge of the bag can be tucked in a little closer.

The main requirement with this system is that the bag feature, not necessarily a full-length zipper, but one that extends at least to the foot area. And incidentally, an opening bag is much faster drying when exposed to the warm sun; and this is an important feature for the distance hiker. Drying time is considerably lessened also if the bag is a dark color, both inside and out.

In order to use the open-bag blanket system, the sleeping bag must be symmetric in its upper and lower halves. Most bags are of the mummy style, and are therefore not appropriate for draping over oneself like a blanket. For two people sleeping beneath an open mummy bag, one person would have to sleep closer toward the head of the tent than the other, and would therefore suffer the brunt of continual drafts at the shoulders. The other person might feel dwarfed. Where there is just one person, the troublesome mummy flap would smother the face, and when the person rolls over, the flap might fall aside, exposing the head, neck and shoulders to the chilling draft.

Bags with less fill material in the lower portion, beneath the person's body, are also unsuitable for using blanket style. One half of the sleeping-bag blanket would contain the standard 1/3 less insulation than the other.

INTERNAL BAFFLES

Most down-filled sleeping bags are constructed with lateral baffles that lack side-to-side compartments. At least some manufacturers would like us to believe that this feature is an asset. They suggest that on a warm night we can shake some of the filler from the top to the sides, and on a cold night, visa versa. In theory, perhaps. In fact, perhaps not. When first you remove a down bag from its stuff-sack, the semi compressed down roves about the insides as gravity dictates. If you use the bag mummy style, and if you crawl into it before the down has had time to fully expand, some of the down is likely to shift uselessly athwartships. This is especially true as the bag ages and loses more of its loft.

Compromising, we buy less expensive gear and improvise as necessary. In this case, each evening before retiring we shake the down bag laterally so as to coax some of the insulation away from the edges (of necessity rather than preference).

THE DOWN BAG

Among the fill materials currently in use, high-fill goose down offers the least weight for the greatest loft. For a sleeping bag rated at 20°F, the weight difference between down and Hollofil insulations, to site one example, is about one pound.

Such a weight difference is of considerable consequence when carried over two and a half thousand miles, especially considering that the extra weight of the synthetic insulation gains the user nothing, 99% of the time.

The current genre of innovative synthetic fills might be slight improvements over Hollofil; nevertheless, they are still heavier than down. Beware the manufacturer's claims of "lightweight performance," and remember the half-loft formula. Beware also of any claims that certain innovative fill materials have greater "effective loft."

The main disadvantages of down are its expense, and its loft degradation when wet. Were I *planning* to sit out a mountain storm I'd choose a bag containing synthetic insulation. I would recommend that inexperienced hikers use this type of bag. And I do not recommend down insulation for use in wet climates, such as those typically encountered along the Appalachian Trail.

I see two prerequisites for using a down bag along the PCT. First, one's tent must feature a suitable awning. See the end of the chapter Rain, page 165, for instructions on drying wet gear during rainy weather. Second, the down-filled sleeping bag, or any other type for that matter, must be protected in a waterproof stuff-sack.

Actually, the down-filled sleeping bag must be protected as though your life depends on it. If the bag becomes quite damp, don't worry; it will still retain your body warmth. But if it becomes soaked through, then you can start worrying, for it will have lost a great deal of its insulation.

Whatever type of bag you choose, you will benefit by carrying it in a waterproof bag. The chapter Sewing, page 194, details how to make one. Failing that, you can buy a waterproof stuff-sack. A single-person down-filled sleeping bag rated to 10°F fits into a sack measuring about 8" diameter by 20" in length. Nevertheless, my homemade variety is half the weight of the commercial ones and a fraction of the cost.

Lastly, you can place a plastic bag inside your stuff-sack, and twist its end closed. The plastic adds considerable weight, but at least it is easily replaced, if a spare is included in an occasional resupply parcels.

We would refrain from carrying an easily punctured waterproof stowbag exposed to the elements, particularly those elements bearing thorns and pointed sticks. If your backpack carries the sleeping bag externally, then you will need to protect the bag, perhaps by rolling your foam pad round it. If you use an expensive and heavy self-inflating (read vulnerable) pad, you must protect both the pad and the sleeping bag stuff-sack. Nevertheless, should either tear or rip, you can effect the necessary repairs using duct tape. If the stuff-sack becomes perforated, you could insert a plastic bag liner at the next opportunity. Suffice it to say, though, that the internal frame pack offers greater protection all around.

WHY DO THEY MAKE SLEEPING BAGS OF GORE-TEX?
(BECAUSE IT'S THERE.)

Sleeping bags made of a micro-porous outer shell are supposedly lighter and warmer. However, they retain far more moisture of insensible (at rest) perspiration. This moisture is then trapped within the insulation. Some manufacturers "solve" this problem by recommending we carry a (heavy) vapor liner. Nevertheless, because these sleeping bags are slower drying, their retained moisture adds weight and diminishes the insulation. Therefore, their overall efficiency seems less. I see little if any advantage to these hyper expensive bags.

THE MATTRESS

Fatigue is the distance hiker's most effective mattress. The footwear chapter, beginning on page 63, suggests why sleeping on the ground is more healthful. For most of the same reasons that shoes are probably detrimental to our feet, mattresses might be likewise to our bodies.

During our two hikes of the PCT Jenny and I slept on a torso-length sheet of ⅜ inch foam, which grew thinner with the passing of weeks. But I've come to relinquish even this as generally unnecessary. When ground insulation is required we now sleep on spare clothing.

MISCELLANEOUS EQUIPMENT

THE WRIST WATCH

If you choose to wear a watch, consider that the band must be long enough to accommodate your wrist as it swells while you are hiking. The difference in the size of my wrist, from when I arise in the mornings at home, to when I retire at night during a through-hike, is 4 holes on the watch band. Also consider that a plastic watch band might irritate the wrist. It might be a good idea to replace the standard band with one riddled in holes, which would improve the ventilation.

During a long hike I like to rise at the first *hint* of dawn. And I have found that I sleep much better knowing that an alarm will awake me at the proper time. In the pre-dawn darkness, if I wear the watch on my wrist, only rarely will I hear its alarm. So instead, each evening when retiring I unlatch the watch and place it near my head.

During our training hikes I use the stopwatch timing feature to measure the duration of our forays. This data I enter into our training log. Also during the training hikes I use the watch's countdown timer, set at 10 minutes. At each rest stop I activate the timer. When the watch beeps, I know it is time to resume walking. This is the recommended mental programming against the propensity to dither at rest stops. However, while on the actual hikes I do not use the timer.

Summary of desirable features:
* Waterproof to at least 6 feet.
* Must show month and date, and day of the week
* Must feature an alarm and a night light.

THE COMPASS

Here's how to determine whether your compass features a quality, minimal-friction bearing. Lay the compass on a table. After the needle has settled, *slowly* rotate the compass base. Determine at what angle the bearing releases and allows the needle to return to magnetic north. Repeat the test in the other direction. If the discrepancy is more than one or two degrees in each direction, (two to four degrees altogether) then consider buying a new compass.

I prefer the types embellished only with the features I need. These are two: a rotating housing and a sapphire jewel bearing.

Even the compass featuring a built-in declination adjustment is of little benefit to the person who cannot remember whether the adjustment is set correctly or not. The problem is that most hikers are never quite sure whether to add or subtract the local magnetic declination. But my mnemonic should settle the matter: Along the PCT, (and the CDT) the compass needle points a little east of true north, as though honoring the AT. On the AT the needle points a little west of true north, as though honoring the PCT.

Incidentally, not everyone knows how to locate north without using a compass. But all hikers should. At night, the two end stars of the Big Dipper, lying generally perpendicular to the handle, point to Polaris: the North Star. Imagine water rushing out of the dipper (down, sideways, or up; depending on the dipper's orientation at the time). And imagine the water traveling across the sky about five times the height of the dipper, to the not-so-bright star, Polaris. From Polaris, drop an imaginary line vertically down to the horizon. There lies true north.

During daylight hours, by attuning our awareness to the sun's position in the sky, and far more significantly, to the direction of shadows as the day waxes and wanes, we will begin to develop an intuitive sense of direction. This is an extremely beneficial skill.

A sighting mirror more than doubles the accuracy of field bearings taken by hand. But the PCT hiker rarely, if ever, requires this degree of accuracy. However, all hikers should know how to take accurate hand-bearings. Those that do not might refer to a book on orienteering.

The two compasses (that I know of) with my recommended features are the Silva type 7NL, (which, when fitted with its lanyard weighs a mere 0.7 ounces) and its clone the Suunto A1000, which weighs nearly the same.

THE KNIFE

Jenny and I were sitting with three hikers near the base of a beautiful little waterfall in the North Cascades. As they swung the conversation to packweight and daily mileages, one women happened to withdraw an astonishingly large folding knife, which she then used to slice a small chunk of cheese. "We don't hike very far each day," she said. And then, unthinkingly, "We're carrying heavy packs, and we just take it easy." (!)

Why does the size of a camper's knife play an important role (second only to that of the backpack) in substantiating the bearer's image? Myself, I carry the diminutive Victorinox Classic. With it's tiny blade I sever cord, slice vegetables, whack resupply boxes down to size for returning items in, and cut packaging tape to length. The scissors I use for cutting adhesive tape, 2nd Skin, moleskin, hangnails and my finger and toenails. I round my trimmed finger nails with the knife's file. And I use the tweezers to remove any slivers and the very occasional wood tick. All this utility costs a mere 0.8 ounces. And I consider that a bargain.

To the knife I have fitted a 7 inch doubled-length of bright-orange parachute cord. This helps locate the wee tool within the confines of the ditty bag, and helps retain the knife in captivity, lest some pre-dawn morning it should sink into oblivion among the pine needles. See page 203 for instructions on sharpening the blade.

WATER BOTTLES

Each PCT hiker might carry a pair of 1-liter water bottles. (Wide-mouth bottles are generally heavier than narrow-mouth ones.) Additionally, south of Cascade Summit each one- or two-person party might carry a water bag with a capacity of two or three gallons. An example would be the Fresh Water Carrier, from Basic Designs. Its capacity is 3 gallons; its weight: 4.1 oz.

The water bottles might best be used for containing filtered water, and the water bag for unfiltered water. The water bag, and the lids of the hard water bottles, must be de-bugged every few weeks—for example by filling them with a solution of iodine, or chlorine bleach. In either case, when the bottles begin growing stubborn splotches of black mold they can be scoured by adding some filtered water and a fistful of clean, formerly dry sand collected away from the trail and water sources. Take care to keep the sand off of the threads, as it might score the seal. Screw on the lid and shake the bottle vigorously. Then rinse the sand out with more filtered water.

Before setting out on the long hike, you would do well to test your water bottles and bag for leakage. This is done by filling them to capacity, and applying pressure. If the plastic bladder can be removed from its nylon shell, do so. Then fill the bladder with water and press firmly against it by hand. Inspect its surface and seams for leakage. If it passes the test, re-assemble it into its protective nylon bag. To test a water bottle, fill it with water, place it on its side on the floor, and place some of your weight on it. If you detect the slightest leakage, return it as defective.

Refer to page 98 for directions on how to open and close a water bottle with a simple twist of the wrist.

MACE

Women hikers traveling alone or with other women might consider carrying mace. The canister can be clipped unobtrusively to the clothing or backpack strap by day, and kept within easy reach during the nights.

We have a friend who, while sailing among the Caribbean isles, was stabbed with a machete. Still functioning, barely, he ridded the midnight assailant from his yacht by spraying him in the face with mace. Needless to say, our friend is a staunch advocate of the little canisters.

SUN HAT

Most people who spend considerable time outdoors have learned the necessity of protecting their skin from the sun's ultraviolet radiation, which in time can induce small patches of hyper sensitive skin. My ears are particularly vulnerable. Having found that a hat does not afford them the needed protection, I often apply skin-colored adhesive strips. Nevertheless, a hat most suitable for backpacking would feature an extra wide brim. And preferably it would also fold to fit inside the backpack.

Sun screen is also of benefit when applied liberally every few hours.

STOVE

When selecting a stove from among the bewildering variety, consider first the fuels in common use.

＊Generally, white gas or Coleman-type fuel is not available en route. And the postal service and the United Parcel Service do not normally handle these volatile liquids. But these fuels are very similar to unleaded gasoline; meaning that you could refill a fuel bottle, and much less expensively, at virtually any gasoline station. However, of the 30 resupply stations listed in the *Handbook's* Resupply chapter, 10 of them lack gasoline stations in their areas.[1] Still, one could anticipate the stations that lack gasoline, and carry additional fuel from the previous ones.

＊Kerosene is quasi-legal to mail. However, many stoves that use it are heavy, and known for producing soot and consuming time and patience.

＊LPG canisters are illegal to air mail. And most mail now travels by air.

＊Stoves that burn natural materials are illegal to use in some backcountry areas and unsafe in most others. This is because while breaking camp in haste, hikers might carelessly dump the smoldering shards onto the forest litter.

In addition to the prospective stove's weight, also of consideration are the weights of its primer and primer container, the weights of its fuel and

---

[1] The stations that **might** not sell unleaded gasoline are Campo, Mt. Laguna, Vermillion Valley Resort, Echo Lake Resort, Burney Falls Camper Services, Hyatt Lake Resort, Crater Lake, Cascade Summit, Olallie Ranger Station, and the Timberline Lodge.

fuel container(s), and the weights of its stowbags and maintenance kits if any.

COOK POT

Two people hiking together might share a 2-quart aluminum kettle with a lid, such as the one made by the Metal Ware Corp. A person cooking independently might need only a 1 quart kettle.

LIDDED BOWL

These are used both for eating and drinking from, and for carrying and storing food. I favor the ones made by Rubbermaid; they are cylindrical in shape and have a capacity of 3 cups. One of them fits neatly inside the above 2 quart cookpot.

SKIS, SNOWSHOES, ICE AXE, CRAMPONS, AND ROPE

Refer to the chapter on snow travel, page 142. Summarily, most hikers would consider carrying an ice axe the entire tri-state distance. My ice axe recommendations are the Cassin (Flash), which weighs 18.25 oz. and measures 25.5" by 9.0"; and the Camp (Jolly), weighing 18 oz. and measuring 25.5" by 9.25".

ZIPPERS

The sawing action of zipper teeth might wear out a coated aluminum slider in a single season's heavy use. A worn slider will slide, but it will not zip. To temporarily cure this malady in the field, reduce the size of the zipper slider's aft-end by crimping it. In lieu of pliers, you might use a pair of rocks. The frequently used zippers, for example on pack pockets and tent netting-doors, might best feature stainless steel or nickel plated sliders, which endure far longer.

MULTIPLE USE

Another technique for reducing gear weight is to use each piece of equipment for more than a single purpose, as illustrated below:

* The hand towel: used for mopping dew off the tent fly, wiping the tent floor, wiping sweat from the brow, scrubbing the body, and when in an aggressive mood, for whacking mosquitoes and biting flies.
* The collapsible Tub: a vessel for laundering clothing, washing hair, transporting water to a distant camp and storing it there, containing water for pump-filtering, and for settling sediment.
* The flashlight: used to illuminate the trail after dusk or before dawn; used while writing in the journal and studying the guide book

at night; and used to identify any pillaging creature and making certain they lack quills before shoeing them away.

* The ice axe: qualifies as fire-fighting tool—satisfying any forest service's equipment requirement; used to dig daily cat holes, to chop steps and to self-arrest; and used occasionally as a tent stake.

FOOTWEAR

They don't know it yet,
but boots might soon become an endangered species

It is better to wear out one's shoes than one's sheets.
—Genoese proverb

To my knowledge, hiking does not cause injuries. Even two-and-a-half-thousand miles of hiking might be harmless. What causes the injuries are the footwear, the load carried, the severe dehydration, the lack of calf-limbering exercises, and the humiliating falls onto the buttocks.

THE MODUS OPERANDI

Our feet were designed to walk shoe-less. How ironic, then, that our footwear is one of the more crucial items in our backpacking inventory. But consider for a moment the disadvantages of wearing shoes or boots.

FOOTWEAR-RELATED STRESS INJURIES

With each footfall, imbalanced pressures are exerted on the structures of the foot. These are transferred, in turn, to the ankle, leg, knee, hip, and up into the lower back. Walking barefoot, these imbalanced forces are exerted by the irregularities of the terrain, but because they vary with each step they tend to nullify one another. A slightly ill fitting shoe or boot transmits a fairly unchanging irregularity with every step. And like a fine-toothed rasp slowly abrading a timber, the continual application of the same imbalanced force might cause a gnawing at the inner workings of the hiker's lower limbs. If the imbalance is pronounced and incessant, and if the affected body parts are unable to adjust and provide the necessary cushioning and protection, an injury might result.

FURTHER DISADVANTAGES

Footwear of any type prevents our feet from carrying their loads naturally. It might twist the bones and toe nails, over-stress the muscles and ligaments, abrade the skin, elevate the temperature, obstruct the ventilation and the sunlight—and consequently encourage fungus to proliferate.

Another disadvantage of footwear is that the soles are normally flat and wider than the soles of our feet, which are curved. On irregular and inclined terrain, flat soles exert a detrimental leverage that torques our ankles many times more than were we walking on the same terrain barefoot, or wearing minimal footwear such as moccasins.

HIKING BAREFOOT

As we walk barefoot, the nerves in the soles of our feet provide our brains with a wealth of tactile information. This sensory data augments our spatial orientation, and as a bonus, it brings us more in tune with the environment. In fact, there is something neolithically sensual about hiking barefoot in a quiet, needle-carpeted forest, on a trail of soft dirt, or on glacier-polished and sun-warmed granite. Those who have not tried it are missing a great deal.

In each of our feet are 126 ligaments that interconnect 26 bones. These have marvelous abilities to adjust to irregular terrain by shifting side to side, twisting, and flexing. But by wearing footwear we restrain much of this beneficial give-and-take action. Footwear therefore increases not only our fatigue, but our risks of sustaining various stress injuries.

Practically every day during a through-hike I remove my shoes and hike barefoot for half-an-hour or so. This is my recommended procedure for toughening ailing feet, both internally and externally. If I am experiencing leg pains, quite likely they will disappear after I walk only a short distance barefoot. Therefore, it seems that those pains are caused, not by the interminable hiking, but mainly by the footwear. So walking barefoot regularly might serve not only as a preventative measure, but perhaps as something of a cure.

In addition to the danger of a stubbing or puncturing injury that could compromise the hike, though, the main drawback of walking barefoot is how substantially it mitigates one's pace. The person walking barefoot must place the feet carefully, and with much less force—almost daintily. Footwear allows one to stomp along the trail with great vigor; and no doubt this jouncing accounts for a percentage of hiking-related injuries.

Assiduously though, when walking barefoot we need to watch each step. Years ago I was hiking barefoot up the calf-deep river coursing the Narrows, in Zion National Park. Gazing at the box-canyon's towering rim, I accidentally kicked a barely-protruding rock. And the painful reminder persisted for two years!

THE BENEFITS OF FOOTWEAR

Primarily because we have misshapen our feet somewhat and weakened our ankles enormously by wearing shoes most of our lives, we must wear protecting footwear most of the time. The artificial cushioning allows us to hike faster over rugged terrain; but again, we need this cushioning probably because throughout our lifetimes our shoes might have weakened the structures of our feet. On the trail, our feet also require protection from sharp rocks, cactus spines, pointed sticks, needle-tipped pine cone scales, and some types of pine needles. Our toes require protection against inadvertently kicking rocks, roots, and stumps. The soles of our feet benefit from the footwear's insulation against snow and frosted ground, and from the searing desert sand. And no doubt they find advantage in the biological barriers against certain parasitic microorganisms that might auger into the bottoms of our feet, for example when unavoidably we step on manure.

DEVICES OF RESTRAINT

Footwear protects our feet and enables us to hike faster, but it also extracts a great deal of energy by restraining the natural biomechanics of our motions, and rhythms of our pace. The interconnections of our ankles and feet bones were designed as working, flexing "joints." With each step they bend and twist. Would we consider wearing supportive and restraining devices on our hips? Of course not. Why, then, do we wear them on the working, articulating joints of our ankles and feet? Simply stated, stiff-soled, high-topped boots seriously compromise the necessary action of these joints. Moreover, the backs of boots and some types of shoes press against the achilles tendons with every step, possibly causing increasingly painful tendonitis.

DISPELLING THE HIKING BOOT MYTH

Most backpackers believe that while hiking rugged terrain they need to wear heavy hiking boots. But I submit that this is a misconception based almost entirely on vogue.

Years ago I hiked hundreds of alpine miles while wearing boots. Sometimes I carried a pair of running shoes to wear around camp, and eventually I began experimenting with hiking in the shoes. This was something unheard of at the time. But the arrangement proved so successful that in the course of a few years I had grown weary of lugging the boots in my pack, where I had been keeping them in reserve. Since then I've hiked most of the PCT twice while wearing running shoes. I use the word "most" because I often wore fabric boots in the High Sierra, in order to trounce steps into the snow while surmounting the passes.

The revolution is not mine alone. Invariably, the occasional shoe-hikers I have met were enthusiastic about having shed their energy-sapping boots.

Most backpackers believe also that while carrying a heavy pack they need to wear stout boots for ankle support. Such logic could be carried only slightly higher to suggest that we use crutches for hip and lower back support. *Indeed, we might have weakened our ankles in the process of living inactive lives, but in all likelihood they were designed to sustain the weights of our bodies and our loads, and to carry us over rough terrain mile after thousands of miles. And in most cases they would readily do so if first strengthened during a pre-hike training regimen.*

Granted, for the individual who spends a great deal of time abutt, and who ventures a short distance into the rugged mountains only a few days a year, stout boots offering maximum ankle support and sole protection might be of benefit. I'm not recommending that the inert person don running shoes and a huge pack, and venture into the High Sierra. Such inattentiveness might be a good recipe for a sprained ankle. But then neither am I suggesting that this person will excel at distance hiking, without first embracing an initially gentle but increasingly rigorous 6 month training program.

Prospective PCT hikers might imagine that because they live reasonably active lives they don't need to train for the long hike. Those who insist on this unrealistic attitude might do best wearing lightweight boots, or perhaps mid-weight, low-cut hiking shoes: boots that stop short of the ankles. Keep in mind that the less a person trains for the long hike, the less capably his or her muscles will wrestle with heavy boots. And boots, high or low topped, generally lack the sole cushioning of a quality running shoe.

FOOTWEAR INERTIA

Besides restraining the natural articulation of the interconnecting members of the ankles and feet, by their mass, boots resist the hiker's exertions at making headway. Imagine you are sitting at a rest stop watching a hiker ambling past. You might notice that, although the hiker is moving ahead at a steady pace, each foot is starting and stopping with each step. Let's examine briefly the kinetics: After the foot taking the step forward contacts the ground, it decelerates to a stop, aided by ground friction. But in order for that foot to take the next step, the forward muscles of the leg are put into action to accelerate the foot ahead, to a speed of roughly twice that of the hiker's. On level ground, the muscular force needed to accelerate the foot depends on the mass of leg, foot and footwear. The heavier the boot, the more energy is required to sustain this continual stopping and starting. To bring the effects into focus, consider that during a day's march of, say, 20 miles, the hiker takes roughly **45,000 steps**. After a long day's march, a pair of boots often feel like a pair of encasing concrete blocks; and for good reason: this is not the fatigue of hiking, but that of wrestling with massive and uncompliant boots, however comfortable and familiar.

Simply put, then, wearing lighter, more flexible footwear facilitates the hiking. The effects are so pronounced that I estimate that each additional 1¾ ounces removed from a boot (3.5 ounces for the pair) will add about a mile to the day's hiking progress. Replace a pair of medium-weight leather boots, which bereft of sealing compound might weigh 3 lb, 3 oz, with a pair of medium weight running shoes, which might weigh 1 lb, 8 oz, and **with no extra effort** find yourself hiking 7½ more miles each and every day. This gain is so astronomical that no distance hiker can afford to ignore its principles. **But remember that the benefits can only be realized after embracing a vigorous pre-hike training regimen designed to strengthen the ankles.**

BRUISING THE FEET

Some backpackers believe that hiking in running shoes while carrying a heavy pack bruises the feet. I once walked behind a fellow who hiked with a peculiar style. Several times a minute he kicked rocks or roots, slipped on mud, or skidded recklessly down intervening snowbanks. But with each blunder he would immediately correct and throw himself adroitly back into balance, as a matter of course and apparently without giving the matter any thought. Considering his curious behavior, I imagined that because he had worn heavy boots for many years, he had grown out of the habit of watching where he was placing his feet. I was wearing running shoes, which offer substantially less protection, and which necessitate stepping more carefully. Just as subconsciously, I was avoiding those rocks and roots, and treading the mud and snow more deliberately, so as not to stumble and slip. In effect, then, the switch from boots to shoes requires an adjustment in hiking style.

One might argue, then, that those hiking in running shoes must spend more time watching where they are stepping, and that they therefore enjoy less time admiring the scenery gliding past. This is backward logic. Boots do not exempt the wearer from maintaining vigilance. Especially on the Appalachian Trail where rocks abound. In southern California, the ongoing danger of a snake bite will teach the hiker to watch his or her every step. And it is this same attentiveness that will prevent the person from kicking rocks and roots, stepping on pointed rocks and sticks, and slipping on mud and snow. With practice the hiker can become adept at moving the eyes constantly from the immediate foreground to the distant scenery.

And speaking of snakes, aren't boots good protection? Not particularly. Rattlesnakes are sensitive to infrared heat radiation; they use this information to help decide where best to strike. Bare legs or pant legs usually emit more infrared than boots do.

HIKING WET FOOTED

Another associated misconception is that leather boots are essential in keeping the feet dry. As discussed in the clothing section, no garment will keep the body dry when it is sweating. As a person hikes hard, the feet sweat, even when the weather is not particularly hot. And a more permeable and lighter-weight shoe (particularly of the type used for running) will allow the perspiration to evaporate, while the grease-soaked leather boot is more likely to contain it.

But aren't boots the footwear of choice when the weather turns cold and rainy? For the distance backpacker, emphatically, no. A grease-soaked boot might deter the pervading water for perhaps a day; maybe two. It depends on the quality of the boots and how much gloppy sealing compound has recently been melted or soaked into them. But eventually the boots are likely to become waterlogged; and when they do, they will have gained considerable mass. And once soaked they will tend to remain soaked for days. And while wearing wet boots, the feet are likely to feel nearly as sodden as if wearing wet running shoes.

What about boots laminated with an inner ply of waterproof-breathable material? Don't they permit the moisture to escape while holding the water at bay? Theoretically, yes. But first, consider that the permeability of Gore-Tex and other such membranes is far less than that of the highly breathable fabrics commonly found in running shoes. More significantly, and regarding leather boots, because the membrane seems to obviate the need to apply sealant, the outer boot material is likely to soak water like a sponge, gaining weight as it does. Then the membrane only inhibits drying by restricting through-ventilation. The user who applies a sealing compound in order to reduce external absorption renders the membrane virtually useless, and the intervening sandwich of leather will only retain the entrapped moisture almost permanently. Such dilemmas can only be justified by daubing them liberally on both sides with hype. Anyway, waterproof-breathable membranes are poorly resistant to chafe, and I suspect that when used in a boot of leather or fabric they begin breaking down, perhaps in less than 50 miles of walking.

For the weekender, wet boots are generally not a serious problem. As a matter of course they can be dried at home. But for the distance hiker, wet boots can be extremely difficult to dry. When running shoes become wet, they don't gain nearly as much weight as boots do. And they dry considerably faster.

Stop and think for a moment that your feet are, for all practical purposes, waterproof. And although you might consider wet feet an adversity of the utmost consequence, generally your feet don't mind being wet, as long as they do not become cold; and as long as they spend their nights comfortably warm and dry. So instead of looking to technology for miracles, (and finding none) let's turn to Mother Nature. Enter the wool sock: so capable of keeping wet feet warm.

THE BENEFITS OF WOOL-BLEND SOCKS

I have found wool-blend socks and running shoes to be the most effective footwear in persistently wet and cold weather. (At least the type of wet and cold found along the PCT.) The only adjustment required seems to be a mental one.

After hiking in wet shoes and socks a few hours, we can remove them, wring out the socks, and put both back on. At day's end we can remove the wet socks and don a pair of dry ones. We can then wring out the wet socks and hang them outside the tent, beneath the awning. In the morning they might not be dry, but in all probability they will be just as wearable. If we have left our sodden shoes outside at night, under the open awning, then by morning we will find them probably much less wet. And if the day's weather proves fine, and if the dew is not on the meadow grass, then our shoes will dry as we tramp along.

Wearing wool-blend socks and running shoes can engender a newfound confidence in hiking during wet weather. Thus attired, no longer need we worry when our feet become soaked, because we know that the shoes will dry fairly quickly. Instead, while squishing along, we might feel almost impervious to the ravages of rain, sloppy snow, and dewey or sodden brush. And we might discover that by leaving the heavy boots at home, we also leave behind a great deal of anxiety that those boots were causing.

Running shoes are less substantial, but accordingly they bring us more in accord with the ways of nature. And nature teaches us to bend to adversity rather than trying to remain stalwart.

Speaking of nature, consider the cost of the traction provided by lug-soled boots. They gouge and chisel the terrain far more than softer shoes do. This is particularly apparent in places where the ground is soft or moist, such as a delicate springtime meadow or a sloped trail.

HIKING IN SNOW

If you reach the base of Forester Pass in early or mid season, you might as well chuck the foregoing discussion on running shoes into the nearest moat. Shoes and wool-blend socks perform well on horizontal and gently inclined snow slopes. And because we hardly mind that our feet become wet we can leave the $80 gaiters at home. Satisfactory gaiters for distance snow-slogging are short, non-waterproof anklets that cover little more than the bothersome gap between shoe and sock, and that therefore prevent snow from entering the shoe or boot. And incidentally, the person needing to improvise might wrap the ankles with strips of material.

But back to running shoes: when the snow steepens and hardens, shoes are out of their intended territory. They do not edge well, and they do not kick adequate steps into hard crust.

I have climbed several snowbound Sierran passes while wearing running shoes: when the snow was soft and the act of kicking steps was not required, and once when my boots were so frozen that despite a prolonged wrestling match I could not struggle them onto my feet. By the term "boots," though, I am not referring to the heavy, leather type. During our second PCT hike I wore fabric boots whenever the going became technically demanding, which typically it did on both sides of the nine high passes of the Muir-trail Sierra. (Again, we were there in early season.) On steep, hard snow the boots performed adequately. Whenever the slope eased, though, I changed eagerly into my running shoes.

The new breed of lighter-weight boots is a boon to the early season Sierra trekker. Those boots that feature steel shanks should perform well on steep and hard snow. And while wearing wool-blend socks, you needn't worry that your nylon-fabric boots are not waterproof. For the distance hiker, dry feet are a myth, remember?

During both our through-hikes of the PCT, Jenny often changed out of her running shoes, and into a pair of "lightweight" boots (which weighed three times as much as her shoes). In these boots she experienced some difficulty while climbing steep, hard snow. This leads to the seemingly incongruous precept that when climbing or descending steep snow, a lighter person needs a correspondingly slightly heavier boot with which to trounce steps.

SENDING YOUR GLACIER STOMPERS HOME

Generally, Tuolumne Meadows heralds the end of the technically demanding snow, and it is here that many through-hikers send their boots home. But be forewarned that there might be a few more steep and snow clad areas in the general vicinity of Sonora Pass. The resupply station beyond that is the Echo Lake Resort. Nevertheless, from wherever you send your snow-boots home in favor of lighter weight shoes, you might still encounter the occasional patch of steep snow. When you do, tighten your laces and forge cautiously ahead, chopping magnum sized steps with your ice axe. If you slip, self-arrest immediately. After regaining composure, resume the traverse. Do not proceed when tired. If you are feeling a little nervous, or are beginning to flag, chop a large stance and enjoy a long rest. If still nervous, chop some more. If terrified, plunge your axe to the hilt and tie yourself to it. If the situation seems in the slightest foreboding, gather your composure, turn around and chop large steps, then once safely on terra firma go find another way. Remember, there is ALWAYS another way; so don't let the summertime-dynamited trail lure you into a potentially lethal situation.

CREEK FORDING FOOTWEAR

One of the hallmarks of the inexperienced backpacker is in leaving boot prints that course through easily avoidable puddles of water and mud. The hiker wearing running shoes is usually careful to avoid stepping in these places. Wet shoes are entirely permissible, but dry ones are far better.

Only in the extreme circumstance will I ford a swift and deep creek while wearing shoes. Usually, my footwear of choice is simply two pairs of socks; preferably dirty ones.

EXPELLING DEBRIS

I lace my shoelaces but loosely. That way I can remove and don the shoes without untying and retying them, for example when dumping bits of gravel or dirt. True, shoes tend to collect more debris than boots do, but then they are far easier to slip off, empty, and to put back on. And here's a tip: During the training regimen you might practice balancing on one leg while looking ahead and upward. Performed every day for a month, this simple exercise could improve your balance a hundred fold. And a well developed sense of balance will hold you in good stead not only when standing one-legged while dumping gravel out of a shoe, but also when balancing across a log spanning a torrent. PCT aspirants take note: **this simple training exercise is extremely important.**

RUNNING SHOES

Even running shoes must offer a degree of lateral heel stiffness (as opposed to ankle support). This helps maintain the shoe's shape as the foot tends to slide off the platform of the sole. The wider the sole the harder it twists and torques the wearer's ankle. And if that ankle pronates (flexes inward) excessively, as many do, then as the sole cants laterally on inclined terrain, the ankle will tend to roll off the sole platform. So when trying on shoes in the store, pay particular attention to the stiffness of their heel counters.

I do not recommend buying state-of-the-art, and therefore inordinately expensive running shoes. There's a great deal of hype out there. In the aftermath of a few disappointments, I look for shoes in the $50 to $60 range. My conclusion is that we distance hikers are not trying to travel at the greatest expense.

LASTING

I have tried to avoid technicalities, preferring the intuitive approach. But here we might do well to learn the three most popular types of construction in boots and running shoes. Before you buy any type of hiking footwear, remove the sock liner (insole) and inspect the lasting. However, this will be infeasible with cheaply made shoes that feature the liners glued in place.

Inside a **board lasted** shoe or boot is a foot-shaped piece of cardboard or other stiff material, glued in place. In the second type, a **combination last**, is a half-length of cardboard covering the aft half of the foot area. Inside a **slip lasted** shoe or boot is fabric, joined by a hand-sewn seam running the length of the shoe. Cardboard lasted shoes and boots are much less costly to manufacture than quality slip lasted ones. The cardboard lasts add stiffness, and they come in various qualities. Some, such as are found in many types of lighter-weight boots, merely abrade and roughen when wet.

Some, such as those found in some types of running shoes, actually begin disintegrating when wet. Moreover, the glues holding the boards in place sometimes dissolve. Bereft of its last, a board-lasted or combination-lasted shoe becomes categorically unwearable, because the upper surface of its midsole is often cratered, reminiscent of volcanic rock. Slip-lasted shoes seem the better choice.

INSOLES

The sock liners that come with today's running shoes and boots are designed to be extremely lightweight and disposable. I recommend temporarily removing them, fitting Spenco™ insoles, then replacing the sock liners atop the insoles. The sock liners might endure a few hundred miles. When they become permanently crushed beneath your heel or the ball of your forefoot, remove them. The Spenco insoles typically last five or six hundred miles. You might include additional pairs in your resupplies.

REFLECTIVE MATERIAL

The reflective material used in many running shoes might alert any night time motorists you might encounter while crossing the highways and byways, but this material is likely to wreak havoc with your photography. In any situation where the fill-in flash comes into play, day or night, its light might rebound from the reflective material of the subject's shoes, and ruin your photo. Ditto with hiking away from a sunset or sunrise. Consider removing the reflective material. Depending on how it was sewn into the shoe, you might try cutting it away. Failing that, you could cover it with duct tape or paint it. Photographers will need to remember to point the camera a little higher, thus truncating the subjects scintillating shoes. And once home you might carefully dab any "arc-welding" spots on your transparencies using a felt-tipped permanent marker.

PROTECTING THE STITCHING

Any exposed stitching on the hiking footwear is susceptible to abrasion. I recommend coating it with 5-minute epoxy, which after it hardens is far more flexible than the slower setting type. While mixing the epoxy, add a small amount of alcohol as a thinner. This allows the mixture to soak into the fabric and stitching. Use a toothpick to dab it on. And smear some also wherever you wish to protect the shoe's or boots' uppers from abrasion, for example where they might chafe against each other near the ankles.

SHOE REQUIREMENTS

The variety of running, hiking and cross-training shoes on the market these days is astounding. And in responding to the competition, the manufacturers are shelling the market with new models annually. The handbook does not recommend the best products, because in most cases there are none. Suffice it to categorize the distance-hiker's qualifications. A suitable hiking shoe would:

✓ Be of moderate cost. (In the $50 range at the time of this writing.)

✓ Be relatively lightweight.

✓ Feature an exaggerated, traction-providing tread.

✓ Provide exemplary heel (not ankle) support.

✓ Afford excellent cushioning.

✓ Feature slip lasting.

On the negative side of the equation, the ideal shoe does not:

✓ Feature a visible cushioning bubble molded into the sole. These might burst on contact with a sharp rock.

✓ Feature uppers made of impermeable plastic, which blocks ventilation.

MAIL ORDER

If while hiking the trail you begin realizing the need for new shoes, and if you haven't included them in a near-future resupply parcel, then at the next way point you might telephone your home base or your favorite mail order shoe retailer. Lacking these, you might try calling Road Runner Sports, at 1-800-551-5558. Relate to the salesperson your shoe requirements, listed above. After you decide among any ensuing recommendations, ask that your choice be sent to you, in care of an upcoming resupply. If the salesperson can't help you decide which type to buy, you might try ordering a pair of Saucony Classic Shadows. However, if you lack a credit card, you might have to hitchhike to the nearest city. I rectify my lack of credit cards with foresight: in this case by including spare shoes in my resupplies. Those shoes that prove unnecessary I send back home for later use, assured that they will function as well off the trail as they would have on it.

THE PROPER SHOE SIZE

Shoes come in approximately ⅓ inch increments, each representing the length of a barlycorn, as decreed in 1305 by King Edward I. A size 10 shoe, then, is the length of 10 barleycorns placed end to end. Thus, our footwear is actually related to our nutrition, albeit remotely.

Notwithstanding, the act of choosing the correct shoe size is confounded by the fact that our feet change size dramatically, depending on the environment, the time of day, and other factors. Our feet change size like accordions, and our shoes change sizes like their hard instrument-cases.

Consider this: Southern California's brain-broiling heat, combined with the continual hiking, is likely to cause your feet to swell a shoe size longer, and two or more sizes wider in the forefoot. And depending on how rigorously you hike, your feet might remain enlarged throughout the summer. If you set off from Campo wearing shoes that fit, then as your feet begin swelling, your cramped, trudging feet are likely to become blistered, trudging ones. Consequently, you **must** plan ahead for expansion.

When trying on shoes, remember that your feet are usually at their largest late in the day. And nearly everyone has one foot slightly larger than the other; so use the longest foot when trying a shoe on for size. While wearing a thick pair of socks, settle on a pair of shoes that leaves a thumb's width between the end of your longest toe and the end of the shoe.

As you try on a shoe, the salesperson might place his or her hand over your instep and squeeze the shoe to feel for excess volume. You might be advised that excess space would allow your foot to drift unfavorably side to side, and forward. Note, however, that your forefoot will probably swell considerably once you have been on the trail a few days. Particularly if those days are hot ones. And be aware that it is inadvisable to fill any gaps in the new shoes with foam inserts, which would hamper ventilation and add unwanted insulation.

Also note that unless your feet are naturally wide, buying EE or EEEE shoes is not recommended. No matter how swollen your feet become, these extra wide shoes might still prove far too roomy in the mid-foot and rear-foot areas. Even when swollen, your feet might wallow in them. Conversely, some brands of shoes are comparatively narrow at the ball of the foot. These are best avoided unless your feet are extremely narrow.

I recommend buying shoes that are comfortably wide in the forefoot, while you wear a thick pair of socks to simulate slightly swollen feet. Then on the trail, when your feet begin swelling in earnest, you can modify the shoes to fit like the proverbial pair of gloves.

MODIFYING YOUR SHOES

After your first few days or weeks on the trail, when your feet begin swelling you must remain acutely aware of how and where blisters are attempting to festoon your feet. Stop every hour or so, (every half-hour during hot weather) remove your shoes and socks, and examine your feet and toes. Before blisters form, but when they seem imminent, apply to the reddened areas a few *breathable-fabric* adhesive strips, such as Band-aids™. Don fresh socks, and consider that the time is ripe for surgery. Not on your feet, but on the shoes. First, cut out their tongues. You accomplish this by jamming the tongue deep into the shoe's toe box, then carefully slicing the intervening tongue-to-uppers stitching. With the tongue done away with, you would then slit the upper forefoot, down the centerline, half an inch toward the tip of the shoe. This half-inch slit allows the shoe's forefoot to expand laterally, creating a little more toe room. After hiking in the shoes awhile, should you feel the need to elongate the forefoot slits, feel free to do so; but only in ½ inch increments. Think twice before slitting all the way to the

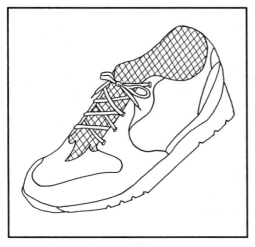

A running shoe, modified to enhance cooling, and to allow more forefoot space.

vicinity of your toe nails, which might then begin snagging the slit with each step. This situation can be most disconcerting, particularly if you are not wearing socks. Rest assured, though, that if you slice too far, you can always break out the contingency needle and thread, and sew a cross-hatch pattern back along the full length of the slice, leaving it plenty wide. No matter how far forward the slit extends, the cross-hatch back-stitching will prevent your toes from grabbing it.

Not to belabor the boot-shoe debate, but the ability to modify shoes to fit like gloves is an advantage not enjoyed by those who wear stout boots.

In perhaps 4,500 miles of hiking with tongue-less and slit-open shoes, the only inconvenience I have noticed was that my feet were usually dirty. But even this might have been an advantage, for I believe that the dura-dirt might have helped toughen my feet. Nevertheless, each evening before retiring, I methodically and vigorously scrubbed my feet, using a wet, or at least a damp wash cloth.

LEG PAINS

Even though running shoes are not designed to handle rugged terrain, scree slopes and the like, they often withstand the punishment surprisingly well. However, like boots, they tend to break down internally, and invisibly. And the result can be a leg pain with no apparent cause. With this in mind, **we would best avoid trying to glean the most mileage from a pair of shoes or boots before switching to a new pair.** Instead, we would send them home long before they begin breaking down internally and causing anonymous problems.

A walking pain does not necessarily emanate from the source of trouble. An ill fitting or broken-down shoe can cause an increasing pain anywhere in the ankle, leg, knee, hip or the lower back. Should you experience pain with each step, suspect your footwear as the cause.

It is folly to ignore a persistent walking pain in hopes that your body or your footwear will adjust. The dictum, "no pain, no gain" has resulted in sports injuries by the tens of thousands. Think of pain as the body's way of signaling a problem, and more importantly, of calling for rectifying **action**.

CARRYING A SPARE PAIR OF SHOES

The thought is so important that it deserves reiterating. When you've been hiking for several days, weeks or months, should you develop a pain somewhere in the lower extremities, a pain that burns with every step, you **must** exchange your footwear for another pair as soon as possible. The chances are excellent that once you have done this, your pain will ameliorate: if not within hours, then within a few days.

For this reason I advocate always carrying an additional pair of shoes, perhaps of a different brand, and also including additional pairs in various resupplies along the way. It has been my experience that many hundreds of miles into the hike I will experience one set of foot, leg and knee complaints while wearing my favorite pair of shoes. Changing into a fresh pair mid day is a genuine pleasure, but within a few hours I might begin experiencing the second set of aches and pains, which have no correlation to the first ones. So when eventually I open a resupply parcel containing a new pair of shoes, I do so with delight.

One might conclude, then, that the act of hiking in running shoes is detrimental to a person's lower extremities. Probably so, but boots are likely to be even more so. Taking into account the unimaginable rigors of continual walking, I consider shoes as merely the more favorable compromise.

AMELIORATING A PAINFUL GAIT

If while hiking you begin developing a painful gait, you would do well to increase the frequency but lessen the intensity of your calf-stretching exercises. Treat a pain with gentle and regular stretching, and with massaging. Also, you might benefit by modifying your shoes further.

A pain in front of the knee, but behind the kneecap might indicate weak thigh muscles. These muscles should have been strengthened with the foot-lift exercises long before the hike. Otherwise, it is not too late to begin them. See page 25 for instructions.

If the pain is alongside the kneecap, it might indicate an over-pronating ankle. To determine if over-pronation might be the problem, try walking on terrain sloped down and away from the painful knee. For example if the left knee hurts, walk on ground sloped down and to the left. If this seems to help, it might indicate a weakness in that ankle. See the ensuing section that discusses orthotics.

If a pain develops on the back side of your calf or heel, try inserting a ¼" thick heel-lifting pad into your shoe. And pay particular attention to your calf-stretching exercises. Otherwise, over the long term the heel pad might allow your calf muscles to shorten, and thereby increase their susceptibility to injury.

There are many ways to enhance a pair of shoes extemporaneously. You can cut wedges of stout foam or cardboard and place them beneath the shoe's insole. You can wad a piece of bandanna and cram that beneath the arch. The point is, don't keep walking; stop and experiment. With imagination, you are far more likely to ad-lib a *temporary* solution to any pain. But remember that these ad-lib methods are only temporary fixes until you can obtain a new pair of shoes.

ORTHOTICS

Years ago I sustained an injury that resulted in an over-pronating ankle. At the onset of our first PCT pre-hike training program I consulted with a sports podiatrist. He cast a pair of plaster molds, one for each foot, and from these ordered a pair of custom orthotics. Invented by George Sheehan, these are removable plastic inserts that fit loosely inside a pair of shoes or boots. They don't provide support beneath the arch, but rather, just behind the arch. I wore the orthotics during my pre-hike training, and eventually determined that the non-injured foot was gaining no benefit from its orthotic. I wore the orthotic in the other shoe the full distances of both our hikes of the PCT, and judged it an unqualified success.

Here's how you can test your feet, as to whether they might benefit from orthotics. Place a piece of paper on the floor. Wet your foot, and step naturally onto the paper. The moisture should leave a foot print. If most of the foot area is visible, but a small area is scooped out at the side, then your arch is probably normal. But if the entire outline of your foot is revealed, your ankle might be over-pronating.

The over-pronator's foot is not flat; it's arch is merely leaning over. This throws the mechanisms of the foot and ankle somewhat out of kilter, and results in abnormal stresses and a reduction in the foot's effectiveness in absorbing shock. An injury notwithstanding, the primary causes of a low arch (flat feet) are a weak set of muscles that maintain the arch's structure and position, or inordinately tight muscles of the outside of the calf. If you judge yourself an over-pronator, consider visiting a sports podiatrist, who would then help you decide whether you might benefit from using orthotics. And once again, pay particular attention to your calf-stretching exercises, as described back on page 27.

As a final note, pronated ankles are not necessarily incapable. Among other examples, the Olympic sprinter Jesse Owens pronated markedly.

THE RAVAGES OF ATHLETE'S FOOT

By my reckoning, the fungus that causes athlete's foot is a key factor in 95% of all the blisters incurred along the PCT. The parasite is ubiquitous in today's society, even though most people don't realize they have it. But it is always present on everyone's skin. Nevertheless, the surest indication of the *infection* is underfoot dead skin that you can scrape away with your fingernails while soaking in the bath, or a lack of foot and toe callous. And these are exactly the malady's most debilitating features. Because athlete's foot consumes callous, it is extremely deleterious to the distance hiker, in the ongoing struggle against blisters.

Athlete's foot is the scourge of the distance hiker; and the battle against it is never ending. I'd recommend that whether you think you have the infection or not, at the onset of your training program, several months in advance of your hike, you commence treating your feet daily. If the infection is serious, apply a **liquid**, or liquid spray antifungal solution containing tolnaftate or clotrimazole. The powders and spray powders are relatively ineffective. If the infection is not acute, use cider vinegar, which sprayed from a plant mister is surprisingly effective. Also, Dr. Bronner's soap works well.

Unconditionally, do not step in a tub or shower, or even on dry concrete, tile, linoleum or carpet, while unshod. This rule applies not only when in motels, but even when in your own home. During the long trek you will encounter the luxury of a shower only rarely; but when you enter a shower stall, you would do well to protect your feet. You might wear ultra-light beach thongs, plastic bags, or maybe only your thickest socks. And after showering and drying your feet carefully, you would do well to apply the anti-fungus medicine or vinegar, carried in a small vile.

BLISTER PREVENTION

Blisters are actually slow burns, the results mainly of chafe. I recommend a four phase process for minimizing them: reduce the athlete's foot infections, walk barefoot when possible (or wear beach thongs in a public place), wear minimal socks, and of course choose shoes that do not constrict the feet.

Blisters are exacerbated by heat, and oftentimes heavy socks act like ovens. For the distance hiker, double layer, padded "blister free" socks can instead be blister makers. And while on the subject of misconceptions, I consider tincture of Benzoin ineffective at toughening the feet.

BLISTER FIRST AID

The product 2nd Skin™ takes The *Handbook's* award as the most innovative backpacking product of the decade. The prospective tri-state hiker would do well to set out carrying 2 boxes of the dressing kits, and to include a kit in one or two resupply parcels. If you find that you are not using the 2nd Skin, so much the better. You can dispense it to blister-footed hikers met on the trail. During our last PCT hike, I used the most 2nd Skin I had used all summer during the final two weeks. My shoes had obliterated, requiring that I borrow Jenny's spare pair, which were three sizes too small for my feet. Sockless and ensconced in their cramped confines, nearly every toe sprouted blisters.

Tape any superficial blisters with breathable-*fabric* adhesive strips, such as Band-aids™ or their less expensive, generic counterparts. Take care not to apply adhesive tape directly to the blister. And carry a roll of white, adhesive tape. This is useful for bandaging blisters, and is the recommended first aid treatment in the extremely unlikely event of a sprained ankle. (Contrary to the almost universal fear, I've not heard of a *well-conditioned* distance hiker spraining an ankle.)

Two or three days after a blister forms, if it becomes painfully bloated with fluid then consider carefully puncturing the blister using a sterilized needle. The fluid would then be blotted with T.P, and the area dabbed with an antiseptic.

If your feet become temporarily disabled by blisters, try removing your socks and all the tape you have plastered onto your feet, and then put your shoes back on. Remember that blisters are heat-chafe burns. Keep your feet as cool as possible, and give them space and ventilation.

FOOT CARE

We commonly neglect our feet during regular personal hygiene, perhaps because they are so far away. Still, these distant relatives deserve the best care and attention. Each of our feet come equipped with some 250,000 sweat glands, which altogether exude ½ to 1 pint of sweat per day, when at rest. The sweating is far more profuse while we are hiking. So keeping our feet ventilated is a major task, and one that is not well addressed by heavy boots. For best results wear lighter weight socks and breathable shoes. Expose your feet to the environment whenever possible, and consider further toughening them by walking a ways barefoot every day. You would do well to wash your feet twice daily, to dry them thoroughly, and to apply the antifungal solution, (vinegar, for example) particularly between the toes and beneath the toenail margins. When necessary, trim the toenails in a slight curve, and not too close. And here's a requirement most people overlook: disinfect your socks. During your training regimen you can sterilize them in a microwave oven, under a watchful eye. Disinfecting them while on the trail is impractical at best; suffice it to wash them often and dry them thoroughly.

ELEVATE THE LEGS WHILE RESTING

On the trail, at each of your hourly rest stops you must remove your shoes and socks as a matter of course. Remember that the act of resting in the seated position, feet flat on the ground, deprives your overtaxed pedal extremities of much of the rest they deserve. This is because as you hike, the leg muscles keep the blood vessels properly sized. Actually, as the muscles flex and relax they pump blood. When you stop and rest, and as your muscles relax they allow the vessels to balloon and the blood to accumulate in them. This vaso-dilation hampers circulation enormously. So instead, when resting try to elevate your feet. Although it might lack dignity, the optimum resting position is the supine, legs elevated and feet propped on or against some object, preferably a cool one.

For the same reason, the conscientious distance hiker sleeps with the legs elevated. The more tired your legs are at the end of the day, the more the blood will pool in them when you stop hiking, and the less the blood will circulate through them. And we must keep in mind that optimum circulation is vital for a restorative night's sleep.

When hiking in arid climes, during the morning rest stops you might place your feet flat against a rock, which will absorb a tremendous amount of your feet's calidity. Failing that, place your feet in the dirt, which in many places acts like a powder in absorbing foot perspiration. Sometimes you can dig them in a ways, letting the cool soil absorb the over-heat. Stir the ground with a stick first, though, to unearth any unsuspecting scorpions.

Before setting off again, air the used socks by securing them to the outside of your pack. Brush the dust and debris from your feet, massage them encouragingly, and change into a fresh pair of socks. Once in place, stretch the socks laterally at the toe areas to give your toes a little more space. And check for wrinkles. An ill-positioned wrinkle can induce a blister in a matter of minutes. Lastly, if the weather is particularly hot, don your second pair of shoes, if wisely you are carrying them.

Jenny and I usually store our day's supply of clean socks roved through the gear webbing loops on top of our packs. We call these our sock bandoliers, and the arrayed socks our trail ordnance. But whenever scraping through overhead brush, we turn and see if the brush might have snatched a sock.

Rob Sweetgall is reported to have walked 11,000 miles through all fifty states in 364 consecutive days. He commented that hot, sensitive feet were his biggest problem. Accordingly, he typically slit open his shoes to enhance their ventilation. Rob asserted that cornstarch worked better than commercial foot powders in absorbing the sweat, and in lubricating his feet and toes inside the shoes. In what he called the "shake and bake" procedure, he placed each foot, one at a time, into a plastic bag that contained a handful of cornstarch.

FOOD
Time-tested recipes, by mice and men

Part of the secret of success in life
is to eat what you like,
and let the food fight it out inside.
—Mark Twain

UNWRAPPING THE FREEZE-DRIED FALLACY
During my first two summers as a professional wilderness instructor I ate mainly freeze-dried foods, as supplied by the company. It became increasingly apparent, though, that those foods were not providing sufficient go-power or mental acuity. Subsequently, I began experimenting exclusively with heavier and more nutritious foods, and soon found that my energy levels and backpacking enjoyment increased. And in the ensuing 20 years of experimenting with different foods while pursuing extended outdoor adventures, I have concluded that the essential strength and restorative effects provided by fresh, wholesome foods more than compensate for their weights.

THE IMMUNITY OF THE WEEKEND HIKER
Generally, freeze-dried food is lightweight, readily available, appealing, tasty and expensive. Therefore, it meets nearly every requirement of *weekend* backpackers, who perhaps unknowingly rely mainly on what nutritional reserves are stored within the cells of their bodies. They can eat freeze-dried meals for a few days while not noticing the subtle internal changes that begin taking place. But during a weekend of strenuous activity they are literally feeding off their own bodies.

Distance hikers, on the other hand, possess but few stored reserves. They have depleted them during the first few weeks of their hikes. Consequently, they need a constant supply of nutrition.

STOKING THE BOILERS WITH QUALITY FUEL
I maintain that inadequate nourishment (combined with overweight backpacks and undertrained bodies) is a major reason that most aspiring PCT through-hikers quit their journeys. Distance-hikers who attempt to subsist on nutritionally deficient foods are like steam locomotives burning rubbish. And this is regrettable because were they to stoke their boilers with quality fuel, they would almost certainly become far more capable. With determination and adequate pre-hike training, most distance hikers have

virtually the same potential. But that potential can only be realized through adequate nutrition.

MAKING THE TRANSITION

The first day of a long journey afoot represents an abrupt transition in lifestyle, both in exercise and diet. As hikers set off from the Mexican border their nutritional requirements suddenly and vastly multiply. But most hikers compensate, not by eating more food of higher quality, but less food of lower quality. Unknowingly, then, they begin draining their nutritional reserves. And the process usually leads to severe deprivation within the ensuing weeks.

Of the body parts affected, the brain is the one preeminent. Sensing an increasing nutritional deficit, as a survival mechanism the mind begins acting subconsciously to rectify the situation. With the passing of days the journey might begin loosing its luster. Reason might begin casting aspersions on the benefits of the wilderness quest, and suggesting instead those of returning to the city, where, incidentally, quality food is readily available. Increasingly, as the mind begins to forfeit its aspirations, it might generate an excuse suitably imaginative to justify quitting the game.

The excuses settled on generally have nothing to do with the problem. Some external aspect is likely to become the scapegoat, and might begin to seem utterly intolerable if not maiming. The hiker imagines him or herself dying a slow death: roasting in the hot sun like a desert straggler, or becoming stranded in the pervasive snow like a member of the Donner party. Blisters might be construed as threatening ruination of the feet. The trail's errant circuity might become intolerable. There might be too much sun and not enough rain, or too much rain and not enough sun. Or perhaps the hiker develops a rekindled passion for a former hobby such as stamp collecting. These are mental ploys, contrived by a brain attempting to direct the body to the supply of nutrients it so desperately needs.

The problem might seem enigmatic at the time, yet the solution is ridiculously uncomplicated. Simply stated, the successful distance hiker must eat quality food, and lots of it.

FOOD AS PACKWEIGHT

Everything in the through-hiker's backpack must impart maximum value. Function, not weight, is the hiker's utmost priority. Light-weightness is also important, but it is entirely subordinate to function. A lightweight, nutritionally empty food (such as a freeze-dried or instant noodle meal) is as useless to the *distance hiker* as a gossamer-weight tent riddled with holes, or a cotton sheet taking the place of a much heavier but warmer sleeping bag.

Rocket fuel is extremely heavy, but it is also packed with potential energy: energy that is more than sufficient to compensate for its weight. And rocket engineers work only with the fuels capable of delivering the most payload the highest and farthest. The wise backpacker does the same.

After the first several weeks on the trail, the hiker who carries and eats heavier but more nutritional food might travel up to twice as many miles each day as the person who carries a slightly lighter pack while subsisting continually on freeze-dried food. And because quality food can power the hiker to the next resupply station in fewer days, not as many days worth of food is required. And carrying the heavier but more potent load, the well-fed backpacker is likely to hike with more enjoyment and élan, and to reach the distant objective in much better condition both mentally and physically.

VIS MEDICATRIX NATURAE
(the healing power of nature)
While traipsing through the backcountry we lack daily access to back yard vegetable gardens and to well stocked supermarkets, and instead we must pre-package most of our food half a year in advance. But occasionally fresh vegetables are available at the resupply stations. If hikers typically recommended that the proprietors stock more of them, then some of them might do so. Nevertheless, what vegetables you encounter, consider buying as many of them as you could fit into your dietary regimen for the ensuing several days. Contrary to the impression of some people, well cared for fresh vegetables and fruits will usually endure for many days, if not weeks.

Just before departing for a long hike, Jenny and I typically place several potatoes in each of our resupply parcels. Previously, at the supermarket we select them individually for robustness. Usually the potatoes arrive at the resupply stations, months later, in fine condition. Some will have budded, and these buds we tear off and discard, as they are said to be toxic. And while on the subject, one should avoid trying to extend the lives of whole potatoes by vacuum-sealing them. They are likely to become unimaginably fetid.

VARIETY
Fresh vegetables, and occasionally some meat might be the adroit backpacker's primary source of nutrients—though they are rarely available. Obviously, though, we will need to include additional sustenance.

As we select these foods, we might keep in mind that of all the aspects of a successful dietary regimen, variety is preeminent. Repetitious fare might eventually become intolerable and all but inedible, no matter how nutritious. In the case of minimal-nutritive foods this is not purely psychological. Our bodies are likely to begin rejecting an over supply of many types of chemicals and inert ingredients.

What follows are some of the distance-hiking foods that Jenny and I have come to favor.

THE BACKPACKER'S POWER FOOD

After years of sampling various processed foods and evaluating the resulting energy boost, if any, we have happened upon what seems a power food *par excellance*. Why and how it works I haven't a clue. I can only report that after we have been on the trail several weeks and have depleted our reserves, this food provides us with many hours of energy. No other meal that we have tried is comparable.

During our first PCT trek we discovered that after eating corn spaghetti our trail performance increased markedly for several hours. At first we thought it coincidental, but the pattern almost invariably repeated itself.

In the ensuing years we experimented further. These experiments proved so successful that during our second PCT hike we ate corn spaghetti on the average of two out of every three dinners. Not once did it fail to provide the energy we needed, and never did we tire of eating it. Had we included more in our resupply parcels we would have eaten it. In fact, during the last third of the hike we were actually rationing our supply, eating the spaghetti only in the late afternoons when we needed major energy boosts for the day's remaining several hours of hiking.

CORN SPAGHETTI

Corn spaghetti is cooked much like wheat spaghetti. Bring a covered pot of water to a boil, using plenty of water. Remove the lid. Break the spaghetti into short lengths and place it into the pot, handful at a time. Bring the water back to a boil, then reduce the stove's heat to prevent boiling over. Stir the mixture often to minimize sticking. When the meal is finished cooking, pour off as much of the starchy liquid as possible. Dilute and save it to drink later if desired; it might be a valuable source of complex-carbohydrate energy. Pour more filtered water into the cook pot to rinse the spaghetti, then pour off most of that water also. Add seasonings, and eat heartily.

JENNY'S TOMATO SPAGHETTI-SAUCE LEATHER

Of the two spaghetti sauces we are most fond of, our favorite is tomato leather. You can make this at home by mixing one small can of tomato paste and one of tomato sauce. Add Italian seasonings, or open a store-bought packet of spaghetti seasoning (select the type containing the least amount of chemicals). Chop and saute some mushrooms, onions or bell peppers, and add them to the sauce. Finally, place the mixture in the food dehydrator (see the following chapter, page 91).

The dehydrator tray would first be covered with a sheet of plastic wrap. Use enough so that the ends overhang the sides of the tray somewhat. Then tape the plastic here and there around its edge to prevent it curling back onto itself and adhering to the sauce. The sauce mixture would be thick enough so that it requires spreading with a spatula to about ¼" thick. Dry the sauce until it is pliable but not yet brittle. Leaving the plastic adhered to the finished leather, roll both in the shape of a tube, then cut it to lengths and seal the pieces in storage bags.

On the trail, while the spaghetti water is coming to a boil, tear a 10-inch square of sauce-leather (half of that for one person) into pieces. Allow the pieces to rehydrate while the spaghetti cooks, by placing them in a cup, adding water, and stirring occasionally. They will rehydrate much faster if instead of soaking them in cold water, you soak them in hot water. Before adding the spaghetti to the boiling water, you might pour off about half a cup of hot water into the sauce-leather cup. This technique also makes a more hearty sauce.

While the leather is rehydrating, add dried embellishments such as turkey sausage or salami, tomatoes, mushrooms, onion, bell pepper, etc. These will rehydrate with the sauce leather.

The alternate seasoning we use is a package mix by Mayacamas called Pesto Sauce Mix. We simply mix it with water and pour it over the cooked spaghetti.

To both of the above we add parmesan cheese to taste.

Bon appetit!

RAY'S WAY-OF-LIFE PORRIDGE

We originated the Way-of-Life recipe while preparing for our first PCT hike. It proved so effective at providing energy and vitality that since then we have eaten it for breakfast nearly every morning—in the woods or at home. It has become, indeed, our way of life.

Our basic Way-of-Life admixture comprises barley, oats, millet, and corn grits, in proportions of 25% each. We buy organically grown grains in their sproutable condition. As a matter of compromise, to speed cooking time and to reduce fuel consumption we crack the grains, using an old-fashioned hand grinder. And after blending the various types into meals, we hermetically package them in heat-sealed, plastic bags.

Most of our breakfasts are experiments. To the basic recipe we add small portions of enlivening ingredients such as triticale, rye, buckwheat, rice, sunflower seeds, sesame seeds, chopped almonds, or pecans. And we further differentiate the breakfasts by adding cinnamon, nutmeg, or almond or vanilla extract. We consider these various additions extremely important in preventing our palates from growing weary of the otherwise repetitious fare.

After bringing four cups of water to a boil we cook 1½ cups of the grain mixture (for two people) for some fifteen minutes, ten minutes if we had soaked the cracked grains in cold water overnight, or even less time if the soaking grains had been slept with. We prefer the grains slightly undercooked: chewy rather than glutinous.

Our usual sweeteners of choice are powdered milk, and raisins or currants, or home-dried fruits such as apple, pear, peach, apricot, pineapple or papaya. And when on the trail we sometimes add jam, honey, or our favorite trail-side delectable in northern climes: huckleberries. It is important to note, though, that sugar, jam or honey will scorch onto the bottom of the pot if added while the grains are cooking.

Incidentally, when in the woods we usually cook the morrow's breakfast immediately after cooking dinner. After eating dinner we place the cooked breakfasts into our lidded bowls, and we "wash" the cook pot (as described in the Hygiene chapter). Breaking camp the following early morning, we set off hiking; then we stop around eight or nine to eat a filling, if cold breakfast.

GRAIN DINNERS

Some of our other trail meals comprise hearty combinations of grains and pulses—the edible seeds of various leguminous crops such as peas, beans or lentils. These meals cook in the same manner and for the same lengths of time as the porridge breakfasts. Our favorites include short-grain, brown rice combined with small white beans, and rice with black-eyed peas. The grains and pulses we purchase in their sproutable condition, then we crack them at home. For seasonings we use home-dehydrated vegetables and thin-sliced turkey ham, seasoned pepper, Vegit, and package mixes such as Chicken Dijon Sauce Blend by Schilling.

CHILI

Another appetizing dinner is home-dehydrated chili, combined with fresh potatoes and home-dried vegetables. Begin by making the chili at home. In a skillet, brown a batch of ground turkey, while stirring in half a package of Carroll Shelby's chili mix, or an equivalent. Spare the salt, which in this case is included separately. After cooking, chop the meat to bits, and place these in the food dehydrator. On another tray in the dehydrator spread the contents of a store-bought package of pre-cooked, frozen vegetables. Another option is to slice potatoes thinly, and place them in the dehydrator. See the following chapter on dehydrating foods, for details on packaging.

During the hike, the meal can be prepared, first by adding water to a quantity of chili and dried vegetables in a lidded bowl. Leave space for expansion; the food will swell to perhaps double its volume as it slowly rehydrates. Place the bowl in your backpack and hike with it for about four hours. When it comes time for dinner, cook the meal for about 10 or 15 minutes.

Turkey franks make a tasty addition to this and many dinner meals; and they are sometimes available at the resupply stations. In a similar vein, if a beef steak is cubed it can be boiled to perfection in a matter of minutes.

JENNY'S NO-COOK HEARTY MEALS

Thus far the *Handbook* has elucidated two exceptional entrees: corn spaghetti and Ray's Way-of-Life porridge. Jenny's No-Cook Hearty Meals constitutes our third culinary innovation. These cookless meals are so effective that when used in conjunction with muesli breakfasts (see below) and the occasional fresh victuals available at stores along the way, they might be of great benefit to those weight-conscious hikers plying the far-flung hinterlands without a stove.

We first discovered the idea fortuitously. One day Jenny added water to the above meal of dehydrated chili and vegetables, in preparation for cooking it later that afternoon. According to our usual practice we hiked about four more hours as the diner soaked. Then we stopped beside the trail to cook it. But while Jenny was making ready the stove I sampled the food. To my surprise I found it edible, even though still somewhat chewy. In fact, cooking it hardly seemed necessary, so we shut down the stove and proceeded with dinner. We have eaten this and other similar meals many times since, and consider the concept very sound.

LUNCHES

Store bought macaroni-and-cheese makes a quick and easily prepared lunch. Occasionally at or near the resupply stations one might find sandwich materials for sale. We enjoy these items, and find them filling and satisfying, but they provide us with ridiculously little go-power.

One of our favorite lunches is home-made muesli mixed with powdered milk and water. Muesli is less time consuming to make than granola because it does not have to bake for two hours.

NUTTY MUESLI
(yields approximately 20 cups)

Combine 4 cups of each: rolled oats, barley flakes, and triticale flakes. Chop them mechanically or by hand until the flakes are smaller but not powdered. Toast them in a dry skillet until slightly brown, being careful not to burn them. When they are nearly toasted, drizzle on 1/4 cup of vegetable oil.

Remove them from the heat, stir in 1 cup of wheat germ or oat bran, 1/2 cup of brown sugar, 1 tsp of almond flavoring, 1/3 cup of shredded coconut, 1 cup of date crumbles, 1/3 cup of pumpkin seeds, 1/3 cup of sunflower seeds, 1 cup of chopped nuts, and one 20 oz, store-bought box of corn flakes. Mix thoroughly, and package.

SNACKS: THE DAY-LONG LUNCH

Trail life for the distance backpacker is practically one long lunch. Regular meals are of primary importance, but except for corn spaghetti, Jenny and I have found that our bodies cannot extract and store enough metabolical wherewithal from foods to fuel five or six hours of strenuous exercise. Like most other hikers, we snack at virtually every rest stop.

GORP

You've addressed your nutritional requirements as recommended above. Now it's time to muster your imagination, and exercise your culinary inventiveness. It's time to conjure your various gorp mixes (trail mixes). During the weeks of making preparations, this is your one opportunity for flair. Gorp is an art form; it should be colorful to look at and fun to eat. You will not be using it as a replacement for breakfast, lunch and dinner. It is merely a trail snack; something to enliven the days—something to make that pancreas dance the tango.

Hard working hikers might carry two cups of gorp per person per day. Peruse the supermarkets for likely ingredients, then at home amass your booty in a large bowl. Stir merrily, then apportion it into paper bags: two cupfuls in each bag. Set the bags aside, make another strafing run through the supermarkets, and repeat the above until you have amassed one bag of gorp per person per day per journey. Such a plethora of junk food will shock your family and friends, and remind you of your summer's commitment. You don't dare quit the hike now.

After lining your resupply parcels in a row against the wall, (and out the door and across the adjacent wall) refer to your selected itinerary (see the chapter beginning on page 208). The itineraries specify the number of days of food you are likely to require between resupply stations. Into each resupply box place its corresponding number of gorp bags. When finished, if desired you might withdraw the gorps from one parcel at a time, and seal them together in plastic. Once at the resupply station you could carefully open the plastic and send it back home, to use the following year; and then you could carry your gorp in the original bags of paper.

VARIETY

It has been our experience that no matter how varied and rich with myriad ingredients were our summer's trail snacks, still we grew tired of what seemed like the same old gorp. And no matter how meticulous you are at choosing the fixings, half way through the hike you too will probably find yourself picking through the tedious gorp and slinging various undesirables to the imaginary chipmunks. One factor in the eventual intolerance might have to do with chemicals contained in the particular food items.

SPONGY CORN CHIPS

If you have included a fair amount of seeds and nuts in your main meals, don't repeat them in your gorp in any noticeable quantities. Also, the ingredients in each bag should be of about the same moisture content. If you add a few prunes with the corn chips, then when you open the bag four months later you are likely to find rock hard prunes and spongy corn chips. Also, keep in mind that the rigors of distance backpacking tend to crush gorp. After being crammed in the bottom of your backpack for 150 miles, those crunchy cereal snacks might be reduced to sugary crumbs.

GORP INGREDIENTS

Possible ingredients for gorp are dried fruit, chopped dates, walnuts, chocolate stars, shredded coconut, almonds, chocolate chips, dried pineapple, raisins, cashews, M&M's (plain and peanut), salted peanuts, spice drops, cashews, jelly beans, and Reeses pieces. And you might be able to buy various pre-mixed gorps in bulk at the supermarkets. For more ideas, wander through the isles, inspecting the chips, crackers, party mixes, dry cereals of corn, and the foods-in-bulk.

TURKEY HAM

Home dried turkey-ham strips are tasty snacks. They should not be dehydrated past the plastic stage. When purchasing a chunk of turkey-ham for using in cooking, though, ask the butcher to machine slice it paper thin. This way the chips will rehydrate much quicker. Used sparingly, they can be used to enliven lunches and dinners.

LEATHERS, ETC.

Fruit leathers are easy to make, and their flavors and texture are excellent. Place the fruits into a blender, and distress them to capacity. Pour the resulting mash onto a plastic coated drying rack, and place it in the food dehydrator.

Home-dried tomato slices are savory munchies, as are those of apples and pears. Dried pineapple is our favorite. Also, one can dehydrate fruit cocktail and compote.

And finally, I don't recommend the hiker exchange a portion of his or her wealth for techno-wonderbars. When considering these products, ignore the catchy names and scrutinize their ingredients. People who believe in these products might also imagine themselves as Popeye eating the magic spinach that supposedly imparts superhuman strength.

DESSERTS

You have eaten dinner and hiked several more hours to dusk, and at last have settled into your stealth camp, quietly and out of sight of the trail. It's time for dessert. You might prepare an instant pudding, mixed with powdered milk. Or maybe you will reward yourself for the high-mileage day by breaking out a package of home-made cookie bars. These can be toothsome additions to your backpacking larder. They can take the form of chocolate chip bars, brownies, or various baked treats sold as package mixes in the supermarkets. Bake them ahead of time and heat-seal them in plastic bags.

HOT AND COLD DRINKS

During our self-propelled journeys, Jenny and I typically forgo the morning hot drink ritual. But a hot cuppa (Australian slang for a hot drink) at day's end provides a welcome ambiance for journal writing. Our hot beverages include Cafix with milk, sweet-milk, and ordinary powdered milk.

My sweet-milk mix is made by blending powdered milk, sugar, cinnamon, nutmeg and cloves. It also makes a delicious milk shake when mixed with ice-cold water, and shaken vigorously.

Another possibility is to make a carbohydrate beverage from powdered milk and a lesser quantity of corn starch.

STEP AT A TIME

The task of preparing the summer's food is a major one. Yet it is considerably facilitated if approached one step at a time—just as is the hike itself. Having read this chapter, you might be in a position to begin experimenting with some of the menus at home, well in advance of the hike. By sampling the menu items ahead of time, you are avoiding the mistake of imagining which foods you might like and which you won't. But remember that your tastes and cravings will probably change considerably once you've been on the trail a few weeks, and as your body's needs for metabolic fuel skyrocket.

FOOD DEHYDRATING

The food dehydrator, to be used during the preparatory stages of each summer's backpacking excursion, would be among the backpacker's more essential items of equipment. Dehydrating and packaging your own provisions is extremely economical. And in your summer's quest it will provide you with food virtually unavailable commercially.

Dehydrating food is a simple matter of extracting much of its moisture. The requirements are two: low heat and ventilation. 100°F is about the optimum, but the variance can be substantial.

While plying the world's three largest oceans, Jenny and I trolled a lure off the sailboat's stern. Lacking refrigeration, whenever we caught a fish larger than what we could eat in the ensuing few days, we sliced the remaining meat and placed it in the tropical sun to dry. One or two days later we had made delicious fish chips. These were our first experiments in food dehydrating.

Here at home we use a wood stove. Adjacent to it stands a simple rack which Jenny built of 1 X 2's, and which supports three trays. Beneath the trays, a fan circulates air through them and disperses the warm air from the stove throughout the house. The stove burns beetle-killed lodgepole pine, abundant in our area. We installed it ourselves, and switched off the electric forced-air heater, hopefully permanently. The wood stove features a glass front, and the ambiance it exudes makes restitution for all those campfires we forego during our long hikes.

In the absence of the above, you can build a wooden box containing a light bulb and a fan. Your local library might have various plans. To construct the drying trays, visit a hardware store and purchase a few window screen kits. The aluminum frames come disassembled and packaged with directions for their assembly. The fiberglass screen is usually sold separately; and is simply scissor-cut to fit. Make the screens first, then construct the drying box according to their size.

BLANCHING

Some books on the subject recommend extending the life of dehydrated foods by steam blanching before drying, or by oven-sterilizing afterward. We refrain from this practice, on the theory that excess heat is detrimental to the food value. We have experienced no spoilage of our dried foods.

TURKEY JERKY

We often enliven our meals with pre-cooked turkey. The turkey ham we slice into quarter-inch thick rashers before placing them on the drying rack. This meat contains preservatives that will insure the turkey jerky's longevity. The chemical preservatives contained in these meats we consider the lesser evil to the bacillus botulism, which is among the most virulent of poisons. Any food that shows evidence of spoilage should be unceremoniously discarded.

STORING DEHYDRATED FOOD

After drying, you might transfer the food onto a handkerchief-size sheet of cheese cloth, which you would then remove and suspend elsewhere until ready for packaging.

Optimum packaging generally eliminates moisture, oxygen, and light. To package dried food, place it on a sheet of brown paper, such as that cut from a grocery sack. Fold the paper to envelop the contents, and tape or tie it closed. Then write the contents on the bag.

When apportioning meals into your resupply boxes, package them together in larger sized plastic bags. During your hike, at the resupply you can then open the plastic bags and mail them back home for future use. Thus, on the trail you have to deal with only the individual paper bags, which are easily incinerated. This technique spares you from carrying to the next and distant resupply station the preponderance of empty plastic bags, which are surprisingly heavy and bulky.

Still, you will probably find yourself using sealed plastic bags to contain seasonings, etc. When cutting one open for the first time, cut only it's corner off, diagonally. To reseal the bag after use, fold the corner down and tape it in place.

STORING HOME-CRACKED GRAINS AND PULSES

Intent on preserving the vitality of our freshly cracked grains, pulses, seeds and nuts, for our first through-hike we packaged the meals using a vacuum bagging machine. This extracted most of the air from the plastic bag, then heat-sealed it closed. We later discovered that during shipping, as the bags jostled against each other they breached the vacuum on about eighty percent of the bags. The problem was that the vacuum bags pressed so mightily against their contents that the rough constituents acted like needles.

Preparing for our second through-hike, we used also a standard heat-sealing machine, without the vacuum. After sealing each bag we inscribed its contents with an indelible pen. And we used a few zip top bags on a daily basis, mindful that they are neither water- nor moisture-proof.

POTABLE WATER

Essential, and sometimes essentially lacking

Basically we are walking waterbags. Our bodies comprise 70% water. Our brains are 75% water and our blood is 90% water. As we hike along the trail we secrete water through respiration, perspiration, and insensible perspiration, and occasionally through urination. Accordingly, we must replace the lost fluids by drinking water at virtually every rest stop. Otherwise, our bodies will extract the moisture they need from our cells, and we will become dehydrated.

DEHYDRATION GREATLY INCREASES THE
RISK OF INCURRING A STRESS INJURY

WATER IS AN ANATOMICAL LUBRICANT

Like oil in the machinery, water lubricates the joints in our bodies. Dehydration increases the friction of motion, and for many reasons it enormously increases our susceptibility to injury.

DEHYDRATION-THICKENED BLOOD

As our blood dehydrates, it thickens. This slows circulation and causes the blood pressure to rise. When the blood slows, it does not carry the fuel to the muscles as well, nor does it carry away their by-products efficiently. Thus, we tire prematurely.

Thicker blood also impedes the brain's activities, by slowing the delivery of nutrients and the removal of its waste products. Furthermore, the dehydrated brain itself is far less capable. Mental and emotional processes begin lagging.

THE PSYCHOLOGY OF THIRST

Now here is the strange part. Ongoing dehydration represses thirst. This is because the sensation of thirst is largely psychological. Drinking a small amount of water often satisfies the psychological need, where even drinking a stomach-full would not adequately rehydrate the body.

Because thirst is psychological, some hikers condition themselves to drinking less water, wrongly assuming that they are conditioning their bodies to needing less water. This is extremely detrimental thinking. Depriving a hard working body of the water it needs not only impedes its efficiency, but subjects it to the risk of a host of physiological disorders. I cannot over emphasize the fact that the hiker who fails to drink adequate quantities of water is placing him or herself at risk.

To know if we are dehydrated we must monitor our urinary output, noting its frequency, volume and color. Heavily colored urine is a sure sign of dehydration. So are headaches and constipation.

HOW MUCH WATER TO DRINK

How much should we drink in order to maintain a clear urinary output? As a guideline, we need to consume ½ liter of water after each one-hour stint of hiking. In hot weather, we would drink far more (see the chapter Hot!). And remember, if you are not producing clear urine, then you need to drink far more water.

THE BEST TREATMENT FOR POTABILITY

The majority of terrain along the PCT features natural water sources located at intervals of five miles or less. Before we discuss techniques for hiking between distant water sources, though, let's consider how best to treat our drinking water against potentially harmful microorganisms.

BYPASS POLLUTED WATER SOURCES

The first defense against microorganisms is in bypassing obviously polluted water sources. The hiker would be imprudent to place too much faith in the purification methods, and to drink of water obviously polluted. For example, no amount of filtering, boiling and adding chemicals will turn stock urine into potable water.

The second line of defense is the application of one or more of the standard water treatment methods: filtering, adding chemicals, and boiling.

CHEMICAL TREATMENTS ARE INHUMANE

Iodine crystals or tablets are effective not only at killing the harmful organisms in the water, but also perhaps the beneficial ones in our bodies. And because distance hikers must drink copiously in order to ward off dehydration, the amount of treatment-chemicals passing through their bodies could indeed be detrimental.

BOILING IS EFFECTIVE BUT INEFFICIENT

Viruses are not removed by filtration, but can be killed by boiling. However, I've not heard of viral infections, such as hepatitis, affecting PCT hikers.

Filtering water and then boiling it is an effective purifying method. The water need only come to a rolling boil; then the heat may be turned off.

But because of the time required to heat, boil and then to cool the water, and because of the fuel consumed, this method is used only occasionally.

THE BENEFITS OF FILTRATION

It is a mistake to place too much faith in a water filter. We would not collect water from a suspect source. And if we feel we must collect water of suspect biological content, we would boil it after filtering it.

In treating water, we are attempting mainly to kill or remove Giardia lamblia. These protozoans are propagated mainly by mammals. The subject is detailed in Giardia, page 111. Any unit that filters water down to 1 or 2 microns will catch most of the Giardia. However, the finer the filtration, the more resistance to water passing through it, meaning that the slower it operates, and the less water it can treat before clogging.

Giardia probably does not inhabit every water source along the PCT. Depending on your immunity, you might drink of most sources without treating the water, and without ill effects. But most of us are not equipped to analyze every source, in order to determine which ones are unsafe.

On the other hand, using a filter does not guarantee you will not contract giardiasis. The filter might be misused or defective, or a few skinny protozoans might slip through. Or you might contract the malady from your dishes, from bathing, and so on. Nevertheless, the assiduous use of a filter will probably increase your chances of staying healthy.

Most backpacking filtration systems are heavy and extremely inconvenient to use. Many of them expend valuable time and energy by requiring the user to operate a hand-pump. To facilitate the procedure I designed the Hiker's Friend Water Filter System. It operates by gravity, freeing the hiker for other tasks. And it is reasonably fast operating. See page 99 for the details.

RECOMMENDED WATER CONTAINERS

I recommend carrying filtered drinking water in one-liter bottles. Additionally, during a long, waterless stretch Jenny and I carry unfiltered water in a three-gallon, nylon covered bladder. When on a long, waterless haul, as we deplete the bottles we refill them from the Hiker's Friend, as filled by the bladder. That way, should the bladder develop a leak, we wouldn't lose as much water.

HOW MUCH WATER TO CARRY

A liter of drinking water carried in the backpack increases the load by approximately 2½ pounds. That is the approximate weight equivalent of five thousand trimmed map borders, three thousand, seven hundred and sixty three sawn-off toothbrush handles, and three superfluous tent stakes. Why do we carry the water? In part, because it represents security. But there is no need to carry too much.

The preferable technique is to rest near water sources, where we would filter water and drink of it copiously. Where sources are not accessible, we would carry enough to enable us to drink freely every hour, and yet that we arrive at the next water source carrying none. This is not difficult to plan, thanks to the information in the guide books. In the rare instances when our water bottles become depleted due to an oversight on our parts, and when the next water source is yet distant, we would accept the ensuing thirst as a part of the experience, and carry on unaffected.

SURVIVAL TIME

How long can a person survive without water? Contemporary medical knowledge has it that, lacking water, a person can walk in 90° temperatures for five days. At 60°, survival is reputedly extended to eight days if the hiker is active, or ten if inactive.

But consider how in 1941 Slavomir Rawicz (RAW-witz) and six other escapees from a Siberian prison, plus one escapee acquired along the way, walked across the Gobi Desert. Their story is described in Slavomir's book *The Long Walk*, (see appendix). Carrying neither food nor water, they walked 6½ days to the first oasis. With only a small mug to carry a pittance of water, they set off again and walked 13 days to an almost dried out creek. From there they began eating the occasional snake. They walked another 9 days to a trickling spring at the edge of the desert. Although two of the party perished, the others survived.

These exceptional people taught us a great deal about the psychology of thirst and survival.

HIKING BETWEEN DISTANT WATER SOURCES

In order to hike with the utmost efficiency between distant water sources we must first nurture a proper mind-set. Proficient distance hikers realize that nature does not always place water to their convenience. Desiccated stretches of terrain occur naturally in the wilds.

We have all heard of individuals and organizations advocating the construction of on-trail amenities, such as wells and water spigots, particularly in those areas "critically lacking" in water. This is incorrect thinking. We are wrong to try to alter nature to suit our whims. As Edward Abbey wrote: "God Bless America. Let's save some of it." Man-made amenities represent civilization's encroachment upon the wilderness. A water well is merely another foot in the door; an excuse to construct another road. And along that road, surely will come nature's helpers: vandals.

So-called wasteland areas that lack water, and that feature rattle-snakes and bothersome weeds, are actually gainful facets of the wilderness gemstone. Hiking in waterless country is a part of the everyday primeval-like backpacking experience. To take this matter to heart is to expand one's wilderness consciousness.

Consider the following scenarios, which emphasize the importance of proper timing.

THE TWENTY MILE WATERLESS STRETCH

Let's suppose that water sources A and B are 20 miles apart. We reach point A mid afternoon, and there we cook, but we do not eat dinner. Instead, we stow the warm dinner carefully in the backpack. Each of us fills a pair of one-liter water bottles with filtered water. Also, we pour a few quarts of unfiltered water into the water bag. After drinking our fill, and bathing, we set off. Hiking a few hours beyond water source A we sit down and enjoy dinner. Refreshed and revitalized, we continue another several miles, purposely into the late afternoon or evening. As dusk approaches we leave the trail and make a pleasant stealth camp, free of the tyranny of water sources. Next morning we arise at dawn and hike to water source B, where we will probably arrive mid-day and not long after having consumed the last of the water in our bottles.

Twenty mile waterless stretches are commonplace along the PCT. Hikers who apply the above technique might find these stretches inconsequential.

THE THIRTY MILE WATERLESS STRETCH

Now let's suppose that water sources A and B are 30 miles apart. We reach point A in the mid to late morning. Near there we bathe, and we filter and fill our pair of two-quart bottles. Additionally, we load our water bag with another gallon per person of unfiltered water. Pressing on, we make a dinner stop in the late afternoon, and cook and eat dinner. Then we carry on with a will into the evening and make a stealth camp away from the trail. Early morning we set off once again, and hike without dallying to water source B, arriving there perhaps in the late afternoon.

THE SIXTY MILE WATERLESS STRETCH

Of course it is not often plausible to time our arrivals at the point A's to coincide with the above scenarios. Suffice it to summarize the technique with a single edict: Hike as far beyond water source A as possible before retiring for the day.

During an exceptionally dry season, hikers would of course bypass any desiccated creeks and springs. Using the above techniques, and carrying more water, they should be able to hike much farther between viable water sources than a mere 30 miles.

SAN FELIPE CREEK

During the majority of years, there might be one place along the PCT that deserves forethought regarding the availability of water. This is San Felipe Creek at Scissors Crossing, located in far-southern California. If you will be starting your trek later in the season, then you might find this creek dry or polluted. Those who live in southern California might consider investigating before beginning their hikes, and possibly stashing water in recycled milk jugs that they would then carry to the next resupply for proper disposal. Those from out of state, upon reaching Scissors Crossing and finding it dry, would either hike one mile northeast along Highway 78 to the marsh at Sentenac Cienaga, which might also be dry, or hitchhike 5 miles southwest to Banner.

OPENING A WATER BOTTLE

Here's an interesting technique for opening a water bottle. Grasp the lid between thumb and forefinger as usual. After loosening the lid with a twist of the wrist, raise only the thumb; leave the finger pressed against the lid. Unscrew the lid using only that finger, as it revolves counter-clockwise round the bottle. When the finger has returned to the starting position, 360° later, grasp the lid once again between the thumb and forefinger, and lift it free. This technique is dozens of times faster to perform than to read about. And it can be reversed when screwing the lid back on.

WATER FILTER

For the Self Propelled

I invented the Hiker's Friend water-filter system in 1987, and Jenny and I have since used it during each of our multi-month wilderness journeys. The system is gravity fed, and therefore it requires little effort. It is comparatively fast acting. And as a package, it is also considerably smaller and lighter than all other systems currently on the market.[2]

You can order the filter bag and filter cartridges in any quantity at a discount from AdventureLore Press.

Preferably, though you can simply make your own. The illustration shows the filter system in use. The filter element is secured inside the coated or laminated nylon filter-bag, which is suspended at head height. A length of clear plastic tubing leads from the protruding element to a container at ground level.

When the bag is filled with water and suspended from a tree branch, not much water trickles through the filter. The weight of the water, alone, is insufficient to create a substantial flow through the high-resistance filter. I solved the problem by adding the syphoning tube. When filled with water, the tube generates the negative hydrostatic pressure-head required to draw water through the filter.

To begin the filtering process, attach the syphoning tube to the filter element, and suck water into it as though it were a straw. Until the element becomes saturated, air bubbles enter the tube. To expel them, raise the tube so that most of its length is above the filter. Bubbles will float upward, and escape. The syphoning process will work with some air in the line, but not as well. When the tube contains only water, lower its free end into a water receptacle. Filtered water will issue forth. And once started, the process becomes self acting.

Note in the illustration that the tubing should J-bend upward before entering the collection receptacle. If the bag is dripping or leaking slightly, unfiltered water might seep down the outside of the tube. The J-bend prevents this from contaminating the filtered water.

---

[2] Note: A few years previously, the author submitted the Hiker's Friend to various companies for manufacture. As might have been expected, rather than pay the minimal royalty, one proprietor changed the idea and began marketing it. But he made his product much heavier and less workable.

The Hiker's Friend water filter system

CAFFEINE

THE MORNING RITUAL
During our PCT hike of '87, when the alarm sounded at 5:30 am Jenny invariably began the day by firing the stove and setting on the coffee pot. We would rise, pack our tackle, then hastily chug 2 cups of cafe-campo before shouldering our packs and setting off, usually by 6:15. As such, we usually spent 45 minutes breaking camp. And we considered this sufficiently expeditious.

RITUAL ABNEGATED
During our most recent PCT hike, the alarm would sound at 4:40. Jenny and I would rise, pack our gear, and set off typically by 5:00. Whereas breaking camp used to take 45 minutes, now released of the coffee rites we were afoot in 20 minutes. And with vascular systems delightfully liberated of caffeine, we began hiking each morning full of expectation; and yes, feeling a little groggy, as nature means us to feel in the early mornings.

COFFEE THE DIURETIC
But by drinking the coffee weren't we helping to saturate our dehydrated bodies? Absolutely not. Coffee is a powerful diuretic. Most of it courses through the body while sucking vital fluids with it. You drink it brown, your kidneys filter out the particulates and solvents, and you pee it clear. But in the process, your body relinquishes some of its fluids for use in flushing the excretory organs. So what little is gained in caffeine is lost in precious body hydration.
Caffeine can stimulate or amplify anxiety. Therefore to an extent it can affect the hiker's abilities to cope with foreboding situations. And considering that dehydration and apprehension do not contribute to the hiker's well being, the trade-off is anything but beneficial.

SQUANDERING TIME
For the distance hiker habituated to the morning brew, foregoing the morning coffee or tea might buy perhaps 25 minutes of extra time, each and every day. This is time that could be used for hiking, or for sleeping in. It is time that would otherwise be squandered, boiling water for coffee, infusing the coffee grounds, letting the concoction steep, cool, and then drinking the brew like an addict.

THE SUBSTITUTE: EXERCISE

Caffeine is a drug. Many people use it to maintain alertness. But we can turn to a more holistic approach, using nutrition as an alternate method of achieving mental acuity and increased physical capacity. Walking produces virtually all the positive effects of caffeine but none of the negative ones. And considering the health benefits to be gained, walking is an excellent substitute.

ALCOHOL

Cascade Summit, a commonly used PCT resupply point, is not far from where Jenny and I live. We stopped by there the other day, and while perusing the trail registers I noticed a rash of complaints about the lack of beer. The little store there is not licensed to sell it, and many hikers had written of their disappointment.

Melodramatics of the wilderness fantasia aside for a moment, distance backpackers spend much of their time thinking of food and drink. It is the lure of the next wayside convenience store or resupply station that often drives them relentlessly onward. And several miles before reaching one they might find themselves acting like horses galloping home to the stables. Indeed, most ramblers revel in pulling into some long anticipated corner of civilization and ordering a round of refreshments.

But in the main, it is also here that the hikers' bodies are the most vulnerable. Typically, the backpack's larder had long since wasted away. Maybe the hikers had been scrimping on nutrients the past few days. And in the morning's stampede, they might have deferred the tasks of filtering and drinking adequate supplies of water.

THE COMMODIOUS BINGE

Making sudden amends with a commodious binge is a sure way to send the deprived organic mechanism into chaos. And it is here that alcohol will wreak its greatest detriments. Alcoholic beverages are powerful diuretics also. They tend to deepen the discharge of urine, leaving the body *severely* dehydrated. In fact, the effects of a hangover are largely those of acute dehydration. This is why today's hiking is less glamorous in the wake of yesterday's six pack.

The dehydrating traits of beer and other alcoholic beverages are extremely detrimental to the distance hiker, who must maintain critical levels of body fluids. Drinking and driving don't mix, and neither do drinking and distance-hiking. Consider saving the booze for an after-hike celebratory blowout, if you must. And meanwhile, enjoy a few nonalcoholic dust cutters.

INJURIES
Identifying and rectifying problems in the legs and feet

THE CAUSES AND PREVENTIONS

Distance hiking, of itself, probably does not cause injuries. Yet a few hikers experience distance-hiking injuries. The disparity? Generally, most of the injuries are the result, not of the distance-hiking, but of a too-rapid transition from a relatively sedentary existence to a very active one. Stress injuries result from pushing our bodies beyond what they are accustomed to, while disregarding the necessary time of adaptation. Yes, our bodies will probably adjust, but not so fast as we might like to think. This is but one reason the pre-hike training regimen is of vital importance. (See Training, page 21.) The longer and less abrupt the changes in our lifestyles, the less our chances of incurring an injury. I recommend six months of training, and consider three months as the absolute minimum.

During both the training and distance hiking programs, we must pay particular attention to the calf-stretching exercises (as described in Stretching, page 27). Strenuous and prolonged hiking places great demand on the calf muscles. Once these muscles grow accustomed to the exertion they will most likely perform their tasks capably and efficiently. Meanwhile, though, they interpret the exertion as antagonistic, and they begin guarding themselves, by contracting. If the exertions are prolonged, the calf muscles are likely to become tighter, and to lose much of their elasticity. Gentle and regular calf stretching encourages suppleness.

During the initial throes of the hike, our bodies struggle to adjust to the physical exertions. And keeping ourselves well hydrated is our best supportive measure. Dehydration robs our bodies of nearly their every defense against injuries. Hiking while severely dehydrated, we are practically asking for a stress injury.

Another way to solicit an injury is to hike vast distances while wearing heavy boots. We laugh at some of the ridiculous inventions of the previous century, at mechanical contrivances that were considered good ideas at the time but that have since fallen out of favor. And I imagine that we will laugh at the stiff footwear that we wore during the twentieth century.

The chapter on footwear, beginning on page 63, discusses footwear-related leg ailments, and what to do about them.

THE TYPES OF STRESS INJURIES

Two types of injuries are not uncommon with distance-hikers: the suddenly torn muscle or tendon, and the gradually stressed one. The hiker who incurs one of them, probably by overlooking the above precautions, might find advantage in the following instructions in anatomy. By gaining a better understanding of the nature and recommended treatment of these injures, one could better decide whether to deal with the injury and remain on the trail, or to detour out of the woods seeking medical attention, or perhaps to indulge in a protracted rest. And remember, the hiker doesn't have to abandon the journey just because of the need to indulge in a few week's rest and recuperation. Perhaps the injury will heal during that time. But remember also that returning to the activity that caused the injury, perhaps by hiking in the same footwear, and allowing dehydration to set in again, will almost certainly cause it again.

THE SUDDENLY TORN MUSCLE OR TENDON

Imagine that you have been on the trail a few months, and that you are in fine health. One early morning you are lumbering along, stiff bodied after a restorative night's rest, when you come to a small creek. You've jumped obstructions like this so many times that the process has become routine; but this time your foot lands slightly off center on a small root that you hadn't noticed. Your body and pack weight crunch down on a crooked, or hyper flexed ankle, and you feel a sharp pain, and hear a faint cracking or popping.

Initially the damage doesn't seem too bad, but it might spread as the days and weeks pass: like a crack spreading across a windshield from a small pit. The unrelenting strain of walking on a seed injury like this can eventually prove temporarily debilitating. A long and timely rest might be the only antidote, and indeed, strained muscles or tendons will almost certainly repair themselves if allowed a prolonged rest.

But if you guard the injury, treading carefully for the next several days, and if you massage the area to encourage circulation, and practice gentle stretching exercises every half-hour or so, the pain might eventually subside. Again, the stretching must be done gently because injured members are extremely vulnerable.

But once again, it is better to strive to prevent this type of injury to begin with. We do this by maintaining adequate muscular elasticity, with hourly stretching and by drinking water copiously.

THE STRESS INJURY

The distance hiker might experience another type of stiffness injury that is more insidious. As the hiking muscles relinquish some of their elasticity, over the hundreds of miles of heavy exertion, the muscles, ligaments, tendons and even the bones begin to sustain minute stress fractures and tears. These infinitesimal cleavages are perfectly normal; our bodies miraculously and constantly repair them without our cognizance. But if the hiker fails to adhere to the daily stretching routine, and if he or she neglects to maintain adequate hydration, the stiffening muscles are likely to transmit increasingly jarring forces until one of those little stress fractures or tears might begin to spread out of control.

ANATOMY AFOOT

In order to self diagnose a walking pain, we need to learn more about our lower extremities.

MUSCLES

Muscles assimilate the energy stored in food, and convert it to mechanical energy. Each muscle comprises a great number of tiny string-like fibers, each no thicker than a hair but capable of lifting 1,000 times its weight. Like bones, muscles grow stronger with use. But unlike bones, increased exercise stimulates the growth of new muscles, as well as new blood vessels. Damage to a muscle is called a strain. Minimally strained muscles will almost certainly repair themselves, particularly if allowed a period of rest.

TENDONS

Muscles exert their pulling force through tendons: lengths of fiber that connect muscles to bones. Tendons are not strengthened or enlarged with use. The tendons of a bodybuilder, for example, are about the same size as those of a weakling. An injury to a tendon is called a strain (the same as with a muscle). More specifically, it's called tendonitis. And like muscles, tendons are capable of repairing themselves in time. However, returning to the same activity that caused the tendonitis will almost surely cause it again. So to safeguard your tendons, keep your muscles well stretched and hydrated.

LIGAMENTS

A sprain is a tearing of a ligament: one of the fibrous bands that connect the bones together at the joints. Ligaments are strengthened somewhat with use. But far more importantly, exercise-increased musculature helps support them. Too much stretching of the wrong kind actually weakens ligaments, increasing the joint's susceptibility to a sprain. A sprain is generally more dangerous than a strain. This is because a weakening or failure of a ligament might cause further damage by leaving the joint improperly aligned. This, in turn, might endanger other parts of the joint, such as the cartilage. A sprain also generally takes longer to heal.

The ankle is the most vulnerable joint to a sprain. And the ligaments on the outside of the ankle are the most susceptible to tearing. Treat a sprain by binding the joint with non-stretchable adhesive tape, while taking great care not to reduce the circulation. If the sprain is serious, consider that continuing with the hike might risk serious complications. Think about heading out, perhaps by hobbling along while using an improvised crutch.

Contrary to popular belief, the best protection against a sprained ankle is not high topped boots, but in *previously having strengthened the muscles and ligaments*. Also, one must be extremely gentle in stretching the ankles laterally, as this might actually weaken the lateral ligaments.

WALKING WITH THE BRAKES ON

The act of walking is an exercise in rapidly flexing then relaxing opposing muscle groups. (See page 29.) Relaxing the muscles quickly is considerably more difficult than flexing them quickly. Therefore, the non proficient hiker might fail to fully relax the muscles during their off cycles. This leads to early fatigue, and possibly to an injury.

SHIN SPLINTS

A shin splint is a strained muscle of the front of the lower leg. Normally it is the result of a set of powerful calf muscles opposing the relatively weak shin muscles. Shin splints sustained while backpacking are most often the result of wearing stiff soled boots while hiking steeply downhill. As each shoe or boot heel first contacts the ground it creates an adverse leverage, pulling on the weaker muscles of the front of the calf. Prevention is the best cure. Strengthening the shin muscles will all but obviate shin splints.

BACKACHE

The most common back ailments have to do with the discs, which separate and cushion the movable vertebrae. During the day's activity the discs lose moisture and shrink. Then at night they reabsorb moisture. As such, the average human is half an inch shorter in the evenings than in the mornings. The backpacker will do well to remember that the spinal disks are not only bearing the weight of the upper body and the backpack, but they are also sustaining the vastly increased loads caused by jouncing along an irregular trail. Unable to withstand the strains imposed on it, a dehydrated disc might partially collapse.

Dehydration radically diminishes the disc's ability to withstand these strains. And this is of particular concern to the backpacker, who battles (or who should battle) dehydration practically every step of the way. Contrary to what the chiropractors might have us believe, a high percentage of back problems are the result of ongoing and acute dehydration.

THE KNEE BRACE

Some hikers wear elastic bands or braces on their knees, to help ameliorate a knee pain. And some doctors recommend this generally unwholesome practice, even knowing that its benefits might be mainly psychological. Of the knee pains experienced by backpackers, the majority are caused by ill fitting footwear. Granted, the pain might be in the knee, but the actual distress is likely to be located in the foot or ankle. As such, the problem is best addressed, not by placing elastic supports on the knee, but by condemning the possibly injurious boots or shoes, and by conditioning the feet and ankles to hiking in well-constructed and lightweight shoes.

If the hiker had actually incurred an injury to the knee, for example through some previous accident, then the best remedy is to strengthen the muscles and ligaments during a gentle and thoroughgoing pre-hike training regimen. Wearing an elastic band as an afterthought is no shortcut to vitality. The band compresses the working members of the joint, possibly making them rasp against one another. And it restricts blood circulation, not only in the knee but in the entire lower leg.

POISON OAK

Learn to recognize poison oak,
especially in early season when leafless.
And carry prescription medicine to treat the dermatitis it might cause.

RETALIATING PLANTS

The Pacific Crest is festooned with scores of isolationist plant varieties capable of retaliating if we so much as touch them. Many examples are based on the cactus theme. Fiddleheads come equipped with hair-like prickly spines, which inflict discomfort to those wading bare legged through patches of these otherwise attractive annuals. Stinging nettles thrive near some creeks. Their tiny needles take the concept one step farther by injecting a toxin that inflicts intense pain. But poison oak can make the discomforts inflicted by the others pale in comparison.

NATURAL IMMUNITY DEGRADED

Almost all people are naturally immune to poison oak, to greater or lesser degrees. In fact, the American Indians are reputedly not allergic to it at all, no doubt the result of their primogenitors having lived around it for millennia. But unfortunately, the Caucasians' immunity is degraded by repeated contacts with the poison. About a third of today's population remains invulnerable to an "average" dose, but almost any of us would suffer typically severe skin irritations if the exposure was prolonged, or if the dose was massive.

Every year a number of PCT hikers suffer the agonizing dermatitis, characterized by oozing blisters and a fiery-itching rash. Many are those who have grappled into the nights, moiling and scratching in agony. And wisely, many were those same ones who temporarily abandoned their quests, and headed out in search of medication. Indeed, if left untreated, the sores are likely to proliferate, and to persist for months.

Another disorder commonly experienced in the out-of-doors resembles a poison oak rash in many respects. This is phototoxic-dermatitis, an itching rash caused by sunburn in combination with a skin allergy to a soap or creme that had been applied. It occurs most commonly to the backs of the fingers and hands. See page 140 for further details.

THE POISON IS IN THE SAP

Poison oak contains a toxic, oily juice that combines with the proteins in human skin immediately on contact. The poison is present in the sap, which is in turn present in the leaves, stems, berries, and roots. Even dead stems are toxic. And the smoke of burning poison oak is extremely pernicious.

HABITAT

Along the crest route, poison oak is found below 5,000 feet throughout much of California. But in all of Oregon and Washington, the PCT hiker will find it only in one area that I can recall: the Columbia River Gorge environs. In the arid climes of southern California, poison oak grows mainly along creek banks, where shade abounds, and where moisture sometimes does.

THE MENACE OF BARE STEMS

Poison oak represents a genuine menace to most distance-hikers, who are likely to encounter the plant during early season when it is leafless. Yet many hikers fail to recognize this perennial. In fact, some don't even watch out for it, failing to realize that its bare stems alone are fully capable of inflicting their malice.

Poison oak is a deciduous shrub; it drops its leaves in autumn. So whenever we reach creek beds, flowing with water or not, we might then begin watching out for small communities of widely scattered bare stems, standing perhaps one or two feet in height. The hallmark of these stems is their characteristic curve. As though hungry for light, most stems are gracefully swept toward the sky.

Whether you are successful in identifying them or not, you would do well to fastidiously avoid touching, setting on, or placing your clothing or equipment onto *any* little bare stems, especially those found in natural drainages. In a few places you might encounter bare stems reaching out across the trail. Cautiously shove them aside using a stick.

THE FOLIAGE

In the springtime the stems begin developing foliage. The leaves burgeon in a variety of shapes and sizes, exhibiting considerable variance among the different kinds. But most often they will be arranged in groups of three. The leaves are oak-like, and greasy or shiny in appearance. And to anyone who has suffered from them, they might seem rather appallingly vibrant in color: green during the summers tending to bright red in the autumn. The stems of poison oak are not thorny, as are those of the raspberry bush, which the novice, hiking down into Grider Canyon toward Seiad Valley for example, might mistake for poison oak. Another California plant often mistaken for poison oak is squaw bush. After crossing I-15, look for a sign referring to a squaw bush as you hike along the abandoned nature trail.

CONTACT

Often you might encounter poison oak growing profusely on both sides of the trail, and sometimes directly on it. If you inadvertently brush against some, depending upon how hard and how much, and upon your sensitivity, the symptoms might emerge not until days later. Having long forgotten the encounter, you might notice an itchy rash that resembles a mosquito bite. But when you scratch it, the itch turns to fire. That fiery sensation means that the rash is probably not a mosquito bite. Instead, it might be a reaction to poison oak. The fiery itch also means that you should not have scratched it. Scratching a poison oak rash can exacerbate it a hundredfold. When trying to sleep, you might find yourself obsessed with the itch. If so, cover the affected area with adhesive tape, against the probability that during the half-consciousness of night you would relinquish your resolve not to scratch.

If you suspect you've touched the noxious weed, break out the small chunk of Fels-Naptha™ soap you might be carrying for such an occasion. Wash the affected parts time and again. This stratagem eliminates much of the remaining transmissible toxins, and perhaps some of your consternation.

CARRY PRESCRIPTION MEDICINE

If you have not experienced the unpleasant effects of poison oak, this is not a good time to assume that you are not allergic to the plant. So carry the appropriate medicine. Over-the-counter cortisone preparations are largely ineffective at treating poison oak reactions. So before leaving home, tell your doctor that you are planning to travel through poison oak country, and that you need a prescription for a topical corticosteroid. Carry a small amount of this ointment all the way to the Oregon Border, and include the occasional sealed packet in your California resupplies.

PARKED ON TROUBLE

In far-southern California we met a fellow who reported having recently hiked out to obtain some medicine for a severe case of poison oak. As we sat before a babbling brook he told me he couldn't remember having touched the plant. I said that this came as no surprise, then pointed out the leafless twigs festooning the area, including the ones he happened to be sitting on.

GIARDIA

I love all waste
And solitary places; where we taste
The pleasure of believing what we see
Is boundless, as we wish our souls to be.
—Shelley; 1792-1822

WHAT IS GIARDIA?

Occurring worldwide, Giardia (gee-AR-de-uh) lamblia, the parasite, causes giardiasis, (gee-ar-DIE-uh-sis) the intestinal infection. When Giardia cysts are ingested by human or animal, they metamorphose into trophozoites, and attach themselves to the small intestine. Once there, they might begin interfering with the host's digestion. Later, the trophozoites encyst, and after the new cysts travel down the colon they are excreted. Thus, the host acts as a reservoir. And if infected stools contaminate a water source, the disease might spread to those humans and animals later drinking therefrom. Thus, the cycle repeats.

WHERE DID GIARDIA ORIGINATE?

It is unlikely that Giardia has surfaced only recently in the chronicles of backcountry travel. Giardiasis, the infection, however, is another matter altogether. Giardia, the parasite, has probably existed as a normal part of the intestinal flora in humans and animals for millennia. Previously, people and animals were reasonably immune to it. Their defense mechanisms produced antibodies that fought off the microbes and staved their effects. But within the past few decades, three factors have probably contributed to the increased risks of contracting giardiasis.

OUR DECREASED IMMUNITY

Being chemically, electrically, and mechanically treated, our municipal water is practically devoid of Giardia. Because at home these microbes are no longer entering our digestive tracts, our bodies have generally quit producing the necessary antibodies. Moreover, by ingesting medicinal antibiotics we have virtually expunged the pre-existing parasites from our bodies. As a result of living in such civil sterility, we have relinquished much of our natural immunities! Also, Giardia cysts might be far more numerous in the backcountry than in years previously, perhaps because humans, livestock, and pack and saddle stock in escalating numbers are polluting the water sources.

Some people believe that the proliferation of Giardia is the result of wild animals eliminating in or near creeks and lakes. The term "beaver fever" is one popular euphemism. Other people believe that humans are mainly responsible for multiplying Giardia, perhaps by burying feces where they later dissolve into the water system. And to other people, the recent outbreak of giardiasis seems attributable to the increased population of grazing livestock, and of pack and saddle stock, which defecates tons of manure in the proximity of creeks and lakes, or which does so in the hoof and boot-rutted trail that every downpour churns into a wash-way of hearty lamblia goulash. If any of these three theories were strictly true, then water coursing down from where beaver, humans and stock could not possibly venture should be free of Giardia. But this is not always the case.

Regardless of the cause, when we venture afield and drink the water, we risk becoming sick. I say *"risk"*, because giardiasis ordinarily does not produce symptoms. More on this in a moment.

BEYOND TREATING OUR DRINKING WATER

Giardia lamblia is ordinarily a water-borne parasite. But the cysts do not require water to survive. Even if we treat our drinking water assiduously, and brush our teeth using filtered water, we can contract the malady. One way is to wash our cook pot, cup and spoon in untreated water. For even after we carefully towel dry the utensils, the Giardia might cling to them. (See page 187, for instructions on waterless dish washing.) And remember that campers can be their own Giardia generators.

THE SYMPTOMS

Giardiasis is commonly asymptomatic. Many hikers, if not most, who remain afield for extended periods become unknowing parasitic hosts without showing significant ill effects. Where clinical manifestations occur, they might do so only weakly or intermittently, depending on the cyst count and the host's immunities.

The symptoms, when they occur, range from flatulence to malabsorption. The hiker might experience increasing diarrhea, nausea, and abdominal pain. The frequent (10 or more times daily) stools might be loose and mucous.

WHEN TO VISIT A DOCTOR

Hikers who begin exhibiting the symptoms of giardiasis have every chance that their bodies will manage to produce the needed antibodies. Those who choose to ride the symptoms out, would do well to increase their intake of water, in order to reduce the malady's dehydrating effects. In any case, I recommend distance-hikers carry a doctor-prescribed medicine, such as metronidazole, (the generic name for Flagyl) but that they use it only as a last resort. And finally, those who endure increasing symptoms might be wise to visit a doctor, in case the ailment is not giardiasis.

Keep in mind that medicines do not improve our natural resistance to the effects of these microorganisms. On the contrary, the antibiotics decrease our immunities and thereby increase our susceptibilities. Also, Giardia cysts are said to be detectable in the stools in less than 50% of the cases. So when seeking medical attention for giardiasis, state your symptoms and circumstances, and suggest that if the doctor agrees with your diagnosis, you might like to try the medication for several days before committing yourself to any expensive, time consuming, and unreliable stool tests. In every likelihood the medicine will ameliorate the symptoms.

RECOMMENDATIONS

Conscientious hikers bury their stools far from trails, campsites and water supplies. And those suffering giardiasis would consider theirs as potent sources of infection. They would do well to sterilize their hands after eliminating, not by washing them in the creek! but perhaps by wiping them with a swab wetted with disinfectant (such as rubbing alcohol carried in a small vial).

Most of the backcountry water is safe to drink, but its clarity is no guarantee. Most hikers treat their drinking water, but some do not. Some of those who do not, contract giardiasis. Conversely, some hikers who assiduously treat their drinking water contract the malady and exhibit its symptoms.

At any rate, prudence suggests we treat all our drinking and dish-washing water and that which we use to brush our teeth. Even then, Giardia might enter our bodies when we swim, bathe, or even when we mop our faces with a creek-dampened towel. No water treatment will insure complete protection. So after taking every precaution, we can only keep the cat hole digging implement accessible.

BEARS

Like winds and sunsets,
wild things were taken for granted
until progress began to do away with them.
Now we face the question
of whether a still-higher standard of living
is worth its costs in things natural, wild and free.
—Aldo Leopold

THE GRIZZLY: CALIFORNIA'S STATE ANIMAL

Although the grizzly was once common in the western and south-western states (and even in northern Mexico), it has long been extirpated from these areas. But it is making something of a return, and now occurs in exceeding small numbers (in PCT environs) in far-northern Washington. Even so, the possibility of a PCT hiker sighting a grizzly is so remote that a relevant treatise is beyond the scope of this book. Suffice it to say this: In 99.8% of the human-grizzly encounters, after apprising the situation the bear will scurry away. Furthermore, all types of bears disdain people in groups; so if you are worried, consider hiking and camping with a few companions while in the far-northern Cascades. Still, I have not heard of a PCT hiker sighting a grizzly.

READING THE PAW PRINT

Rarely, you might encounter the track of an *uncommonly* large black bear. How do you discern its species? The grizzly's front paw print shows long claw marks that extend two and a half times the length of its toe pad. That of the American black bear might show claw marks, but they are much shorter. A bear's rear foot pad is shaped roughly triangularly, its apex pointing aft. If you find a large track with a generally triangular pad pointing forward, and which lacks claw marks, you are probably looking at the track of a cougar. The shape of a Sasquatch track is as yet a matter of conjecture.

BLACK BEAR TERRITORY

Along the Pacific Crest, the black bear ranges from the Canadian border to Walker Pass (just beyond the southern reaches of the Sierra), and is slowly spreading south. If Walker Pass seems quite southerly, imagine how the proprietor of a small store, located between Inyokern and Ridgecrest—far out in the Mojave Desert—felt when a bear reputedly wandered into his store and began pillaging the merchandise.

TWO TYPES OF BLACK BEAR

The black bear is not always black. It can also be blond, cinnamon, reddish, and brown. Despite the coloration, the species can be divided roughly in half. The two types, the wild bear and the park bear, are as different as day and night.

WILD BLACKIE

The "wild" variety of black bear occurs generally outside of national parks. Every hunting season it becomes prey to myriad big-game hunters, and often their hounds. Thus, outside of national parks the black bear has not shed its innate fear of humans. If surprised unaware by a hiker it will probably bolt away into the woods at astonishing speed, often smashing asunder large branches and bowling down small trees happening in its path. Should the bear in question be a cub or yearling, though, it might stop and stare curiously for a few moments before scurrying away to hide behind a tree.

Hikers take note: **Left alone**, the *wild* black bear poses not the slightest danger to you, nor menace to your supplies. Your only precaution is to avoid giving a sow the false notion that you are preying upon her cub. Even so, anywhere along the PCT, distance hikers would do well to follow the precautions that follow on page 117.

PARK BLACKIE

Inside national parks, where hunting is generally not permitted, the black bear can become a genuine nuisance. In Yosemite Valley, where I lived for 11 years, there seems to be an unlimited supply of bears. No matter how many are hauled away, others take their places. Whether they come from inside the park, as yearlings and adolescents, or from outside the park, is perhaps a matter of some speculation. Suffice it to say, though, that inside the national parks, bears tend to gravitate to the nearest black hole of outback civilization. And there they commence raiding campsites and vehicles with virtual impunity. Being constantly hungry, insatiably curious, and remarkably intelligent, they readily adapt to the endowment of so-called protectionism. They becomes "tame."

Lacking morals, the bear hasn't the slightest qualm about stealing food, or objects containing or resembling it. Therefore, as the bear struggles to interlace with society it becomes an increasing menace, sometimes even a hazard. And when finally its havoc wreaking becomes intolerable, the rangers break out their bear traps.

Trapped bruin is drugged and ear-tagged or body painted, then towed away in its wheeled coach. Most usually, a custodian of the natural world relocates pitiable bruin to some far away forest, and releases it back to the wilds. But bruin now realizes that a better life is ordained for it. Straightway it descends to the nearest outpost and resumes pillaging, perhaps only to be shot on sight. How do we know? The ear tags and body paint.

Outside of national parks, bears are hunted to the ends of the earth. Inside the parks, the protectorates relocate them to the outside.

DANGEROUS TO HIKERS?

Rarely, a park bear injures a tourist stupidly trying to feed it. This accident occurs because by nature, bestial voracity overrides restraint. Notwithstanding, the adept PCT hiker would do well to remember that even though powerfully muscled and armed with claws and incisors, blackie has no appetite for humans. It has never eaten one, nor does it intend to do so at some future date. The park bear wants only your food. And it wants it bad.

And considering that about only one in fifty campers will defend their stores, it usually meets with considerable success.

PROTECTING YOUR FOOD

Because the NPS has not been able to exert dominion over the park bear, despite the agency's best efforts, it has turned to its only scapegoat: the backcountry visitor. Rangers cannot fine the bear for stealing our food, so instead they fine us for suffering the bear to steal our food. The fine is up to $500 for not bear-bagging our food. Unable to solve the bear problems, the "authorities" are demanding that we hikers solve them.

They instruct us that while in the backcountry we are to suspend our food from contrived overhead wires, or to place our stores in metal boxes. Because the wires and boxes exist only in designated camps, the rangers are effectively corralling us into known, and therefore easily regulated sites. But imagine the irony! The ticket-bestowing rangers deem camper agglomeration a great convenience; and so do the prowling bears.

Concerning designated campsites that lack bear wires or boxes, official literature depicts various methods of suspending food from tree branches, so many feet above the ground and so many feet out from the tree trunk. This is conservation?—killing a tree branch by sawing into its bark with a thin line hoisting a load of stores?

Nevertheless, I reckon that many bears of the national park back-country owe their health to gullible hikers trusting in these systems. Bruin is incredibly resourceful at retrieving comestibles; and the nights are long. I've seen the results of scores of intriguing bags eventually plucked from high in the air. Even lost one myself years ago, hung so high that the bear would have needed a step ladder to reach it. But reach it, it did, and the massive branch supporting my haversack narrowly missed smashing both me and my tent. Alas, new bear-bagging techniques come up into vogue as fast as they go down, while the food bags, and the branches supporting them, mainly go down.

Many experienced national park backcountry visitors have realized the futility of bear-proofing their supplies. Some of these folks may wish to consider the methods I use in an attempt to outwit the ravenous bear.

We begin by examining our mistakes. But first, consider that the park bear associates us with the food logically in our possession. And it has learned that hikers exhibit a universal stereotyped behavior. Almost without exception:

⊗ They camp in designated sites, every one of which lies on the bear's nightly marauding route.

⊗ They advertise their presence with a campfire, the smoke of which sends an olfactory signal clearer than any siren.

⊗ They cook food, the aroma being a thousand times more alluring than mere smoke.

⊗ They hang their food in sight as though advertising it.

⊗ They act terrified at the bear's intrusion and readily back off, recognizing the bear's dominance and giving it free reign.

Were I a bear roving in search of plunder, I could not imagine a scenario more conducive to success. In fact, after a time I might begin thinking myself illustrious and well respected.

But because I and my stealth-camping (page 177) contingency are hikers, not bears, we must turn the tables. Otherwise, the results, as thousands of campers have learned, are unlikely to fall to our advantage.

In avoiding bears, first we need to assess where they are likely to be found. They are not ubiquitous. In season, and in the backcountry, the park bear will be found almost exclusively within range of the designated campsites, which, in turn, are invariably located near sources of water. Second, we must consider that in the wilds, bear maraudings in the presence of humans are strictly nighttime activities.

These premises reduce the task of avoiding the bear to the simple matter of avoiding camping in the target zones, populated by the hoards of unenlightened campers acting as bait. Therefore:

☺ We refrain from sleeping within miles of the nearest designated site.

☺ We do not advertise our impromptu camps with campfires.

☺ We avoid cooking and eating our evening meals and scrubbing our utensils within miles of where we sleep.

☺ And some of us might not suspend our stores—both because we would harm the tree branches by doing so, and also because by following the above, there might be no need to.

In PCT environs I sleep with my food, prepared to guard it without compromise. At night I keep my flashlight near at hand, lest I take a blind swat at porkie. When in national parks I observe the foregoing precautions, and I camp with a small pile of fist-sized stones lying outside the tent door. And I do not suffer the misconception that my nocturnal bliss is inviolate; I fall asleep prepared to rise and assert my position.

In years past, while camping in Yosemite I learned the effectiveness of taking a firm stand. When awakened by intruding, powerful, but readily daunted bruin I would rise. Not backing off an inch, I would begin hollering and hurling stones, first in the bear's direction, then should it require more prodding, reasonably gently at its well-padded body—being careful to avoid striking its face. Not once did my atypical behavior fail to prompt bruin to mosey reluctantly away in search of happier hunting grounds. However, I am not suggesting the reader follow suit. Throwing rocks at bears could elicit an undesirable reaction. Furthermore, many camp bears in the backcountry are accustomed to hiker's acts of mock aggression, and are no longer daunted by them. Here, I am merely describing what has worked for me. And once again, I have found no need to deal with bear mauradings while stealth camping.

A further word is in order: Once blackie has procured your food the tables are irrevocably turned. Consider the joke on you, and in the interests of well being, do not attempt to steal it back.

Blackie can become belligerent in the late autumn while preparing to lie torpid for the winter. But by then we PCT hikers will have long since gone. Nevertheless, I might mention that in the late season, and at established campsites, as a last resort to persuade the camper to yield the food blackie might charge, only to stop a few meters short. When the matter concerns food, black bear aggression is almost always a bluff. Back off a ways, taking your food with you, and in all probability the bear will acquiesce. If not, examine the creature more carefully. It might be a ranger in disguise.

SNAKES

Travel teaches toleration.
—Benjamin Disraeli

THE GOPHER SNAKE

Sizeable, but harmless to the hiker who leaves it alone, the gopher snake (also called the bull snake) resides throughout much of California, Oregon and Washington—from sea level to 9,000 feet. Left to itself, this non-poisonous snake behaves impassively. When confronted, though, it might hiss, flatten its head, and vibrate its tail defensively. And it is well known for biting a molester.

Because the gopher snake shows patterns of darker blotches on its back and sides, inexperienced hikers regularly mistake it for the rattlesnake. To the contrary, the gopher snake is one of our most highly regarded reptiles. And as a bonus perhaps, like the California kingsnake it occasionally feeds on rattlesnakes.

During your through-hike of the PCT you might encounter the occasional gopher snake stretched across the trail, hoping in vain that you won't notice it. If so compelled, it might pose nervously for a close-up photograph. But no doubt it would rather you get on with your quest and leave it alone.

THE RATTLESNAKE

Among a dozen or more interesting species of snakes common to the PCT environs, the only venomous one is the rattlesnake. In its many subspecies, the rattler occurs widely throughout California, Oregon and Washington, from sea level to 11,000 feet. As a PCT hiker, you can expect to encounter rattlers only rarely; although they exist in many sections along the full length of the trail. In particular, they might be found in rocky or brushy areas, along creeks, or in lower forests. You are unlikely to meet with one in red-fir or sub-alpine forests, or in alpine areas. Their presence and populations generally vary according to those of their prey.

STEWARDS OF THE NICHE

All snakes are of great benefit to their local ecology, and rattlesnakes are no exception. But some people imagine that by culling the rattlesnake population, however insignificantly, they are encouraging the gopher snake to assume the greater prevalence within the same niche: making the wilderness a safer place for those hikers who follow. The consummate outdoor enthusiast, though, is by nature a staunch conservationist. However, we trod on ants and myriad other insects. And emphatically, most of us slap mosquitoes and biting flies caught drilling into our flesh. But of course, in most of these examples the killing is usually inadvertent, unavoidable, or done in self defense.

CHARACTERISTICS

But back to the theme. Forget its markings for a moment. The rattler is characterized predominately by the flattish, triangular-shaped head, wide in the jowls and fashioned improbably onto a thin neck. This is the viper look. And most (but not all) rattlesnakes come equipped with a set of tail rattles.

BELLIGERENT?

In the wilds, rattlesnakes are not warlike toward humans. The size ratio is to their genuine disadvantage, and instinctively they avoid threatening species. So don't expect to be charged by one. Once identified by a human armed with a stick or a few rocks, the rattlesnake becomes extremely vulnerable. So instead, its *primary* defense is to remain concealed.

The notion that rattlesnakes are aggressive is entirely fallacious. But a few of its attributes spell danger to hikers. One: its infrequency. After you have hiked weeks without seeing one, your guard will be down. Two: its camouflage. And three: almost invariably the rattler will lie still initially, in hopes that you won't notice it. This defense ploy can allow you to approach within striking range, unaware of the snake's presence. Contrary to popular belief, the snake doesn't become angry or aggressive. But if so required it can defend itself by exercising its ultimate recourse. And it does not always rattle first before striking. If you step too close too quickly, it might strike without warning.

THE DANGEROUS ENCOUNTER

Furthermore, the rattler exhibits one foible, which will, or at least which should keep your nerves on edge throughout most of California. It's a torpid beast, especially after feasting on a succulent lizard, mouse, vole, rabbit, ground squirrel or bird. And frankly, it would sooner curl up and enjoy a nice nap, and leave the world to its predicaments. Like most people, it spends much of its time in a state of inattentiveness.

And here you come, galumphing down the trail with your mind in the clouds. And there lies the snake, fortuitously off the trail in a comfortable bed of dry weeds beneath a shading bush. As with any potentially lethal encounter, time is of the essence; especially for the underdog. And we may be assured that the snake endures by far the greatest peril. Statistically, for every person that suffers a bite, thousands of rattlers are killed. Fortune, it seems, favors the colossal.

Nevertheless, as you approach the snake unawares, it dozes. Closer you tramp. Suddenly the snake awakens to your vibrations, which signal danger. It lies very still, attempting to safeguard itself by remaining unobserved. But in the flurry of the next few moments, still you come. To protect itself, the snake finally coils instinctively and begins buzzing. Enlightened, you stop short and immediately step back. After buzzing a while, the snake retreats a short ways, but surprisingly with little sense of urgency.

The snake is now yours; to destroy with a large rock lobbed casually onto its midriff, or to walk away from, allowing it to enjoy life, as we hope it did you.

CONQUERING THE FEAR

Once identified, the snake poses little danger to the person who exercises caution. In fact, I recommend hassling a rattlesnake once in your life, as an exercise in dealing with your inner fear rather than to automatically flee. Demonstrate to yourself that a rattlesnake is not an insidious creature of revulsion. After accessing your exit, from a safe distance you might toss a few rocks at the snake—not at its body, which is sluggish, but at its head, which will easily duck your salvos with lightning-fast reflexes. By taking the aggressive stand you will enhance your confidence beyond measure.

Fear the rattler? No. Remain vigilant and respectful of it? Yes indeed!

CLOSE ENCOUNTERS

Like nature's many other variables, snakes appear in numbers that vary year to year. In most seasons, hikers encounter few. During our two through-hikes of the PCT, I imagine that Jenny and I might have walked past scores of rattlers, unaware. During our first PCT hike we met with 6 rattlers. One was "monstrous" in size and another was merely huge. In the desert we came upon a large Mojave green rattlesnake, the most venomous species. During our second through-hike we encountered 8 rattlers. A small one was lying on the trail, coiled in the sleeping position (as opposed to the striking one). Obliviously, I stepped over it; toes on one side, heel on the other. Straightway Jenny called out. I stopped and turned in time to see and hear a vibrating set of rattlers disappear down the steep slope and into the brush, buzzing as it went. On another occasion I was again in the lead; we were hiking a shovel-cut trail, ornamented with underbrush. Suddenly a sporadic buzzing emanated only 18 inches from my bare leg. I leapt ahead and Jenny stopped short. Peering low into the bushes we saw a sizeable rattler lying between us.

In both of the preceding instances the snakes had me within easy range; yet they forewent the opportunity of lashing out. And many other hikers have similar stories. These certainly do not prove that rattlers don't strike, but they do illustrate the fact that rattlers don't always strike.

THE CHANCES OF BEING BITTEN

In the U.S, an estimated 8,000 venomous bites are sustained each year, **most** without trips to the hospital. Only about a dozen are fatal, to children, mostly. In other words, your chances of being killed on the PCT by a rattlesnake are virtually zilch. I have not heard of a PCT hiker being bitten by a rattlesnake, although my experiences hardly suggest dismissing the possibility. Still, the subject is prone to overdramatization.

FIRST AID TREATMENT

Should a rattler strike you, do not cut or suction. (Most doctors experienced with snake bites recommend against snake bite kits.) Use no ice or tourniquet. If you like, apply an ace bandage above the bite. Your single most important action is simply to remain calm. Move away, lay down, and *relax for awhile.* Above all else, keep a firm grip on a positive attitude. To fear the worst is to summon the worst. Consider that some types of rattlesnakes are far less venomous than others; those of Oregon and Washington, particularly. Consider that the snake might have injected only a minimum of poison. And remember that in 25% to 50% of all cases involving poisonous snake bites, no venom is injected whatsoever. How will you know? Envenomation usually causes immediate swelling and pain, and within 10 to 15 minutes, edema: an *excessive* accumulation of serous fluid in the immediate tissues. However, symptoms of envenomation immediately following the bite of a Mojave green rattlesnake (easily distinguished by its pale green color) should be construed as a medical emergency.

Rattlesnake venom digests cell tissues. Badly damaged tissues do not recover; they die and slough off, or they might need to be surgically removed if they become gangrenous. Very serious bites might require skin grafts.

HIKING IN SNAKE COUNTRY

In snake country walk attentively. Scan the trail eight or ten feet ahead. Where the trail is overbrushed, probe ahead with a stick. For those hikers wishing to take every precaution, snake chaps are well worth considering. They are available from Leonard Rue Enterprises, 138 Millbrook Rd, Blairstown, NJ 07825.

TICKS

THE TICK DESCRIBED

Occurring in hundreds of species, the tick is flat, roundish, and eight legged. A parasitic arthropod, it feeds on the blood of mammals, but is food to none. It feeds only once during each of the three phases of its two year life cycle: first, as a 6-legged larvae, then a year later as an 8-legged nymph, and finally several months later as an adult. It lives in brush, weeds, leaf litter and duff. Awaiting a meal, it is attracted by heat, movement, and by carbon dioxide exuded by animals. It does not fly or jump, but instead simply reaches out and climbs aboard. After securing a suitable host, the tick will usually crawl around while examining the menu for several hours before biting. This is often the astute hiker's saving grace. During the bloodletting, the tick injects saliva into the host's blood stream. If infected, the saliva can transmit a number of diseases.

THE FUTILE SEARCH

In parts of southern California where ticks are the most abundant along the PCT, it is not uncommon for the hiker to pick 20 to 50 adult ticks from the clothing and body each day. In suitable conditions, a mere 100 yards of trail can produce similar results. One of the hiker's defenses against adult ticks is to habitually search his or her clothing after scraping through each section of brush. Light-colored clothing enhances success considerably. As a precaution, those hiking with a buddy would do well to regularly inspect each-other's underarms and divested back-sides, paying particular attention to the back of the necks. Before crawling into your sleeping bag, inspect your body carefully.

The overwhelming majority of the ticks discovered are adult ticks, generally measuring ¼-inch across at the most. The larvae are not much of a concern because they are not known to transmit disease. **But the pin-head sized nymphs, which are far more likely to transmit disease, are so tiny that only rarely are they detected.** *Because the nymphs are small and difficult to detect—especially on a hairy arm or leg, merely looking for them is ineffective protection. For this reason, hikers would do well to physically protect their bodies and extremities.* Typically, ticks will try to crawl under the clothing. But they generally lack the power to force their way under the snug-fitting elastic bands of socks, pant legs, arm cuffs, and waist-bands. And they are usually stopped by form-fitting Lycra. As protection for the lower body I recommend light-colored Lycra pants that overlap light-colored socks. At each rest stop, the hiker would peel back the Lycra pant-legs and inspect carefully for any "wandering freckles."

As an aside, Lycra supposedly shreds, as its wearer scrapes through pernicious brush. This is generally incorrect. In fact, many double-stretch fabrics are surprisingly durable. But please note that despite my recommending Lycra pants and shorts for backcountry hiking, I strongly recommend the hiker don more appropriate attire when approaching outposts of civilization. The woods and the towns are two different worlds; what works in one rarely does so in the other.

If Lycra is not the apparel that best expresses your individuality, then consider wearing long pants with their leg cuffs tucked into your socks. Remember that loose fitting pant-legs provide perfect concealment for any hungry ticks wandering about your legs. Therefore, in tick country you would remove the trousers regularly in order to inspect for ticks.

REPELLENTS

DEET is the active ingredient in most insect repellents. When applied to the skin or clothing it reputedly reduces the number of ticks crawling unseen on your body and clothing by about 75%. Permethrin supposedly reduces them by almost 100%. Permethrin doesn't repel the ticks, it kills them. It is a remarkable chemical that can be sprayed on shoes, clothing, and even on your backpack. It is poorly absorbed into the skin (to the hiker's decided advantage) and it is almost totally deactivated by the enzymes in skin.

Duranon (formerly called Permanone) contains 0.5% permethrin. Currently it is the tick "repellent" of choice. The solvent used is water; the pressurized sprays do not contain chlorofluorocarbons; and the chemical is biodegradable. The manufacturer claims that permethrin repellent chemically binds to natural and synthetic clothing fibers, and that it remains effective for up to two weeks following application. When dry it is odorless, colorless, non-staining and non-reactive. Permethrin also kills black flies, mosquitoes, midges and lice on contact.

Presently, the main disadvantage of the Duranon "repellent" is the size and weight of the can that contains it. Thus, I recommend one or both of the following tactics:

A) Include a can in your running resupply box. (Note that pressurized aerosols are illegal to air mail. But it will probably not travel by air over such a short distance.) At the resupply station, spray your clothing and backpack, then mail the running resupply two weeks ahead.

B) Or buy a bottle of liquid permethrin, which comes in extremely concentrated form. Pour a tiny amount into a small spray bottle (of the type used for DEET). Then top off the bottle with water.

Permethrin products are available from Leonard Rue Enterprises, 138 Millbrook Rd, Blairstown, NJ 07825 (908) 362-6616. The company also sells insect-repellent saturated netting jackets, guaranteed snake-proof chaps, bear repellent (Capsaicin, which reputedly causes an immediate and vigorous retreat), and a wealth of photography accessories and wildlife books. Request a copy of their interesting catalogue.

TICK REMOVAL

The remedies of daubing an embedded tick with petroleum jelly or alcohol, or heating its derriere, are unreliable. If you find a tick that has embedded into your skin, use tweezers to grasp the tick as close to your skin as possible. If you lack tweezers, cover the tick with a piece of plastic bag, as a biological barrier protecting your fingers from infection. Pull steadily but gently, without twisting, until the tick lets go. Take great care not to crush or puncture the tick, or to contaminate your skin with its fluids. If you pull too forcefully, the tick's mouth parts might break away and remain embedded, possibly causing irritation and infection. After removing the tick, disinfect your skin, and wash your hands thoroughly with soap and water.

RECOGNIZING EARLY SYMPTOMS

Presently the PCT hiker bitten by a tick is unlikely to become ill. *Most* ticks en route do not yet carry any of the nine tick-borne diseases found in other parts of the country. Nevertheless, because of the seriousness of the diseases possibly transmitted, and because recovery depends almost entirely on early detection and treatment, the hiker would do well to recognize the early symptoms of at least the two most prevalent diseases: Rocky Mountain spotted fever and Lyme disease.

ROCKY MOUNTAIN SPOTTED FEVER

Endemic throughout the continental U.S, and especially prevalent on the Atlantic seaboard, this is perhaps the most serious of tick borne diseases. Its rickettsia are transmitted by the wood tick and the dog tick. The initial symptoms are most often a high fever, headache, chills and severe fatigue. More characteristically, though, a *spotted* rash often develops (hence the name) initially on the subject's hands and feet. If you begin suffering these symptoms, start a course of oral antibiotics, and head for the nearest doctor.

LYME DISEASE

Lyme disease was first chronicled in Europe in the early 1900s. Most likely it was prevalent before that, although probably it was misdiagnosed. Today we know it is endemic to every continent except Antarctica.

In the western states, the disease is transmitted by the western black-legged tick, also known as the Pacific tick. This is the counterpart of the deer tick of the northeast and upper midwest states. Presently, along the PCT only 1% to 5% of the western black-legged ticks carry Lyme.

Following the bite, which usually goes unnoticed, the earliest evidence of infection (in only 60% of the cases) is a skin rash at or near the bite. The rash is most likely to appear about a week after the bite. In the next several days it might expand, growing into an ever-widening red circle. However, there are many variations. Along with the rash, or sometimes in its absence, the patient might experience flu-like symptoms: fever, malaise, headache and possibly a profound sense of fatigue. Even if not treated, these symptoms, including the rash, usually disappear within a week or ten days. But the disease generally progresses unperceived, until resurfacing later and possibly causing acute and chronic health problems.

Doctors can treat Lyme disease at any stage, but the earlier they begin the treatment the better the patient's outlook for a full recovery. Let the amateur-in-the-field take note, however, that the diagnosis is usually based purely on the symptoms; for in the disease's early stages, blood tests rarely confirm the presence of Lyme. Antibiotics are the treatment of choice. Doxycycline or amoxicillin plus probenecid are preferred over tetracycline or penicillin. Before setting out on the PCT, consider asking your doctor for a prescription, so that in the unlikely event you should notice any burgeoning symptoms, you might initiate treatment while hiking out of the woods seeking medical assistance.

And remember: dark-brown clothes are the tick's allies.

MOSQUITOES

*The use of traveling
is to regulate imagination by reality,
and instead of thinking how things may be,
to see them as they are.*
—Samuel Johnson

Imagine us setting off across the High Sierra, early in the season, while intentionally carrying inadequate clothing. Cold would rule our alpine existence, and if we survive this hypothetical ordeal, we would probably complain emphatically of the cold.

Now imagine we are setting off into the mountains at the height of mosquito hatching season, carrying only a few bottles of bug repellent as protection against the voracious hoards. We would be practically inviting mosquitoes to rule our lives for that span of time.

When venturing into the wilds we need to take along clothing that will suitably protect us from whatever adverse elements we are likely to encounter. For cold weather we would carry insulating clothing; for desert travel, clothes that protect us from intense ultraviolet radiation; for rain, rain wear; and during those seasons when the biting and flying insects are particularly voracious, we would carry bug-proof clothing and netting.

POPULATIONS VARY YEAR TO YEAR

Just as some years are more rainy than others, and some yield more snow, some years are buggier. Often, PCT hikers encounter minimal mosquitoes and biting flies; but in some years they come across them in disconcerting droves. Most types of mosquitoes hatch in water, and their populations vary according to the precipitation of the previous winter and spring. But some types of mosquitoes hatch on the underside of branches, for example of the buck brush of central Oregon. In season, these pests are well represented in most years, and far from the nearest pond or lake.

DEET

For the distance hiker who plies the backcountry for weeks and months on end during a particularly buggy year, insect repellent is **not** adequate protection. DEET is a powerful toxicant. Six hours after applying it, 50% of it will have absorbed through the skin, and most of that will have entered the blood system. 10% to 15% of each dose can be recovered from the urine. *The Handbook* stresses the distinction between techniques suitable for weekend hikers and those for distance hikers. And this is one of them. The weekend hiker might use DEET with impunity. After several weeks of such abuse, though, the bodies and minds of most distance hikers might begin rebelling. It is when reaching this stage of mental intolerance that they begin not only to loathe the repellent, but also to suffer from the bugs. One of the side effects of the repellent seems to be a lessening of one's ability to endure mentally the buzzing hoards, and physically their bites.

PROTECTIVE CLOTHING

So instead, we distance hikers need to emulate our forbearers, who were perhaps fortunate in lacking these modern chemicals. We do this by wearing clothing that physically blocks the biting insects from reaching our skin. My recommended bug-proof wardrobe comprises these items:

✓ A lightweight, breathable nylon shell-jacket, used also on occasion to shunt the breeze. The wrists are of elastic.

✓ Pants similar to the above, with elastic pant cuffs.

✓ A loose-fitting head net that extends below the shoulders, and that features one flap extending 18 inches down the back and one extending the same distance down the chest.

✓ Net mittens that extend half way up the forearms. Elastic cuffs hold the mitts in place. The mitts can be lose-fitting cylinders that lack thumb protuberances.

✓ Net stockings, extending upward to below the knees, and worn over the regular socks.

Again, these items must fit loosely. Some types of biting flies cannot bite through the nylon or the netting, but mosquitos can readily insert their long proboscises. The function of the garments is primarily to distance them.

THE COLORS OF CHOICE

Color plays a key role. Light colors minimize the absorption of solar radiation; they are cooler and therefore more tolerable to wear. This is a genuine consideration when hiking exposed to the sun's incandescence, which only adds to the metabolical heat generated by strenuous hiking. Also, flying and biting insects are often far less attracted to lighter colors. To my chagrin, I have noticed this many times as Jenny and I have sat together, she wearing light colored clothing and I wearing dark. Furthermore, the person wearing lighter colored garments can more effectively check for the presence of ticks.

Having said that, though, a black face-net is a little more transparent than a light-colored one. This is because the black material absorbs more of the scattered light, reflected by the fibers.

SOURCES OF PROTECTIVE CLOTHING

Where do you obtain these garments? You would make them yourself, of course! And fortunately this is not difficult. Refer to the chapter on Sewing, page 194.

WHY TAKE CHANCES?

Once again, this gear is necessary only in years when the insects are particularly numerous. During some years, headnets and net mittens are not needed; but during others, they are. So why take chances? The garments are lightweight, and categorically useful when needed. And my advice is to carry them.

PSYCHOLOGICAL?

Most of us have suffered various lecturers extolling the virtues of mosquito forbearance. "Just ignore them," we are instructed, "it's all psychological." As with wintry or desert weather, I admit that psychology plays an important role; but so does protective clothing.

REPELLENT

In addition to our bug-protective wardrobe, still we might want to carry some repellent, applied infrequently and sparingly. Studies have shown that a 35% solution of DEET is actually more effective than a 95% or a 100% one. And most of the inert ingredients have the benefit of not absorbing into the skin. Eschew the "long lasting" repellents, which contain a molasses-like substance; in the long term these can be extremely uncomfortable on the skin. The spray pump is a convenient applicator, but much of the atomized chemical is lost to the air. One's face must not be sprayed, and what repellent (and its residues) remain on the skin must be washed off before retiring at night. If water is scarce, one can wipe as much off as possible using a damp hand-towel.

DEET dissolves many types of plastic, such as that of eyeglasses and wrist watches. And beware: in quantity, it immediately destroys the internal membranes of expensive Gore-Tex and other waterproof-breathable garments.

THE PSYCHOLOGICAL ITCH

By scratching insect bites, we only increase the annoyance, and damage our skin in the process, at the risk of inducing a serious infection. Resisting the itching is definitely a psychological battle.

REVENGE

As we hike from one place to another during mosquito season we might find that the bugs at either place are about the same in number. What a coincidence. In fact, the throngs might be one and the same. An entourage of voracious mosquitoes is likely to follow its host close behind and seemingly to the ends of the earth. In lieu of netting and repellent, how do we find relief? Stop and kill the bloodthirsty buggers to the last insect, then hike on. Flattened mosquitoes have a marvelous way of leaving a person alone. And often their replacements are slow in coming.

But there is an easier way. Spray Permethrin on your clothing and your backpack. It kills insects that land on it. Refer to page 124 for the details. Generally, I shun the use of chemicals in the backcountry, but this type of revenge I find irresistible.

CREEK FORDING

Setting out on the voyage to Ithaca
You must pray that the way be long,
Full of adventures and experiences.
—Constantine Peter Cavafy

Throughout a life of backpacking, hiking, climbing, and kayaking adventures, I've acquired reasonable experience fording creeks and rivers. The result is an enormous respect for the power of moving water.

As fledgling professionals in charge of various wilderness programs, we instructors experimented with every technique we could think of related to using ropes as safety devices when crossing creeks and rivers.

Initially, we scheduled arriving bus loads of students to disembark at the bank of some daunting river. After unloading, we instructed the students to line up, to lock elbows, and not to let go. Then we marched them mid-torso deep across the swift-flowing river. Usually this technique was effective. But sometimes a student did let go, only to be swept downriver at great peril. So before the beginning of one course we set a floating safety line, angling obliquely across the river and downstream, out of sight of the students. Sure enough, one fellow let go of the gang. And soon we discovered to our horror that our safety rope acted instead like a spider's web, trapping the student. The director dove headlong into the river, swam to the student's rescue, and pried him bodily off the rope.

TRIAL AND ERROR

In the ensuing years we experimented further. We tried wading a river while holding a rope's knotted loop; only to find that the rope-drag drastically compromised the wader's balance and concentration. We installed sky-lines over creeks, tree-to-tree, and experimented with various tensions and heights of rigging them. At first we affixed the students to a sky-line using long lanyards and carabiners. This proved dangerous, because the stretching sky-line offered but little balance, yet the taut lanyard tended to drag the wader headlong into the water. Then we tried using the sky-line only for hands-on balance; but again because of the stretch factor, not only did the ropes fail to provide hardly any support, but in pulling the waders upstream they radically threatened their balance.

We set Tyrolean traverses: pairs of taut ropes, across which students hauled themselves while hanging connected to the ropes with harnesses and carabiners. And we constructed complicated rope latticeworks, as make-shift bridges. Both of these techniques seemed contrived because they first required that someone swim across the river, towing a pilot line. And this was genuinely perilous. Furthermore, the weight of even one person hanging on the block-and-tackle-stretched ropes elongated them beyond their elastic limits, and ruined them.

A ROPED DROWNING

A friend of mine and his climbing partner had completed a technically difficult ascent of the Leaning Tower, in Yosemite. After climbing down the Tower's back side, they decided to descend to the valley via a route that led across Bridalveil Creek. The precipitous falls were immediately downstream, and the creek bed comprised polished bedrock, made slippery with algae. But I imagine that their recent climb had left them feeling almost invincible, because just as though climbing rock, my friend waded in, his climbing rope knotted to his harness. The rope led back to his partner who was seated on the riverbank in the standard belay position. Within seconds my friend found himself a swimmer, for the powerful current had wrenched his feet and legs downriver while the taut rope held his waist fast. The belay rope, originally meant as a safety device, now acted instead as a drowning mechanism. The torrent's force, coupled with that of the opposing climbing rope, submerged the fellow to the riverbed; yet his belayer could not pay slack because of the nearby waterfall. The fellow who was belaying later related to me that the force on the rope was unimaginable. Nevertheless, he secured the rope to his belay anchors, then rigged a system that climbers use to haul bags of water, food and bivouac equipment up precipices. And after a protracted struggle, he managed to winch the body out of the water.

THE LESSONS

These and many other experiences have taught that the combination of a river, a rope, and a wader or swimmer is a recipe for disaster. Preeminently, the rope encourages a dangerous undertaking that judgement alone would not corroborate. And a raging torrent will search out a backpacker's weaknesses. The slightest stumble and the wader becomes prey. We have all heard and read instructions to use a rope with which to safeguard a creek crossing. The fact is, a rope tends to drown a creek crosser. The force exerted by the rope acts against the counter force of the current. Thus, the rope actually tends to drag the victim into the water. And even in a river not so swift, the strain on a rope tied to a submerged victim will render him or her incapable of untying it. And depending on the current, even the strongest belayer might be unable to haul him or her out of the water.

CREEK CROSSINGS ALONG THE PCT

Creek and river fordings are unavoidable facets of the PCT experience. And they are not necessarily undesirable. Most are reasonably benign and present little danger, and theoretically all of the unfordable torrents have bridges. Still, floods and avalanches have a way of relocating "reliable" bridges. Also, when the days are generally cloudless and the sun is melting the high mountain snowpack at a prodigious rate, the early season PCT hiker can expect to encounter a number of bridgeless and potentially dangerous torrents.

If I seem to be daunting the reader, so much the better. Many hikers lose their lives in creeks and rivers every year. In Yosemite alone, typically a dozen or more people drown each season. So remember that the water is usually deeper (due to refraction of light), colder, and more swift than they might appear from shore. No matter how swift the current, the boundary layer effect (page 162) permits algae to grow on the riverbed. And some types of algae are transparent. I've learned that creek-crossing skills are entirely subordinate to a respect of the power of flowing water. And I hope some of this healthy respect will propagate, and provide you with more than adequate margins of safety as you hike the PCT.

NURTURING A SENSE OF BALANCE

Many creeks along the way are bridged naturally by fallen timbers or rocks. Negotiating either, often requires an adroit sense of balance. But balance is not an innate skill. Like riding a bicycle, it has to be developed. The details are located on page 71. This is important material, which I hope you will study and practice. It could spare you a severe dunking.

THE BALANCING STAFF

When approaching a creek, half a mile back I begin looking for a suitable, *ad hoc* fording staff: a branch that I can use as an aid to balance. Should campers cease from burning fording staffs, we might find these sticks well represented on both sides of nearly every creek, major or minor. But alas, firewood has long ago become a scarce commodity at the creek-side campsites, and fording staffs are fair game. I encourage recycling them by carrying them well beyond the campsites and depositing them alongside the trail for use by those coming the other way.

UNLATCHING THE BACKPACK'S WAIST STRAP

Before taking the first step across any creek, large or small, unlatch the buckle of your backpack's waist belt. Thus unbound, should you slip and fall in, you might rid yourself of the overbearing pack. Drill this rule into your mind. It applies also when traversing precipitous terrain and steep snowbanks.

BEWARE OF VERGLAS

As you step gingerly out onto a rock or log, assume that it is slippery. Wet logs are often coated in slime. Also, the early morning's diffused light might not reveal the glimmer of often-present verglas: condensed and frozen dew coating the creek's proximate objects. To jump might be to plunge.

THE NATURAL BRIDGE

If a raging creek is bridged by a fallen tree, think twice before sauntering across. You might lose your balance and blemish an otherwise uneventful day. Instead, consider straddling the log. Your feet dangling below will contribute greatly to balance. And you might be able to squeeze the log between your legs. This position is far more secure, and it allows you to scooch across, a few inches at a time. To increase stability, remove your pack and place it laterally on the log ahead of you. Scoot ahead, shoving your pack as you go. With the pack off your back, your center of gravity is much lower. And in the highly unlikely event that the pack falls by the board, at least you will not go with it. One caution: before placing your weight on a log, make sure it doesn't roll.

THE FORD

Often, the most expeditious method of fording a creek is simply to remove the shoes, and wade across. Some hikers wade creeks in windsurfing shoes or booties. I've found, though, that 95% of the fords do not require them, so I prefer to hike unencumbered of their weight. After removing my shoes and tying them to my pack, I might don a second pair of dirty socks. The socks provide adequate cushioning and protection, they provide slightly more friction, and they insulate my feet somewhat against the crushing cold. Once at the creek's far side, I sit down, remove the socks, wring them out and hang them on my pack to dry. Then I don a fresh pair of socks and my dry shoes.

However, if the ford is imposing, as a safety precaution I wear the shoes.

RECONNOITERING THE BEST FORDING

Consider that a creek might offer better fording up or downstream of the trail. Jenny and I have often reconnoitered a mile or more up or downstream searching for a safe position to attempt a wade. And we once walked downriver 5 miles before finding a place that barely afforded a safe wading. Where the PCT disappears into a raging creek and emerges from the far side, realize that you are following a trail built primarily for equestrian travel. Your safest crossing probably lies somewhere up or downstream. Upstream is usually best.

WADING TECHNIQUES

I had a friend that lost his life while backpacking in King's Canyon. As he waded across Bubbs Creek, only mid-calf deep, he discovered (we can be sure) that the polished creek-bed was greased with algae. He slipped; found himself manacled to his own backpack—strapped tightly to his torso and loaded with heavy climbing gear—and was dragged eventually over a series of cascades.

Of all the safety precautions for creek crossing, the one preeminent is that of staying on your feet. Do not assume that you can swim a raging torrent. If the water is too swift and deep to wade, and the bottom too slippery, then you must not assume that in a last ditch effort you will be able to swim across.

So build your wading experience one day at a time, and always conservatively. The more creeks you wade, the better you will be able to judge their attendant dangers. When unsure, wade into a creek slowly while carrying a stout balancing stick. Test the waters. Is the riverbed dangerously slippery? Is the water much deeper than it appeared from shore? Is the current more swift? As you proceed ahead, step by cautious step, don't place your weight onto your next foot until it has explored the bottom by feel and found secure footing. Keep your gaze fixed on the far shore, to prevent the water's motion from disrupting your equilibrium. But don't focus on the far shore as being your objective, lest it deprive you of judgement. Instead, anchor your mind on your present situation. Feel the current pressing strongly against your legs. Feel it trying to wrench your foot away as you lift it free to take the next step. And maintain control. If you seem the slightest insecure, turn back; and once again, carefully, step by calculated step, work your way back to the shore you departed from. Returning is easier, because you've practiced the moves, and you know the ground.

Otherwise, before you reach the half-way point, access your strength. If you are tiring, consider turning back. Fatigue is composure's worst enemy.

Having nearly reached the far shore, you might find to your dismay that the water ahead deepens and becomes more swift than expected. This is often the case at the outside bend of a river, where the water's centrifugal force drives it into the far bank. And this can be a most dangerous situation; so do not let the shore tempt you into bolting for it. Prudence might dictate you turn back and search for a better fording. I've done this many times.

CONSIDER THE PERILS

Before starting across any creek, via a log, a series of rocks, or a wade, stop and consider the perils. If the risks seem genuine then back off and search afield for another way.

The on-route creeks tend to vary year to year, as to which are the more prodigious, and to which happen to feature naturally placed log bridges. As a through-hiker, you are likely to meet with your first challenges north of Tuolumne Meadows. The creeks that gave us the most trouble during our first through-hike where not the same ones that daunted us during our second hike. So I will not provide a list of possible widow makers, on which you might feast any surplus anxieties. But keep in mind that both our through-hikes were early season ones. And this is one of several reasons the *Handbook* discourages early-season PCT trekking.

MAN-MADE BRIDGES

Typically, the PCT will approach a daunting creek, only to disappear into it and emerge from its far side. And you might stand there looking at a potential drowning: yours. Or perhaps you will stand there fuming at the government's failure in providing hikers with a suitable bridge. Consider, though, that every time the wilds are "improved," civilization thereby thrusts its voracious maws a little deeper into the erstwhile pristine wilderness. Should we construct stalwart bridges across every creek? How about benches and water faucets every few miles? How about a five-foot wide trail, well groomed and leading to huts at 10 mile intervals? And how about power lines and roads to the huts, so hut-keepers could provide nutritious meals?

Instead, we might benefit the most by leaving the wilderness to its own devices, and laboring to improve ourselves. When confronted with a swollen creek, rather than seeing an absent bridge, we need to see the challenge of finding a safe way across, somewhere upstream perhaps. A bridge might allow us to cross safely, and it might save us considerable time hiking upstream to circumvent the torrent, but it does not strengthen us. It does not better prepare us for the next bridgeless ford, ahead. I suggest that complaining about a lack of bridges (or about blow-downs, overbrush, poor trail routing, etc.) only weakens us. Why? Because it reinforces our insecurities.

Security is confidence, not in the condition of the paths we travel, but in ourselves. And no bridge can carry us over the river of our own impatience and insecurities.

LIGHTNING

May the warp be the white light of morning,
May the weft be the red light of evening,
May the fringes be the falling rain,
May the border be the standing rainbow.
Thus weave for us a garment of brightness.
—Song of the Sky Loom (Tewa Indians)

THE MECHANICS

A thunderstorm builds intense electrical charges. The upper part of a thundercloud becomes positively charged, while its lower part, negatively. Lightning is the sudden relieving of these pent-up electrical potentials. The most common type of bolt travels from the cloud's upper part to its lower. The other type, and the one we are concerned with, travels from the ground to the cloud's lower regions.

In the U.S. alone, lightning kills about 100 people a year. In most instances of people struck by lightning, the electrical shock induces ventricular fibrillation, and the victim's heart ceases pumping. In many instances, the person has every chance of recovery if someone is present who is capable of administering CPR (cardiopulmonary resuscitation).

Lightning strikes in a highly random fashion. Microseconds before a ground-to-cloud bolt, the cloud sends down an electrical structure resembling the roots of a tree. Seemingly as a matter of chance, the root nearest the ground will close the circuit and become the chosen path. In the immediate vicinity of this root, the highest grounded object will attract it.

Thunder is the supersonic shock wave, caused by the lightning bolt ramming air away from the discharge. Thunder travels approximately one mile in five seconds. To estimate the bolt's distance in miles, count the seconds between the flash and the thunder, and divide by five.

THE BENEFITS

As the lightning bolt rips though the sky it breaks loose nitrogen. Twenty million lightning storms annually deposit some 100 million tons of nitrogen on soil and plants, as brought to the earth by rainfall. Nitrogen comprises some four-fifths of the atmosphere, and it is the sustenance of growth for the world's flora. So when standing at the base of a colossal tree, consider that its mass came largely from the nitrogen and carbon dioxide in the air.

DANGER TO HIKERS

Lightning represents a genuine threat to hikers, especially as they travel the high mountains in the afternoons, when thunderstorms are more prevalent. A bolt can strike virtually anywhere, purely as a matter of chance. But when Thor is hurling his mighty charges in our vicinity we can take a few precautions that might vastly reduce our chances of acting as targets.

First, *we would not wait for a lightning storm to develop before taking action.* If the sky is foreboding, and if the route ahead ascends to an exposed position, we would stop hiking early in the afternoon. And no matter how hard the rainfall, we would not sit beneath a sheltering tree during a thunderstorm. If a bolt should strike that tree, at best we might be knocked unconscious.

If we happen to be plying an exposed ridge above tree line, we would commence a descent at the earliest hint of a lightning storm. If we find ourselves cliffed, we would descend as far as we could from the ridge, and then crouch low; but we would not lay down. We would stoop on our feet, allowing our shoes to provide some electrical insulation. Our pack stays, umbrella shaft and ice axe might indeed attract lightning if we are carrying them. So we would set them aside.

Keep in mind that the vast majority of hikers and climbers who have experienced a sizzling, cracking or buzzing in their hats or jackets have come away safely. Some think that this slow discharge means that lightning is not about to strike. Nevertheless, in such a situation we would be wise not to tempt fate by standing up until the buzzing ceases.

I've experienced heavy static charges many times. Once, a few of us sat huddled beneath a tarp during an intense electrical storm in the wee hours of the morning on Colorado's Continental Divide. We watched an eery-green, crackling ball of swirling energy climb the arm of one fellow, moil about his beard, then descend his other arm before wafting away into the night.

Finally, we wouldn't carry our umbrellas deployed when the air is electrically charged. Once, while hiking in the desert, umbrellas held overhead for their shade from the blazing sun, Jenny and I walked beneath a set of high-tension power-lines, and the umbrellas began sizzling and crackling. So I suppose that it is not impossible to be struck by lightning during a clear day.

HOT!

I walked in a desert.
And I cried:
"Ah, God, take me from this place!"
A voice said: "It is no desert."
I cried: "Well, but—
The sand, the heat, the vacant horizon."
A voice said: "It is no desert."
—Stephen Crane

Hiking in a torrid environment can be pleasant and rewarding for the person who has learned the requisite skills. Concerning desert trekking, the skill is singular. It is regulating body temperature.

Arabs wear heavy clothing primarily to protect themselves from the powerful ultraviolet radiation, and secondarily to insulate themselves from the intense heat. Obviously, while wearing this insulation they must be very careful not to over-exert. Otherwise, metabolic heat generated by their muscles would convert their garments to kilns.

We distance hikers would do as well to protect our skin from the sunlight. But we cannot wear heavy clothing while exercising strenuously. Instead, we regulate our body temperatures primarily by wearing loose, lightweight clothing, perhaps by carrying a shading umbrella, and by drinking water copiously. The umbrella and lightweight clothing protect us from the sun's ultraviolet radiation, and the fluids provide for ample perspiration. Sweat evaporating on our skin is our primary method of preventing overheating. And incidentally, a sweat that drips profusely is inefficient, and suggests an overpowering of the cooling mechanisms. When this happens, desert trekkers might do well to seek shade and to rest.

Some experienced desert trekkers begin hiking when the morning is light enough to reveal the presence of any rattlesnakes. Typically they might hike until the day warms to a temperature that seems intolerably hot, and rather than battle the afternoon sun they might rest in the shade, reading or napping until late afternoon. Setting off again, they would hike until the ambient light of day is no longer sufficient for them to remain on guard for snakes.

But I have found that while hiking beneath an umbrella, and while carrying lots of water and drinking of it profusely, I can hike throughout the day.

WHERE ARE THE HOT SPOTS?

The Pacific Crest Trail crosses a few desert regions, primarily in far-southern California. For example, the terrain between the Mexican border and the flanks of Mt. Laguna can be quite warm. The stretch between Chariot Canyon and Barrel Springs might be the hike's most torrid. The Agua Dulce and Tehachapi environs might be hot, as might certain regions around Castella, farther north.

HOW MUCH WATER TO CARRY

Jenny and I have distance hiked in 120°F weather in the Mojave Desert. After several days of trial and error we learned that the weight of water, which we finally learned to carry, was inconsequential compared with its value in sustaining life. Initially we tried powerhiking between water sources, carrying very little water and traveling swift-footed. But when our bodies became severely dehydrated we suffered. After one particularly desiccating jaunt we reached a water source and gulped five quarts of water, each.

Eventually we learned to carry ample water, and it was then that we resumed hiking as usual, despite the heat. In 120° heat we drank three gallons of water per person per 24 hours. In 105° heat we consumed about two gallons each.

The desert hiker might also refrain from consuming diuretics, such as coffee, tea, and alcohol. These fluids extract water from the body, rather than add to it.

PHOTO-DERMATITIS

Photoallergertic and phototoxic contact dermatitis are maladies commonly experienced by those distance hiking in California. These skin problems are manifested as exaggerated sunburns, following the application, or the ingestion, of some chemical. The skin reacts to the chemical by becoming far more reactive to ultraviolet radiation. The chemical might be contained in a soap, shampoo, hand lotion, insect repellent, or ironically even in the sunblock cream. Rarely, the offending agent could be contained in a food or drink.

When spending a great deal of time exposed to strong sunlight, should your nose or ears break out in blisters, this is probably just a severe sunburn, and an indication that your sun-hat and topical cream are not performing as imagined. The treatment of choice is to dab the affected areas liberally with antiseptic, and then to cover them with skin-colored, cloth adhesive strips. But be extremely careful when removing the strips; otherwise they might peel away the blistered skin.

Should your hands break out in itching patches, either in the absence of a rash, or more likely in blisters that resemble a poison oak reaction, then you might be experiencing the initial throes of photo-dermatitis. Rinse the affected parts repeatedly and gently in cold water. Use no soap. For relief, try applying Cortaid(tm) ointment, or the equivalent. Then don clothing that covers the affected area. To protect the hands, for example, you might wear a thin pair of light-colored socks. The malady can persist for weeks or months; so consider ahead of time that prevention is the best cure. **Keep your skin protected from the sun.** This is particularly applicable while traversing the scintillating, early season snow fields.

One of the more effective shields for use in extreme hot weather is an umbrella covered with a sheet of reflective-silver mylar, cut from a Space® Blanket for example, and taped in place around its perimeter.

HEAT EXHAUSTION

Heat exhaustion is a comparatively minor disorder, but if not treated it can be a precursor to heat stroke. The symptoms of heat exhaustion might be a gradual weakness, dizziness, nausea, anxiety, or faintness. In the majority of cases, dehydration is the predominant factor. The remedy for heat exhaustion is to seek shade, to lay down flat on the ground, and to replace lost fluids.

Prevention is the cure of choice. The adroit hiker avoids reaching the stage of heat exhaustion by drinking water copiously, perhaps by carrying a mylar-covered umbrella, and also perhaps by eating some salty food.

As you hike, if water is abundant then consider wearing a wet towel or shirt atop your head, or on the nape of your neck. If you are rationing water, try drinking a small quantity of it mixed with flavoring crystals such as Wylers or Tang. In the evening you might cook an appetizer of Chinese noodles, for example, which might taste good for the salt.

NIGHT HIKING

Jenny and I enjoy hiking far into the evenings, sometimes very far into them. Yet we consider walking through the desert at night impractical. The mitigated pace and the chances of stepping in pot holes are only minor inconveniences. What disturbs us is the possibility of encountering green rattlesnakes. In the desert at night, virtually every stick lying on the ground poses as a snake, to the gradual ablation of our nerves. And usually, a full moon only worsens the situation by casting suspicious shadows over the creosote bushes. A flashlight might obviate many inconvenient moments, but at no little weight and expense, and considerable ecological impact.

While camping in the desert, inspect the surrounding area for what appears to be scorpion holes. Scorpions are found in southern California's deserts, chaparral and woodlands below about 7,000 feet. They can be attracted to the heat of a camper's sleeping bag. Their stings are not lethal, but they make poor bedfellows.

SNOWPACK

Every land has its own special rhythm.
Unless the traveler takes the time to learn the rhythm
he or she will remain an outsider there always.
—Juliette De Baircli Levy

COMMON MISCONCEPTIONS REGARDING SNOWPACK

Many prospective PCT hikers mistakenly believe that the trail in southern California leads almost exclusively through arid climes. They might imagine that for the first several weeks of their through-hikes, snow will be encountered only rarely, and that the first guaranteed snow will be in the High Sierra. Hikers following the *Handbook's* itineraries might find this to be generally true. But those who set out from the Mexican border too early in the season might encounter dozens of miles of snowpack blanketing the flanks of Mt. Laguna, reached in a mere three or four days after setting out from Campo. April storms that deposit a few feet of snow on this mountain are commonplace. Farther along, the expansive snowpack obscuring much of the trail on Mt. San Jacinto, 175 miles into the hike, can be as daunting as that found in the Sierra. Improbable though it might seem, few early-season hikers manage to punch through it. Most find themselves reluctantly circumventing the PCT-San Jacinto's upper reaches. Next, from the intervening desert the trail addresses the San Bernardino mountains, which also harbor early season snow. And after another stint of desert trekking, the trail over the San Gabriel mountains can offer protracted, early season snow trudging.

Simply put, then, prior to the advent of the *Handbook's* itineraries, most aspiring through-hikers began their journeys too early in the season. Thinking in terms of a 6 or 7 month trek, they were trying to avoid not only the late-spring torridity of the deserts, but the early-winter snowfall in the North Cascades. But they overlooked the fact that early-season winter-like conditions normally exist in far-Southern California, inescapably sandwiched between the deserts.

Typically, those who began too early toiled needlessly. And many of those who admitted temporary defeat found themselves waylaid somewhere en route, waiting for the snowpack to abate, and perhaps wishing they had waited, instead, at home.

Another common misconception is that during a year of heavy snowpack it is not possible to hike the PCT. It is true that in almost any year, hikers traversing the High Sierra during early June encounter a great deal of snow. For them, it matters little how deep the snow is. They walk atop it, sinking in a ways, but certainly not all the way to the ground.

But June is normally a sunny month in the Sierra. And when it is, the usually intense sunshine melts the snowpack rapidly. Those traversing the High Sierra in July walk *mostly* on bare ground. Even in years of extreme snowpack, most is gone by mid July.

It is also true, though, that the early-winter snowfall of the North Cascades comes much earlier in some years than normally. Any through-hike of the PCT is a series of compromises, and we feel that in most years, the *Handbook's* itineraries represent the optimum concessions.

Yet another mistake commonly made by hikers is to telephone various ranger headquarters, and ask what are the current snow conditions in their districts along the PCT. Virtually the only way the office staff would know about current conditions is that by happenstance some hiker had recently stumbled into their office and reported them. But because most headquarters are located at considerable distances from the PCT, such occurrences are unlikely. Furthermore, rangers are well known for ultra-conservatism. In early season, their almost standard reply will probably be that the trail is snowpacked, extremely dangerous, and essentially closed.

SNOWPACK: A DAUNTING IMPEDIMENT?

The majority of prospective through-hikers consider snowpack as the PCT's most daunting impediment. And indeed, hiking in soft snow can be analogous with canoeing in molasses. And make no mistake, it can be dangerous. Often, though, half-hearted backpackers appoint snowpack as a scapegoat of convenience. They might use its existence as an excuse to justify wilful detours or untimely terminations of their journeys.

It is a fact that alpine snowpack represents the inherent dangers of hypothermia, of avalanche, and of falling on a steep slope. But it is also true that snowpack is not automatically dangerous. Usually, it is a repulsive obstacle only when the inexperienced mind declares it so.

I consider alpine snowpack as one of nature's most beautiful compositions, lending spectacle and beauty to the mountains and high forests. Blanketed in its wintry splendor, the wilderness is enjoyed only by the privileged few. The winter highlander feels awash in primordiality. The snowpacked landscape is pristine, void of sound but never quiet, tranquil but never still. And it is virtually free of mosquitos and biting flies. Often it is made to seem far less imposing by the dainty tracks of small animals, and heartening furrows of big game. These remind us that life does indeed thrive in the alpine winter wonderland.

To tread slowly and methodically across some vast glacial-like expanse can be a humbling but mind escalating experience. At times it can seem almost as though we are trespassing Mother Earth's inner sanctum. When the snowpack steepens and hardens at long last, the winter mountaineer eagerly draws the ice axe, and sallies forth into a playground of unparalleled grandeur. Alpine air beneath one's heels has a way of intensifying reality; and no scene on earth is more sublime, more rewarding than the sudden view over some hard-won spine of the frozen High Sierra.

THE ANNUAL COLLECTION OF TRAIL COMMANDOS

Typically each year, PCT hikers set off from the Mexican Border too early in the season. Those that negotiate any snow on Mt. Laguna are almost guaranteed to meet with extensive snowpack farther on, blanketing Mt. San Jacinto. Those that are rebuffed tend to congregate in the town of Idyllwild, after bailing off the snow-blotched Desert Divide. And there, less than 175 miles from their ecstatic beginnings, they await the snow's melting from the trail that traverses the upper flanks of Mt. San Jacinto. Nearly each morning finds a few of them trudging up the Slide Trail toward the impacted PCT. And as likely as not, midday finds them shuffling back down in defeat. As the days pass, and as patience gives way to restlessness, hikers begin abandoning their cast-iron intents to adhere strictly to the trail. One by one, they embark in small groups along the Black Mountain road, which rejoins the PCT northwest of Fuller Ridge.

The strange part is that these hikers are not daunted by deleterious, physical effects of the snow. Instead, they are rebuffed mainly because of its presence.

THE TWO BASIC TYPES OF SNOW

The Eskimo (Inuit) language reputedly contains a hundred words that differentiate the various types of snow. The more civilized we have become, the more we have relinquished our wilderness vocabulary, it seems. To illustrate the ultimate in obtuseness: every spring, southern Californians of various descriptions drive from their sultry cities and into the mountains, where if afforded the opportunity, they often rush from their cars and leap gleefully out onto some beckoning snowfield, in some cases only to slide helplessly to their high-speed deaths against trees and rocks far below. Snow can be soft and yielding, or it can be frozen hard.

THE TEST

Rarely does danger publish itself, else it would not be danger. One method of determining if a steep patch of snow is soft and compliant, or if instead it is dangerously hard, is to probe it with an ice axe. However, the most common method is to step out onto it. But before making this potentially lethal test, the hiker MUST assume a hardness and slipperiness akin to an uplifted ice skating rink. Even under a blazing sun. Every PCT aspirant can plan on encountering at least one such slope, if not hundreds. And it takes only one false step to spell disaster.

SCHOOLING IN THE PROPER TECHNIQUES

Before setting out on the long quest, if you are not competent and well practiced with the techniques of ice axe self-arrest (stopping a bodyslide by digging in with the pick of the ice axe) you would do well to enroll in a certified class that teaches and **practices** the standard ice axe techniques. Reading the book *Mountaineering: Freedom of the Hills* (The Mountaineers; 5th edition, 1992) is highly recommended, but reading alone will not suffice. Only by practicing repeatedly will you acquire the requisite reflex actions. And it is the reflexes, not the mere knowledge, that can save your life.

As a bonus, practicing with the axe builds confidence in negotiating steeper snow. And confidence greatly dispels the notion that snowfields are nature's anathemas.

THOSE LACKING TRAINING

If you cannot fit snow training into your schedule, then unless the previous winter deposited exceptionally little snow, you must not plan on hiking through the Sierra as part of your through-hike. Instead, you would plan on detouring around them. And even so, you would still need to carry an ice axe with which to chop the occasional steps, for you might find it nearly impossible to avoid every dangerously inclined patch of snow. These typically occur sporadically all the way to the Canadian border. In some places the only way to avoid them is to turn back and search for a way around. So, again, if you are wholly inexperienced at snow climbing, you might be subjecting yourself to considerable risk.

THOSE HIKING IN EARLY SEASON

If you are ignoring the *Handbook's* itineraries by starting the hike before mid April, and if you are not an experienced winter mountaineer, then you might consider the following: You might encounter miles of relatively benign snow on Mt. Laguna (the guide book's map A7). Farther north, you would leave the trail at the Pines to Palms highway, (map B5) and hike the highway's shoulder[3] to Idyllwild. You would follow the Black Mountain Road, and rejoin the trail at the northwest terminus of Fuller Ridge (map B10). From there you would follow the trail on through the San

---

[3] Here, I am reluctantly recommending hiking along a highway, and only as an alternate to the possibly dangerous, early-season snow slopes on the mountain. Still, the recommendation illustrates my "supple-aspen" philosophy of not doggedly following the trail when and where the hiker's own judgement might recommend otherwise.

Bernardino mountains, carrying an ice axe with which to chop large steps and to safeguard yourself across any occasional patches of snow between the Mission Creek Trail Camp and the Coon Creek Jumpoff (map C4). After following the trail all the way to Wright Mountain, (map D3) you would take the Acorn Canyon trail leading down to Wrightwood. Road walking would then take you to Big Pines (map D4) and along the Angeles Crest Highway to Islip Saddle, (map D6). The PCT ahead should now be generally snow-free all the way to the High Sierra, so proceed to Walker Pass, (map G1). There, you would decide whether to avoid the High Sierra by hiking the Owens Valley, or whether instead you might hitchhike out of the mountains to indulge in a long respite, while allowing much of the snowpack to melt.

The hike through the Owens Valley can be an interesting one. Because of the plethora of side roads, one can largely avoid the busy highway. And there are a number of hot springs along the way, as well as many friendly Californians.

Again for the **early-season**, non mountaineering trekker, the question as to where to rejoin the PCT would be an enigma. By bypassing the High Sierra you are pulling ahead of the season, as it were, rather than traversing the mountains slowly and allowing the snow farther north to melt. Often, those who hike or hitchhike around the Sierra, (with plans to return later) and who rejoin the trail much farther north, encounter almost as much snow there as they would have in the Sierra. So don't feel pressed for time. The trail ahead is likely to be largely snowbound (in a normal year) practically all the way to Canada, and there is nowhere you can jump ahead to in early season, where the trail will be extensively snow free.

If you feel you must jump ahead, though, consider that Tuolumne Meadows might not be the best place to rejoin the trail. Aside from the snow, the route through northern Yosemite is fraught with possibly dangerous, early season torrents. So instead you might aim for Sonora Pass (map J1). Back on track, you would use your ice axe to cautiously negotiate any occasional and steep snowfields on the southern exposures of Sonora Peak. Then above Wolf Creek Lake you would descend a snowfield into the East Fork Carson River drainage. Subsequent to that, the trail remains below 10,000 feet.

Those *inexperienced*, **early-season** hikers proceeding from Walker Pass to Kennedy Meadows might indulge in a vacation, and allow the Sierra Nevadan snowpack to melt. Since the days would be growing longer, and the sun climbing higher in the sky, the snowpack would fast be melting. When you feel you've waited long enough, proceed ahead to Cottonwood Pass (map G13). If this area is still snowpacked, then you can assume that so are the remaining eight high-passes. That being the case, you would leave the trail, hike down to the Horseshoe Meadows trailhead, and hitchhike down to the town of Lone Pine for another extended layover.

Once again, the depth, pervasiveness, and density of the snowpack in the vicinity of Cottonwood Pass, (map G13) and for the next few miles beyond, are entirely indicative of the pervading High Sierran snowpack. What you encounter there is generally what you can expect to encounter sporadically during the next few weeks to Tuolumne.

THOSE THAT HAVE HIKED THE PCT TO TUOLUMNE

If you have hiked the PCT to Tuolumne, then beyond there you will probably encounter little snow. However, the southwest declivity of Benson Pass (map I4) might be snowpacked, as might the Seavey Pass environs, (map I5). In both instances the trail might be obscured for a ways, and you might need to navigate using map and compass; but this is easily, if cautiously, done. As mentioned earlier, although snow is not the problem for the early season hiker, the snowmelt runoff might be. The chapter on Creek Fording, page 131, details the considerations.

CRAMPONS

Imagine you are a neophyte pilot, launching a motorless hang glider from a lofty seaside cliff, and flying far over an ocean void. Such a flight would be as effortless as it would be perilous. Now imagine you are a novice mountaineer strapping on a pair of crampons and venturing temeritously across a steep and frozen void of snow. Both activities would be fairly easy, and both would be extremely dangerous.

Crampons fail in many ways, mostly through misuse; and it is the novice who is most prone to misusing them. In order for crampons to function, obviously the wearer must remain upright. A hiker wearing crampons can lose balance through vertigo, or stumble on an unnoticed object, or catch a crampon prong on the other crampon, its strap, on a pant leg or gaiter. A crampon strap can work loose, or a tooth or other metal component can fracture. Moreover, if the snow is wet and sticky, it can glob onto the bottom of the crampons and accumulate with every step until you are walking, not on perforating spikes, but on slippery snowballs.

Once you fall onto hard, steep snow, whether wearing crampons or not, the laws of physics suggest that you will immediately accelerate downward. Plummeting down the slope is not a favorable time to deliberate the proper techniques. Well practiced, lightening-fast reflexes are your only hope of avoiding the rocks below. So you initiate speedy self-arrest, using your ... crampons? Nope. Touch those spikes to the snow and you are likely to cartwheel wildly out of control. With your gloved hands? Nope. A stick, walking staff or ski pole? Sorry, those feeble implements would probably snap like toothpicks. Ok, prudently you were carrying an ice axe in the self-arrest posture, and WHAM, you sink in the pick, while keeping your crampons clear of the surface. Shards of ice rooster-tail down the frozen declivity a short ways, and you drag securely to a halt.

I consider crampons unnecessary on the PCT, even though Jenny and I could have used them dozens of times during our latest, early-season through-hike. Our ice axes proved utter necessities, though. Using mine, I chopped the steps—several hundred altogether—that obviated our need for crampons. I figure that the time and energy I expended chopping steps was more than compensated for by not carrying the crampons.

SNOWSHOES

Rent a pair of snowshoes, take them to a grassy or snowy park, and bumble around on them for a few hours. Or maybe it'll only take a few minutes to convince you of the difficulty of winning inspiriting mileage while wearing the clumsy devices. Now consider that while following the *Handbook's* itineraries you are likely to hike on bare ground throughout most of the summer. Also bear in mind that most of the snowbound PCT is too steep and sloped for productive snowshoe travel. Historically, those who have included snowshoes in their hiking inventory carried them strapped to their already overloaded packs 99.9% of the way to wherever they sent their snowshoes home.

For two winters I taught courses and led trips based partly on snowshoe travel in Colorado. There, the powder often falls cold and fluffy, and it accumulates deeply. Furthermore, it tends to remain in that condition. Fall off your snowshoes while in the high mountains of wintry Colorado, and your pack might pile-drive your body head first and practically out of sight. And when eventually you struggle a ski pole beneath your inverted self, a hefty shove might only prod it downward to your utmost reach. In those conditions, snowshoes or skis are essential.

THE CALIFORNIA CRUD

But out here in the sunnier west, we are concerned more with a concoction known as the California crud. (With four terms now, we are slowly gaining on the Inuit.) Along the PCT, the snow falls generally in large flakes, which begin metamorphosing soon after landing, if not before.

Heavily laden, the west coast hiker sometimes sinks in to the crotch, especially during late afternoon when the sun has been softening the crud all day. At night, though, if the sky is clear (allowing radiant cooling) the terrain begins yielding its heat, and the soft snow might begin freezing—from the surface down. In the early mornings, this frozen crust might support the weights of you and your pal, Pack. And this is the appropriate time to boogie, to shake a leg, to get out of Dodge while the getting is good. Let the snowshoers sleep in, while you make miles of tracks: barely indented ones.

SNOW CLIMBING

Typically, you will be traveling uphill during the early morning, making for the next high pass. And as the morning should grow warmer, it does not—because higher is colder, and the two effects tend to nullify one another. But when the mountain steepens, and you attain the technical heights, the snow becomes suitably sun-softened, and allows you to kick perfectly adequate footholds. However, in the shady places you might need to chop a few steps. Gaining the crest at last, you indulge in a well deserved and purposefully long rest, thinking of those who will be sweating up the dusty and manure-spackled switchbacks later in the summer, and who will do the same while traveling down the other side. If the weather is favorable you might eat an early lunch, allowing the snow-clad declivity ahead to soften as much as possible, and bearing in mind that the act of descending hard-crusted snow can be far more difficult than climbing it.

DESCENDING A SNOW SLOPE

The prudent novice will resist the urge to glissade down the far slope, or far more dangerously, to slide down the slope while seated on a ground sheet or a poncho. Save those stunts for later in life: possibly for the last few minutes of it. You labored mightily up one side of the pass, and even though you therefore deserve to slide down the other, you would do well to exercise better judgement.

And before setting off down this slope, which drops out of sight, you might consider that any alluring tracks left by recent predecessors might lead you straightway on eternity's last ride. The people ahead descended the slope safely, or so it appears. But those tracks mean nothing to you. Snow conditions change; maybe the people passed through here late in the afternoon when the snow was soft. And now, because the day has not yet warmed, maybe the slope is still frozen. A visual inspection is not the ultimate test, remember? And consider that snow conditions are rarely similar on both sides of a major pass. They can be as different as day and night.

So exercising the utmost in distrust, you proceed gingerly ahead. If the snow is hard—if it resists your kicking adequate steps—then you would return to the crest and enjoy another protracted respite. Step chopping with the ice axe is not particularly difficult when traveling uphill, but it is not as practical when going steeply down. Leaning over in order to whack at the slope places you in an ungainly position. And precariously perched, the momentum of axe swinging might threaten your equilibrium. You could do it, but it might not be worth the trouble.

If the snow is soft, though, you would proceed cautiously, assessing the avalanche hazard. No doubt you've practiced the plunge step, locking the knee and letting your body weight pile-drive the heel into the snow with each step.

At the slope's base you might come to a lake, albeit one frozen over. Even though you might be post-holing laboriously by now, (foot suddenly breaking through the hard crust, and leg plunging deeply into the snow) while paralleling the shore at a safe distance you would do well to resist the temptation to venture onto the ice. True, it might be easier to walk on, as long as it supported your weight. But any boot prints out there mean only that some fool was blessed with astronomical luck. Even considering that the ice had obviously held his or her weight, it might have since softened.

BRAIN LOCK

By far the most dangerous aspect of snow climbing and descending is a phenomena I call brain lock. Remember the cartoons of the coyote forever chasing the road runner? The road runner zooms off a cliff and into space (after all, it *is* a bird), and the unthinking coyote pursues. Suddenly realizing that something is dreadfully amiss, the coyote stops, somehow suspended in mid air. It ponders for a few pregnant moments, gives the audience that look of utter dismay, and ... drops into the abyss.

The point is: despite the actual circumstances, a person does not drop until the brain decides the time is right.

As an example, I was leading a group of students down a snowfield, in which our boots were imprinting only slightly. The slope gradually steepened the farther we went, but still it did not seem inclined steeply enough to warrant stopping to withdraw our ice axes. The students were ambling blithely along, emulating my lack of concern. Then one fellow reported, "Hey, this is getting steep." At that instant five of them went down like bowling pins. They slid a few dozen feet into the talus, but not fast enough to sustain major damage. The others held fast, and together we traversed off the slope.

Brain lock can suddenly wrench a person from Heaven, and hurl them into hell. I've witnessed the phenomena many times, and have noticed that the effect is virtually irreversible. Once the mind forfeits its acuity, it is likely to remain padlocked until the situation resolves itself, for better or worse. Yet imagine the irony of the situation: You traverse a dangerous slope, knowing that if you fall you would likely plummet to your death, and suddenly, brain lock—an involuntary mechanism designed to keep you from having to deal with reality—almost makes you faint! This sounds absurd, but it is entirely representative.

As another example, I was cruising solo near the Continental Divide in the Colorado Rockies, planning to meet with students farther on. By intent I came upon a snow slope. The snow was in excellent condition, so I began boot-skiing cautiously down it. Farther down the steepening mountainside I happened upon a most unexpected scene. Someone was lying impinged on the slope, clinched in the self-arrest position. Three others were seated in the talus, 50 feet safely off to one side. All were equipped with ice axes, and wore stout mountain boots. Obviously, the person on the snow was brain locked and in serious trouble. I wasted no time in reaching her, and within moments had escorted her safely off the slope.

The foursome had been out sporting on the snow. Perhaps one person had been teaching the others the basics of the ice axe self-arrest, then together they had climbed the slope. Reaching higher climes, someone might have panicked. My dictionary defines panic as a sudden, overpowering, and often contagious terror. How true. Perhaps one person had become frightened, the mental infection had no doubt spread to the others, and suddenly all four found themselves in serious trouble. Three had managed to traverse to safety. But each lacked the courage to return and help the woman, who lay frozen in abject terror. A life might have been saved that day; the woman might have ultimately lost strength, and tobogganed at break-neck speed several hundred feet into the boulders. But the fact that I came bounding along, completely unaffected by the steepness and exposure, (a skill acquired through years of experience) illustrates that brain lock has little to do with reality. Her reality was that the situation was beyond her capacity. But the fact that she was able to walk off the slope while clinging to me for safety tells us that, physically, she could have done likewise without my help.

I cite these examples merely to instill the novice reader with an understanding of what dangers might be associated with innocuous-looking snow slopes.

How do you anticipate brain lock, and how do you prevent it? Early one morning Jenny and I were descending snow-bound Fire Creek Pass, in the North Cascades. A hundred miles earlier I had consigned my trail ragged shoes to a trash can, and in order to avoid hitchhiking to civilization I had appropriated Jenny's spare shoes, and had slit them all manner of ways, enlarging them to accommodate my feet. Needless to say, those shoes did not perform well on steep and hard snow. My feet were so crammed into them that the uppers bulged over both sides of the soles, rendering the soles fairly inaccessible for edging. Part way down from the pass we came to a steep and crusted slope, which was inconvenient to circumvent, as often they are. Exuding confidence despite our lack of safety gear, I began leading across; and Jenny followed. The farther we traversed, though, the harder became the snow's surface. To hack each minuscule step, I slashed repeatedly with my blunt shoes. Probably I could have done better wearing roller skates. Nevertheless, a scant few dozen feet from the ever steepening far side, I deemed the slope too dangerous to proceed. Had I slipped, Jenny might have panicked and done likewise. Feeling a brain lock hovering menacingly overhead, I clinched my resolve and *matter-of-factly* told Jenny that we were turning around. Now here was the strange part. Reversing those steps required twice the time. And the scant footholds we had carved now seemed frightfully insecure. We circumvented the slope by climbing around it, and I went away with an increased distrust of those shoes.

The point is, brain lock can strike anyone, regardless of experience. Realize, though, that the danger lies primarily within. So remember my advice to maintain a level head. When in a dire situation, do not give up. And by all means carry an ice axe.

MORE TYPES OF SNOWPACK

Hard-crusted snow will begin melting in the day's heat. And as it does, your boots are likely to begin sinking into it more deeply, until by late afternoon you might be floundering. And having descended the high-mountain pass, you are now approaching the zone delineating snow and terra boggy. It is here that the going is usually the most trying.

Snowpack melts in two ways. One, it metamorphoses into slush; and two, it sublimates, or simply "evaporates". Either way, as the melting snowpack becomes less cohesive it might lose the strength necessary to support your weight.

A snowfield's greatest rate of melting occurs generally around its margins. When descending a snowfield and approaching its margin, which can be from one foot wide to several hundred, be prepared to begin sinking in to the fundaments, and to wallow ahead. Conversely, when you first climb onto a late-season snowfield, plan to flounder a ways, until you manage to negotiate the weakener margins. And here we need to exercise a little more caution. As our feet break through the crust, we risk twisting an ankle on unseen rocks or logs lying concealed beneath.

Novices, hiking up a trail and reaching the first snow, commence struggling with innumerable patches of it. Imagining that snow is to be avoided where possible, and figuring that the greater snowfields beyond are in the same rotten condition, they might deem a retreat as the more prudent course of action. In short, they turn tail and head for warmer climes.

But let's remember that during springtime the snow is least amenable to walking upon at the **lower** elevations, where it is melting and sublimating the fastest. And it is usually in this transition zone that the hiker will expend the most energy for the least forward gain. But take heart; the transition zone yields many clues as to the best places to walk.

Following a person's boot tracks, we can readily assess his or her experience, as to how well the snow was being read. And according to the person's ability to read the snow, we can guess the person's disposition toward hiking in it. Basically, the people who consistently step in all the wrong places are those who consider snow a major obstacle.

Jenny and I were climbing toward Donohue Pass, our ninth and final snow-bound pass in the High Sierra that year. Coming the other way, a fellow bedecked in a stunning array of techno-gear stumbled onto the scene. His bedraggled countenance brought to mind that of Maurice Hertzog on his descent from Annapurna. "There's too much snow up there," he informed us in a tone presumably designed to daunt us into turning back. "I'm headed out."

This fellow was typical of the half-dozen we had met, practically all of whom were complaining of the snow, and withdrawing from it. And indeed, we had encountered far more snow than I'd foreseen. But of the three times we had hiked the John Muir Trail section of the PCT, including once in the late summer when the trail was entirely snow free, Jenny and I were now making our best time. Essentially, we carried relatively lightweight packs; and diligently we adhered to the following techniques, which I had developed over the years.

PLYING THE TRANSITION ZONES

While adhering to any of the *Handbook's* itineraries you will be traveling the Sierra Nevada in late June. This is a time of coalescing for the snowpack, regardless of its depth. What follows applies only to late-June and early July conditions. It does NOT apply to those of winter.

When descending a snowfield and approaching its margins, you would begin looking ahead for the following clues. Soon you might begin sinking in much deeper, and by carefully choosing the route ahead you might avoid a great deal of bumbling.

Clue #1: Look for willows or other branches barely protruding from the surface, or scan ahead for a darkened hint of buried branches. The heat of these plants has probably desiccated the substrate, and weakened it considerably. Avoid these areas as though they were booby traps.

As you hike near the snow's transition zone, yet as you are still managing to keep your boots upon or fairly near the surface, observe the boot tracks of those who proceeded you. Notice how they course more or less directly ahead, and therefore how they lead repeatedly into barely protruding patches of willow. You, on the other hand, deviate around the bushes, and the previous hiker's multitude of attendant post holes.

Clue #2: The transition zone might be hundreds of yards broad. In it, pick a line that keeps the most distance from trees. And try to stay uphill from trees, where possible. A tree gives off heat, which slowly melts the surrounding snow. The ensuing moisture will flow imperceptibly downhill-not near the ground as one might expect, but actually as a horizontal profusion, which weakens the snowpack as it goes. To step onto this weakened snow is to posthole into it.

Clue #3: Again in the transition zone, watch for subtle, shallow, linear depressions in the snow's surface. These might indicate melt troughs, caused by the snow's gradual melting by the heat of trees or rocks. Moisture is effusing downhill, and is probably weakening the stratum as it goes. Hence the sagging, slight depression.

Clue #4: In any type of snow, avoid the margins around protruding, or noticeably underlying, rocks. As do trees, rocks transmit the earth's heat, which melts the surrounding snow. The resulting void, often covered, is known as a moat. Generally, the larger the rock, the more capacious its moat. If you have not inadvertently fallen waist deep into hidden moats at least ten times, then you have not yet qualified for the Cosmos-is-avenging-me merit badge. Those who have seen gaping moats as large as dump trucks might not wish to qualify for the badge.

Clue #5: This is the most important of all. At some distance from the edges of the snowfields, from one to twenty feet or so, and at some minimum snow depths, from a few inches to several feet, you might see visible, if very subtle transition lines delineating the more solidified snowpack and the desiccated, weakened snow. The weaker snow is often somewhat more crystalline in appearance. And it is sometimes the slightest more yellowish in color. By avoiding the crystalline where possible, you might be amazed at how much swifter you can travel over the transition.

Innumerable times during our recent trek, noticing a crystalline margin I stepped only a few inches to one side of it (and to one side of someone's post-hole) and thereby avoided sinking in. Time and again we bore away only slightly to circumvent patches of desiccated snow riddled with the post holes of our recent predecessors. To me, those folks seemed almost blind.

Keep in mind, though, that no matter how assiduously you adhere to these recommendations, you might still wallow a fair amount. Faced with acres of unavoidable, rotten and thigh-deep snow, it's time to change your priorities. Switch off the speedometer. Banish the urge for forward progress from your mind. Instead, mitigate your pace and concentrate **intensely** on your cardiovascular mechanism. Think of a soft snowfield as a steep hill. If it seems you are clawing ahead at a mere snail's pace, then you haven't yet relinquished your ongoing crusade for speed and distance. Using brute force is a sign of impatience, and will deplete you in short order. Instead, proceed thoughtfully and in control. And when you finally achieve the proper pace and mind set, the miles will begin passing underfoot.

BACK TO THE INUIT

Snowflakes fall from the sky in an infinite variety of forms, sizes, temperatures and densities. As a result, some snowpacks are much more dense than others. And once a snowpack is in place, depending on winter's effects, the individual crystals will begin to metamorphose. While traipsing through even the lightest powder of a ten foot depth, you will walk not on the ground. Whether the snow is five feet deep or twenty is largely inconsequential; what matters most is its consistency: how deeply your boots sink in with each step.

To this point my essays have discussed mid-season snowpack: snow in which the hiker's boots imprint only from one to twelve inches or so, and that usually freezes at night, particularly in the alpine highlands. In no way, though, can the *early season* PCT aspirant assume a preceding winter of compact snow, however copious or scant.

But even the most powdery snowpack will begin coalescing during late May and early June (depending on the elevation), when the season progresses and the sun ascends toward its solstice. So the snow's condition is not a matter of luck, but of the hiker's timing. Thus, through-hikers who set out from Kennedy Meadows too early in the season might find themselves constantly wallowing.

USING SKIS

The question of using skis is generally self deciding. If you are considering skiing through the Sierra early in the season, then your mountain-skiing proficiency must be of a standard to allow you to decide for yourself. Keep in mind, though, that the skier must weigh the inconvenience of a self rescue in the not-so-unlikely event of a twisted knee.

I've skied in the mountains a great deal, and while carrying a backpack. But typically in the spring, when the snow has coalesced, invariably I've left my boards behind in order to save weight. Of course, many times I'd longed for a pair of skis to swish down several miles of pristine PCT snowpack. But virtually all aspects of life are trade-offs, and even 10 miles of glory would not seem to justify the inconvenience of carrying the skis.

USING SNOWSHOES

For nearly all PCT aspirants, using skis will be out of the question. If you are planning an **early-season** hike, here's how to determine whether you are likely to need snowshoes:

The snow conditions you encounter on the higher flanks of Mt. San Jacinto represent the tip of an iceberg, as pertaining to the reasonably similar conditions in the Sierra Nevada, standing away to the north. The type of snow you encounter on Mt. San Jacinto will probably resemble the type you find later in the Sierra.

The *Handbook's* itineraries are shaped to avoid most of the sno during a normal year. Hence, those hikers following the itineraries unlikely to need snowshoes. But those planning to begin their hike ahead of the itineraries, for example because they consider themselves winter mountaineers, and because they revel in snow travel, a few weeks before beginning their hikes they might telephone the ranger station in Idyllwild. Rather than ask how deeply the snow blankets Mt. San Jacinto, they would ask how deeply hikers are sinking into it, in the vicinity of, say, the Slide Trail's juncture with the PCT. If the ranger reports that the snow up there is so compact that climbers are walking on top of it, without sinking in, then the early season hikers might not find use for snowshoes for the entire season. But also they must consider that ranger reports of trail conditions are not always accurate.

If, at the other extreme, the reports are that hikers are wallowing, the early season hikers might consider the advantages, not of equipping themselves with snowshoes, but of delaying their journeys to coincide with the *Handbook's* itineraries, in order to allow the snow to coalesce, if not to melt altogether.

Snowshoes are marvelous tools for negotiating powdery, **wintry,** and not too steeply inclined snowfields. In many places along the high PCT, though, the steeply tilted slopes are unsuitable for using snowshoes. Furthermore, we must remember that California's snowpack in almost any year begins coalescing during the early Spring. And as it does, it begins obviating the need for snowshoes. So once again, if you are distance-hiking in snow that requires the continual use of snowshoes, then you are there too early in the season.

In any case, you might consider the traverse of Mt. San Jacinto as a test of the waters. When you've negotiated this mountain's snowpack, then you will be able to anticipate the upcoming conditions in the Sierra.

SAN JACINTO EARLY-SEASON DIRECTIONS

After climbing 1,000 feet above Saddle Junction on Mt. San Jacinto, if the trail is snow-bound you might have difficulty finding where the PCT forks left from the Mt. San Jacinto summit trail. If so, traverse west to the drop-off, and inspect the distant, (usually sunny) slope to the northwest. There you should see the PCT snaking across the mountain. Beyond Deer Springs Campground, the *early season* trekker will likely encounter the route-finding crux of the San Jacinto traverse, if not of the entire PCT. The guide book's map depicts the trail with reasonable accuracy. Once you reach ⌐est of Fuller Ridge, traverse along it, keeping a hundred feet or so ⌐astern declivity.

FOLLOWING A VAGUE TRAIL

ving partially or mostly snowbound trail, look for arrayed vise linear indentation in the snow's surface. Also look for logs, for signs of the understory having been brushed, or the overhead tree branches having been cut. If the slope is inclined, look for old shovel cuts. Rather than search for the trail at your feet, look ahead; it might show more clearly. Where the land is covered in patchy snowdrifts, one method of losing the trail is to leave it and walk around a drift. So instead, climb each snowbank, and from its apex look ahead. As per the railroad effect, the trail might be far more readily discerned in the distance while you are standing over it.

SKI POLES

Wielding a pair of ski poles seems to be the current trendy hiking style. "It's a total body workout," we are instructed. Veneering the affectation, I suspect, is the intent to publish oneself as a proficient mountain skier in training. Frankly, I don't think many distance hikers have time for this sort of pretense.

Ski poles would serve as third and forth legs, helping the adventurous arthropod maintain balance on rocky terrain. But most hikers don't require that much support. A ski pole would be a good rattlesnake poker, or were it strong enough, it would vastly enhance balance when fording a creek. But then, so would a stout stick or two, found lying about.

Alas, some mountaineering equipment salespeople (trying to sell gear, but not necessarily the *right* kind of gear) and some uninformed hikers are known for recommending the use of crampons and ski poles in combination, (instead of *maybe* crampons and certainly an ice axe). Should the hiker fall down and accelerate wildly down a steep slope, the efforts of self-arresting could snap a pair of ski poles like match sticks.

THE ICE AXE

Accidents involving hikers sliding out of control down steep snowfields are not uncommon in the Sierra and the Cascades. And they are often serious or fatal. Furthermore, almost invariably they involve people who had not bothered to learn and practice the simple techniques of ice axe self-arrest.

So I recommend, first, that all PCT aspirants enroll in a school that teaches and practices the ice axe self-arrest; and second, that all PCT through-hikers carry a light-weight axe (less than 20 ounces) the full tri-state distance. If the axe proves unnecessary, then you have erred on the safe side. As likely as not, though, you might encounter at least one, if not several, steeply inclined patches of snow, blocking the trail. However, when you reach Belden Town, if the trail has been entirely free of snow since you last descended past the 10,000 foot level, then you might consider mailing your axe home. In that case, though, you would ask whoever is handling your resupplies to keep the axe handy, should you need it returned for use in northern Washington.

We need to dispel the obsolete notion that the ice axe must be of a comfortable length for use as a walking cane—as though technical alpinism induces premature geriatrics. We ounceophobic distance hikers view a waist-high shaft as inordinately heavy. And besides, the act of walking along while clanging the axe on the ground with every other step not only blunts the shaft point, but it frightens away the Hobbits. In actual use on steep snow slopes, the modern, shorter ice axe performs nearly as well as the old, heavy style. I much prefer the new models.

AXE TERMINOLOGY

The bottom (pointy) end of the shaft is called ... the point. The curved, step-chopping and daily cat-hole digging blade, at right angles to the handle, is the adze (pronounced "adds"). Opposite the adze is the long, narrow blade called the pick: used for self-arrest. Think of the pick as resembling the pick-axe, used in the gold-rush era.

When not in use, the axe is normally stowed on the outside of the backpack, and in such a way that it won't snag overhead branches, and that it won't mortally wound the owner should he or she step in a steaming mass of horse manure, only to slip and fall in more. What an indecorous end! So think of the pick as fate's fickle finger, and keep it pointed away from your body.

Ideally, the hiker would be able to withdraw the axe quickly without having to unharness the backpack—like a knight-errant withdrawing a saber from its scabbard at the sight of an approaching ticket-bearing protectorate in green trousers. Lack of acuity being what it is, a safety tool that is a bother to get at might be taken to hand only when urgently needed. But by then the need might be too urgent. And you wouldn't want your carcass to suffer the humiliation of being found at the bottom of some narrow but long, and glistening defile, with your ice axe affixed inaccessible to your backpack. And finally, after you have been on the trail a few months you might find that Mother Nature can beckon suddenly and with vehemence. The toilet paper can wait, but that cat hole might need digging on the spur of the moment.

Finally, I recommend using a wrist loop that attaches to the axe. You can improvise one by tying a length of cord or thin webbing, which in this case is called a lanyard, to the head of the axe. I will explain the necessity anecdotally.

Having descended one of the technical passes of the High Sierra, Jenny and I were snowfield cruising. The early morning snowpack was hard, and the present inclination inconsequential. When *both* of my feet post-holed through crust, I tripped and went kefoffer over teakettle. Brushing myself off, chagrined, I marched over to collect my ice axe, which had catapulted through the air. I explained to Jenny that because the terrain was nearly level I had intentionally rid myself of the danger of landing on the axe. Nevertheless, I determined to exercise better control, on the theory that tossing away one's axe during a fall is unbefitting conduct in the high mountains.

A few days later I went down again, and lost the axe for the second time. Incredulous, I asked myself, "how could an experienced mountaineer lose grip on his axe while falling down on level terrain?" The answer occurred to me eventually. Experienced mortals are still mortal.

So take it from this experienced mortal. Should you fall unexpectedly on a steep snow slope, your body's uncontrolled reflex could relieve you of your safety implement in a flash. As a precaution when on a steep snowfield, fasten the axe to your wrist with a lanyard.

ROPE

A 20 foot length of 7-millimeter climbing rope would be an excellent safety feature for two people traveling the snowbound Sierra together, but **only** if one is experienced and the other not. If both people are inexperienced, a rope is just as likely to double the danger, for if one person slips, the rope might wrench the other person off balance. On two occasions I caught Jenny as we descended frozen snow on Glen Pass. Both times she lost footing and began to slide off what seemed the edge of the world. But before she could self-arrest I stopped her with the rope. And in neither instance did I need to dig-in my axe. The rope was merely another of my husbandly methods of leaving little to chance.

EARLY SEASON CONDITIONS
ON THE NINE HIGH PASSES OF THE SIERRA

For those winter mountaineers traversing the High Sierra in **early season**, the following descriptions might apply.

1) COTTONWOOD PASS qualifies as one of the PCT's high passes in every regard except one: the trail does not climb up, over, and down it. Instead, it almost levels out at 11,000+ feet, and remains at that elevation for several miles. Once again, the snow conditions there are entirely indicative of those of the alpine regions ahead. Your progress through this area will suggest how you can expect to progress over the ensuing passes en route to Tuolumne Meadows. If you are bogging down and post holing knee-deep or deeper with every step, then consider the advantages of bombing off to Lone Pine, and allowing the Sierran snowpack to coalesce.

2) FORESTER PASS ranks not only as the highest, but also as the most technical of the PCT's passes. The upper reaches of the trail ascending its south side were largely blasted from sheer granite. When snow plastered, this section can be dangerous. This is mainly because the blasted-out trail often becomes inundated with steep snow, and you might find yourself

kicking steps across it, as several hundred feet of thin air waft beneath your heels. Seventy feet below the pass the trail crosses a steep couloir, notoriously coated in snow and ice, and corniced at the top during early season. In favorable conditions this traverse is easy. But before mid June it might call for extensive use of an ice axe, with which to chop steps.

It should be noted that during winter, mountaineers normally take a line that climbs instead to the high saddle 1/8 mile east of Forester Pass, mid-way between Forester Pass and Junction Peak. This route avoids the blasted-out switchbacks and the possibly treacherous couloir. I have no experience with this route, but should someone require an option, it might be a good one.

The northeast slope of Forester Pass is much less daunting. The early season hiker has two options. If deep snow pervades, consider descending almost directly down the fall line, angling slightly to your left (direction given while facing out). Although the terrain below is hidden, this slope leads to the frozen lake. If the snow is largely absent, then the route of preference is the trail, which avoids the steep scree below.

3) GLEN PASS provides us with a daunting, but surprisingly easy romp up its south side. Early season trekkers wend steeply up the slope a few hundred feet left of the actual pass. Near the top, they traverse right to the exposed ridge crest.

The opposite side presents us with a classic North Cascades type of snowfield: steep, unbroken, and expansive. Because this is a true north face, it receives little morning sunshine. Therefore, if the Sierran snowpack has coalesced, then the snow plastering the north slope of Glen Pass might be quite compact in the early morning. Proceed down and to the right (directions given for someone facing outward), and with the utmost caution.

4) PINCHOT PASS is technically uncomplicated, although it might require a small amount of step chopping while climbing its southeast side. The descent is a walk-down.

5) MATHER PASS is relatively short, but in early season it can be daunting. When plastered, its southeast face is a steep snow field of questionable stability. Most early season travelers do not attempt to follow the buried trail. Instead, they take a line left of the lake. Those climbing the pass during winter-like conditions, should keep to the left (facing into the precipice) to avoid the steep slabs hanging beneath the notch.

If Forester Pass is the most dangerous in early season, then Mather is a close second. If the snow is deep, and if slabs of rock are protruding to your right, and steep sentinels are jutting overhead, then you might imagine yourself on some desperate mission. However, if you have surmounted Forester Pass, then you are sure to succeed on Mather Pass.

The descent is straightforward if one chooses the easier ways among the ledges and slopes. We once encountered fresh bear tracks climbing the unbroken snow slope on the northwest side of this pass. To our amazement the tracks led to the crest.

6) MUIR PASS is a walk-up, and a walk-back-down the other side. During early season, this area provides rewarding winter-like travel amid spectacular scenery.

7) SELDEN PASS is more than a thousand feet lower than Muir Pass. If you've reached this point, then you have climbed the most arduous passes, save one. This pass generally lacks technical difficulties.

8) SILVER PASS: ditto the above.

9) DONOHUE PASS in early season will probably stand as your last reminder of the grandeur that is the High Sierra, and of the arduous passages among them. Unlike its kin to the south, Donohue is reasonably accessible; so the way might lie graced with the tracks of many predecessors. As for the approach, the PCT "High Trail" is far easier than the Muir or the River Trail, because of its exposure to the snow-melting sun. Beyond Thousand Island Lake, if the trail is buried then you would do well to keep one eye on your compass and the other on your map. The way ahead way might be fraught with the constantly diverging paths of those who had erred before you.

The descent is straightforward, but some who have tried to short cut from 10,800 feet to 10,400 feet have slid all the way to the hospital. So take heed. And enjoy.

COLD!

Revelling in the alpine winter wonderland, safely

Who would true valor see, let him come hither;
One here will constant be, come wind, come weather.
There's no discouragement shall make him once relent
His first avowed intent to be a pilgrim.
—John Bunyan, 1628-1688

There might be times during the summer's trek when you might imagine that the seasons have run amok. Winter-like conditions can strike at most places along the way, and in summertime. But you need not find yourself unprepared; particularly with a better understanding of how insulating clothing functions. And after you become more competent in cold-weather hiking techniques, you are likely to move ahead with far less anxiety, whatever the weather.

AIR AND WATER

Consider first that air is an exceptional heat insulator, and that water is an excellent heat conductor. These two substances lie at virtually opposite ends of the scale of thermal conductivity. And both are the backpacker's cold-weather companions.

THE BOUNDARY LAYER

Air and water are fluids. Microscopically, they adhere to most surfaces as though glued. The phenomenon is known as the boundary layer effect. No matter how hard water is sprayed at a dirty car, for example, the vehicle will come away sheathed in a film of dirt. In order to clean the car we must physically wipe the film away. This is because the water's micro-thin boundary layer, which is attached to the car's wetted surface, is so well attached that more water is incapable of moving it away.

AIR-TRAPPING FIBERS

The insulation capacity of any low-density material depends on the air it contains. The tiny fibers capture the air in boundary layers, restraining its movement. (Incidentally, this is why mosquito netting is far less breathable than it appears.)

Furthermore, it is the air, not the materials, that insulates. Equal thicknesses of Thinsulate, 700 fill prime northern goose down, shredded and crumpled newspapers, and #000 steel wool would provide virtually identical insulation. As long as the fill remains low density, the individual fibers neither conduct nor insulate appreciably. This is because they are too thin to conduct heat. Their only function, then, is to trap the tiny pockets of air-

-the insulator. Thus, if a garment or sleeping bag is to be warm, it must have loft (thickness).

WATER EXTRACTS BODY HEAT LIKE A SPONGE

When protected from the wind, pockets of air next to your body provide insulation. Water against your skin extracts body heat. Imagine the difference between walking in 40 degree air, and swimming in 40 degree water. One would be tolerable, the other would not.

EXERCISE STAVES OFF HYPOTHERMIA

The hiker's working muscles generate a tremendous amount of heat. This heat is the result of the combustion of metabolism. Food and oxygen combine chemically within the muscles, which then produce work. Mechanically, the body translates this work into the desired locomotion.

The heat produced by hard-working muscles far exceeds what is needed for personal warmth, even on a cold day. The blood ducts excess heat away to other parts of the body, to be disposed of by radiation, conduction, and evaporation.

It is important to note that the process of heavy metabolism requires great quantities of water. Water must be available to the hard working muscle cells, and quantities of water must be present in the cells in other parts of the body. Some water is also needed to be exuded from the pores as sweat. Sweat is one of the primary mechanisms of dispersing excess metabolic heat. But even at rest, the body loses about 1½ pints of water a day, in the form of insensible perspiration.

SWEAT IS THE COLD WEATHER HIKER'S ENEMY

Categorically, sweat is the nemesis of the hiker's insulating wardrobe. As the hiker's body temperature vaporizes the exuding perspiration, the vapor migrates outward through the clothing. If the day is cold, then in all likelihood the vapor will reach the dew point before it leaves the clothing. As such, it condenses back into water, and is straightway back-absorbed by the clothing. If the hiker is wearing wicking garments, so in vogue these days, they will wick the condensed moisture directly back to the skin, where it then begins affecting the body's evaporative processes.

USE TWO SEPARATE WARDROBES

In cold weather, hikers need to use two separate wardrobes: a hiking wardrobe and a resting wardrobe. The hiking clothing would be thin and lightweight. They would minimize sweat and allow excess body heat to diffuse into the atmosphere. Conversely, the resting clothing (normally worn only while resting) would comprise heavier garments designed to provide insulation and protection from the wind chill. At each rest stop, preferably at a place sheltered from the elements, the hikers would remove the sweat-dampened, lighter-weight garments, and hang them to air-dry. Then they would quickly don the heavier clothing, carried readily accessible in the backpacks. Just before recommencing the journey, they would remove (usually reluctantly) the warm clothing, don the lightweight, damp, and now decidedly frigid hiking clothing, and stow the resting wardrobe back into the pack. Very soon the hiking wardrobe would warm to body temperatures, and within a few minutes the metabolical processes would begin counteracting the encroaching chill.

Recapitulating, during cold weather, **hikers must be extremely careful to not sweat-soak their insulating clothing,** which is saved mainly for periods of inactivity.

Cotton fibers absorb water. As such, they are much slower drying. We have all heard the backpacker's slogan: "cotton kills," and most of us are aware of the dangers of wearing sweat-soaked cotton. Synthetic fibers absorb very little moisture, meaning, not that they are warmer when wet, but simply that they are generally faster drying. Sweat-dampened garments of high-tech materials are nearly as dangerous as cotton ones, if worn while resting.

COLD AND ALTITUDE ACCELERATE DEHYDRATION

In alpine conditions, hikers must be particularly careful to avoid dehydration. As they breathe cold air, their lungs exude additional moisture used to warm the air. And breathing heavily in cold air exacerbates the moisture losses. Furthermore, water's vapor pressure is lower at higher altitudes, resulting in increased evaporation within the lungs. The resulting dehydration hampers circulation and the body's ability to warm its extremities. Therefore, drinking water copiously is essential in preserving body warmth while hiking in wintry, alpine climes.

THE PIERCING WIND

In his book *The Long Walk*, Slavomir Rawicz describes how he and six companions broke out of a Siberian labor camp and walked 4,000 miles to freedom. At one point he writes:

"We scooped the snow away down to the tree roots and cleared a space a couple of yards square. We built up the snow around into a solid low wall. Kilemenos cut branches with his axe and we laid them on top in a close mesh, piling on more snow to complete the roof. It was a lesson we had learned the hard way in Siberia: Get out of the wind, because the wind is the killer."

RAIN

Designs for dealing with the deluge

An ancient gaffer once I knew,
Who puffed a pipe
    And tossed a tankard;
He claimed a hundred years
    And two,
And for a dozen more he hankered;
So o'er a pint I asked how he
Had kept his timbers tight together;
He grinned and answered:
    "It maun be
Because I likes all kinds o' weather.

"For every morn when I get up
I lights me clay pipe wi' a cinder,
And as me mug o' tea I sup
I looks from out the cottage winder;
And if it's shade or if it's shine
Or wind or snow befit to freeze me,
I always say: 'well, now, that's fine...
    It's just the sort o' day
        To please me.'

"For I have found it wise in life
To take the luck
    The way it's coming;
A wake, a worry or a wife—
Just carry on and keep a-humming.
And so I lights me pipe o'clay,
And though the morn
    On blizzard borders,
I chuckle in me guts and say:
    'It's just the day the doctor orders.'"

A mighty good philosophy
    Thought I,
And leads to longer living,
To make the best of things that be,
And take the weather
    Of God's giving;
And though the sky be ashen grey,
And winds be edged
    And sleet be slanting,
Heap faggots on the fire and say:
"It's just the kind of day
    I'm wanting."
        —R. Service; Contentment

THE RAIN PARKA

    Distance backpacking can be extremely hard on a rain parka. Where the pack straps bear against the jacket they might abrade its waterproof-breathable membrane. (This is another advantage of wearing the parka backward, as described on page 167.) Thus, despite the parka's necessity, for the through-hiker its lifetime is about one season. After that, the jacket might begin leaking. For this reason, I recommend leaving the $400 rain parka at home. A through-hike of the PCT might ruin it.

    Still, we distance backpackers are hardly in a position to compromise function. If anyone needs a high-performance parka it is us. But in this case, high performance does not necessarily mean extraordinary cost. Those who buy hyper-expensive parkas might be investing in their self-images by surrounding themselves with neon-visible evidence of money spent, but they are probably not keeping themselves any dryer than if they wore less expensive, but equally functional garments. Arguably, the majority of technology resides in the fabric. It does not comprise the dazzling colors, the pit zips, the plethora of cargo pockets and their zippers and storm flaps, the mesh liners, velcro tabs, loops and bookmarks plastered everywhere about the garments. And in particular, the technology does not reside in the brazen logos. In my considered opinion, logos on parkas are child-like medallions of imagined bravado; like tin sheriff's badges kids like to wear while playing cowboys. Also, designer seams crisscrossing the fabric are potential leaks. They might make the parka far more colorful and appealing in the advertisements and in the stores, but in the field they are little more than extraneous plumbing.

TWO TYPES OF WATERPROOF-BREATHABLE FABRICS

The through-hiker's model parka is made from a waterproof-breathable fabric. Two-ply (two-layer) is made by bonding a layer of nylon fabric to the plastic membrane. The mills leave it to the manufacturers to protect the vulnerable membrane's other side. This protection is accomplished by sewing a nylon liner into the garment. In the store this liner gives the parka a nice feel. And in the field, when perspiration condenses on the membrane's inner surface the liner acts as a buffer. But that buffer actually reduces the membrane's ability to transfer vapor, by reducing the temperature gradient across it.

Three-ply waterproof-breathable fabrics are made by sandwiching and adhering the vulnerable membrane between two outer, protecting layers of nylon. Three-ply garments do not sell as well in the shops probably because they are not as expensive, nor do they look and feel as luxurious as their two-ply counterparts fitted with liners. Nonetheless, three-ply is my choice for a rain parka. Parkas made from it are far less complicated and therefore less expensive. Presently, I know of only one parka made of three-ply Gore-tex. This is the Vagabond parka, sold by Campmor.

HEAT IS A PRODUCT OF WORK

A car's motor burns fuel, generates power and therefore heat, and is cooled by its radiator. If the engine becomes hot, does that mean it is working too hard? No, it indicates only that it is working, and most likely as designed. If the motor's thermostat should malfunction, blocking the flow of coolant, though, the engine would probably boil over and eventually self destruct.

In like manner, human muscles burn fuel, they generate power, and therefore they produce heat. Sweat exuding from glands acts as their main coolant. Does the presence of sweat indicate that the hiker is working too hard? Again, not at all. But if we curtail the body's natural cooling mechanisms, heat prostration might result.

Imagine driving at normal speed up a steep hill in weather so cold that your car's engine remains cool to the touch. The ambient temperature would have to be well below zero. The situation is similar with your body. If you were wearing only shoes, shorts, and a light shirt, and running at a good clip up a long, steep hill, the air temperature would have to be well below freezing to prevent you from breaking into a sweat. And no matter what type of garment you put on, it would interfere with your natural cooling mechanisms.

A space suit attempts to maintain the astronaut's temperature by enveloping him or her in an intricate network of small-diameter plastic tubing, sewn into thin undergarments. Through this tubing, a thermostat-controlled electric pump circulates coolant. Thus, the astronaut's sweat is minimized.

But for those of us bound to an earthly existence, sweat is our mechanism of venting excess heat. By interfering with this process we impede our body's efficiency, and mitigate our ability to perform the desired tasks.

THE POACHED WIENERWURST

Imagine you are hiking steeply uphill while carrying a heavy pack. The day is cold and breezy, and you are wearing a $50 wicking garment beneath a $370 waterproof-breathable parka. Breaking into a sweat, your body begins attempting to vent the excess heat generated by metabolism. You respond by opening the parka's pit zips, as suggested by the manufacturer. To little avail: The muscles of your upper back are generating much of the heat, and they are above the pit zips. Because heat rises, this heat cannot vent out the pit zips. The same holds true with much of the excess heat being carried away from the legs by the blood, and brought near the surface at the upper body. Sweat begins wicking into your inner garment. Some manages to evaporate and find its way out the parka's scant openings and micro-pores; the remainder condenses on the garments inner surface. The result: you soon feel like a $2.25 poached Wienerwurst.

The solution is to stow the expensive parka into your pack, (preferably *before* breaking into a sweat), and hike on. At the next rest stop, remove the undergarment, don an insulating jacket, and put the shell-parka back on. Indeed, the high-techery works well when worn at rest.

WEARING THE PARKA OR SWEATER BACKWARD

If piercing winds suggest you wear the parka while hiking, one solution is to wear it backward. Leaving the jacket open in the back ventilates your hard working shoulder and back muscles, which are already over-insulated by the backpack. Wearing the parka backward greatly mitigates sweating during blustery weather. And if the day warms, you can remove the parka without having to stop and unharness the backpack. Instead, you can simply slide the parka off your arms. To stow it, fold and drape it over the lower portion of a shoulder-strap, beneath your arm. If the day chills again, withdraw the parka and don it backward, again without having to first remove the backpack.

To gain more protection from the elements, again while hiking, proceed as follows: Remove one arm from the backward-worn parka, and withdraw that same arm from its shoulder strap. The hip belt and the other shoulder strap will secure the backpack in place. Insert that arm into the parka sleeve, and into the pack strap. Repeat the procedure for the other arm. The packstraps would now be atop the parka sleeves, pinning them in place. Next, unfasten the waist belt, and refasten it over the top of the parka.

To gain a great deal more ventilation, remove one arm from the parka, and fold the garment inward, and diagonally across the front of your body, tucking in the sleeve as well. The sleeve that remains on your other arm would be on the windward side of your body.

DESIRABLE FEATURES IN A PARKA

The hiker's parka should not feature supplementary insulation. As you hike in the rain while carrying a backpack and wearing the rain parka, any further insulation might induce you to sweat copiously. And the sweat will absorb into the parka's filling, increasing its weight and decreasing its suitability. Sweat-soaked insulating garments are generally unserviceable at camp. If the insulating garments are separate entities, though, they can be used more favorably, and only when necessary.

The parka should fit well in its shoulder girdle and hood. Otherwise, as you jounce along the trail your pack might drag the back of your parka slowly up your back. And this in turn might shove the hood down over your eyes.

When selecting a rain parka, choose one with a full-length, front-opening zipper. The sleeves should extend well beyond your wrists, in order to cover your mittened hands. And the parka would extend well below your waistline. Also, it must fit loosely, especially about the shoulders.

The parka's every seam must be factory sealed. On a parka made of a two-layer micro-porous material and a liner, look for faint impressions of the sealing tape, inside. The seams that are not taped, (those at the cuffs, emblems, reinforcement and color panels, etc.) will need to be sealed by hand. Self-fabric seams at the arm cuffs and waist hem, and that are not seam sealed, will collect water, to the hiker's disadvantage.

RAIN PANTS

The types of protective garments suitable for the torso are generally not the same as those for the lower appendages. The legs and buttocks are much less demanding in terms of temperature control. And they don't sweat as copiously when their muscles are producing heat; instead they rely on the circulatory system to duct much of the heat away.

I suppose that during extremely persistent and heavy rainfall the *hard working* distance-hiker might somehow benefit by wearing trousers of micro-porous fabric. But in my experience rain pants have yet to prove their worth. Lycra shorts and wicking-fabric pants are my choice for leg protection. And during rainy weather this is especially so. Unless noticeably articulated, (curved at the knees) rain pants are prone to binding at the knees with each step. This is especially true when they are wet inside, which is likely to be the case after you have walked in them awhile. Incidentally, the shabby genteel's way of articulating the fabric is simply to safety pin a generous tuck into it just above each knee. This helps prevent the pant leg from binding against the skin at the knee. Nevertheless, once at camp, the rain pants will probably be wet, both inside and out, and you might be faced with the difficulty of drying them. The parka shares this problem; but for the sleeves it opens wide for airing.

Except in the worst of conditions, rain pants might be an overkill. Your legs will generally carry you along more efficiently if allowed the breathing room they're accustomed to. Lightly clad and working hard, they'll not mind the wet. In fact, if the day is not frigid and the wind not blustery, then you might consider hiking bare legged during rainy weather. That way, you might arrive at camp with a pack full of dry clothing suitable for wearing once you are comfortably sprawled inside the tent. And after hanging your fast-drying shorts to dry beneath the awning, your worries will be over.

If the day is rainy and cold, though, then you might hike more comfortably wearing pants of Lycra or of a wicking fabric. If colder still, then you might wear a combination. But remember that the garments you soak by hiking in during rainy weather are likely to be unsuitable for wearing in camp. However, should the storm persist into the next day, you can don these damp garments, assured that they will again perform favorably.

If the wind is slanting rain in powerful gusts, then you might decide to don your mosquito/wind pants over your wicking-fabric ones. Made of thin, highly breathable nylon, not only will they effectively shunt the wind, but they will dry quickly when afforded the opportunity.

FOOTWEAR

Footwear suitable for distance-hiking during rainy weather comprises socks blended of wool and synthetic, and lightweight, breathable shoes or low-cut boots. This is discussed in detail in the Footwear chapter, page 63.

MITTENS

During rainy weather, if your hands become chilled then you could don fleece mittens, or keep your hands ensconced within your pockets, or tuck them beneath your parka. During both of my hikes of the PCT I carried a pair of home-made Gore-Tex shells, sized to cover my fleece mittens. The shells' weights are infinitesimal. But alas, I did not use them. Still, I recommend them for protecting the fleece mitts during stormy weather. Lacking shells, when the mittens become wet you can remove them and ring them out, or sling them vigorously to extract some of the water, then put them back on. They will be quick to dry when their time comes.

THE RAIN HAT

The parka's hood will normally provide adequate insulation for your head. If it does not, you could wear a skull cap inside the hood. Oftentimes, a rain/sun hat will improve your lot by allowing you to douse the parka's hood. This improves ventilation of your upper back, shoulder girdle, and neck, where ventilation is needed. While wearing the parka backward, though, wearing its hood is impractical. The brimmed hat is the substitute of choice, and it would also shelter the eyeglasses, helping to keep them clear.

UMBRELLA

Appropriate clothing is the hiker's first protective measure against rain. The umbrella is the second measure. The umbrella is not a substitute for a rain parka. Rather, it is a complement to it. The two would be used in conjunction. During our second PCT through-hike, Jenny and I each carried an umbrella the entire distance, and with considerable success. I had sewn loops of webbing to our pack straps. (See the following figure.) These loops secured the handles of the umbrellas and supported the umbrellas overhead. Without some sort of supportive arrangement, the umbrella would probably not be worth including in the backpacking inventory, for the hiker would soon tire of holding it overhead.

Carrying an umbrella while hiking is practical only if you can reach up and douse it whenever a gust of wind strikes. Umbrellas are fragile mechanisms, and they require guarding. Comically, though, on one or two occasions a gust suddenly wrenched my umbrella from its shoulder loop and launched it high into the air, sending me in pursuit.

While desert hiking, the umbrella will shield its user from much of the sun's harmful ultraviolet radiation. It also blocks much, but certainly not all, of the sun's heat. And it will block a great deal more if covered with a sheet of reflective mylar.

On a cold day, one of the prime advantages of an umbrella is the shelter it provides. We can sit down to rest, place the umbrella close in front

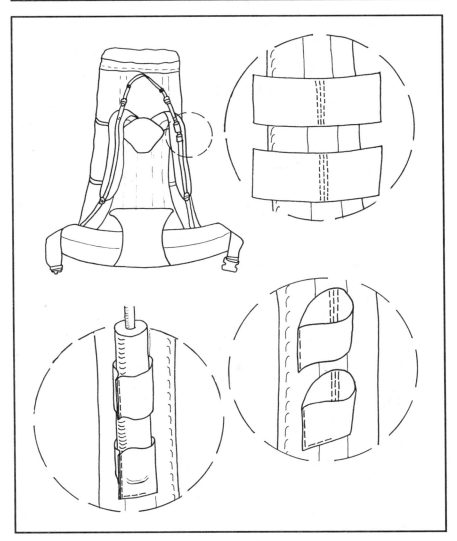

The pack-strap umbrella attachment

of us to block the wind, and feel almost as though we were inside a tent. The protection it affords is that good. And during rainy weather we can crouch beneath tree branches, where the ground is less wet, and by placing the umbrella in front of us we block much of the wind and rain. Furthermore, in the late afternoon when we are cooking, the umbrella can shield the stove in like manner.

While backpacking in pouring rain, when we need to withdraw an item from the pack, the umbrella held overhead prevents rain from entering the pack's open access. Also in pouring rain, the umbrella allows us to sit down and rest where the area is devoid of natural shelter.

If you choose to carry an umbrella on your journey, before setting out you might fortify its construction. Notice around its perimeter where the seams terminate at the tine ends. These terminating seams are stress points, and are prone to pulling apart. Consider applying reinforcing patches of duct tape to them, and then stitching the tape to the umbrella's fabric, using a sewing machine or an awl. Furthermore, if your umbrella's handle is J-shaped, cut off the curved portion using a saw, and file the plastic smooth. Not only does this reduce weight, but it allows you to fit the straight part of the plastic handle into its home-made pack-strap holder.

During my initial experiments, the shoulder strap umbrella-holding arrangement seemed inadequate. Because the pack strap is not a fixed object, whenever I shifted the strap, the umbrella overhead also shifted. And when I cinched the pack's waist belt, the shoulder strap slackened and the umbrella slouched to one side. But after using the system awhile I learned the knack of putting the umbrella where I wanted it, by simply adjusting the tension of the waist belt.

Should the weather prove sloppy, day after day, then your brolly might seem like a tool of the trade. But if the season is fine, then you might remain suspiciously unconvinced of its merits as you walk for weeks in cloudless weather. But when the rains come at last, you might pull out your umbrella--ceremoniously, and with a wry grin if anyone is watching--and you will probably be glad you did not send it home.

During exceptionally rainy weather, at day's end we will still be wet. The umbrella doesn't keep us perfectly dry, but it does keep us much happier.

PACK COVER

Ludicrously, despite the skyrocketing price of packs these days, hardly any are waterproof. And my ongoing series of experiments have demonstrated the futility of trying to seal the seams. The standard "solution" is to fit the pack with a waterproof rain cover. Oddly, many of the commercially available pack covers seem ill designed. Most leak profusely. And those that are baggy might flog violently in strong wind. The simplest, and most readily improvised system is to invert a stout plastic garbage bag over your pack, and wrap it in place with a few lengths of cord. This covering is far better than nothing, until you scrape past a tree branch and breach the plastic. Nonetheless, I've seen plastic-bag pack-covers travel remarkable distances. Their main disadvantage is that they block access to the pack's contents. For these reasons, I recommend sewing your own pack cover. Refer to the details beginning on page 194.

We can use the covers to protect our packs from rain or dew, should they not fit inside the tent. And incidentally, if the packs will not fit inside the tent, then we would place them within reach of the tent's doorway, so that we might awaken to the sounds of any pillaging animals.

We can also use our pack covers, or our rain hats, as pads to sit on during rest stops. This practice thwarts those wretched globs of evergreen balsam that are difficult to detect on the ground, and even more difficult to remove from our Lycra or wicking-fabric pants.

WET WEATHER HIKING STRATEGY

Hiking in wet weather is a skill. Therefore, only by practicing it will we gain proficiency. Generally, the concept is to dress lightly and to hike briskly, to rest frequently but briefly, to eat often, and then at day's end to pitch the tent, remove the wet clothing, and crawl straightway into the sleeping bag. And unfortunately, if you are not carrying an awning—either sewn to your tent or placed loosely over its doorway—then you are not adequately equipped to distance-hike during *extended* and copious periods of rain. See page 175.

While hiking in rainy weather we constantly look for trailside protective objects (usually tree branches) that would shield us from rain and wind. If and when we find such a sheltering object we might stop and sit down to enjoy a 10 minute respite. If natural shelters are lacking, and if the tree branches are leaking through, then we might stop every 45 minutes and sit gingerly on our packs while holding the umbrellas overhead. After munching a few snacks we will move on before the onset of any pervading chills. While lightly dressed we must abbreviate our rests, for as we sit still, the chill will start penetrating our bodies, and by the time we finally notice that we have grown cold, we might have grown deeply cold.

When hiking minimally dressed during cold, rainy weather we are operating metabolically. Consequently, at each of our rest stops we might consider ourselves in a red-alert situation. **Hypothermia lurks around the bend.** The person who falls asleep while lightly dressed might soon be cold, dead meat. I'm not suggesting that hiking in rainy weather is dangerous. Far from it. Freeway driving isn't particularly dangerous as long as the motorist possesses and exercises the appropriate skills. So once again, we keep the rest periods frequent but brief. And if we tire, or become chilled, and especially if we begin shivering, we make camp. Refer to the excellent treatise on hypothermia in either volume of the PCT guide books (Schaffer, et. al, Wilderness Press).

When hiking during inclement weather we will do well to snack at frequent intervals. At least in theory this helps to maintain an elevated metabolism, and to ward off the preliminaries of hypothermia at our abridged rest stops. Rarely will our larder include extra munchies, but we might borrow them from our next day's rations. The idea is to eat more food during foul weather, unless tent bound. If the storm clears, then we will have less food to see us through the better weather; but we can cope with that easily enough. But if the foul weather persists, then we could call a temporary halt, declare a partial layover day or two, and relax in our tents. If we actually deplete our supply of food, we might bring to mind George Hassler Johnson, who walked from Chicago to New York in 1926. He covered 578 miles in 20 days, averaging nearly 29 miles per day. And not once during his journey did he eat.

While distance hiking in rainy weather we might do well to resist the urge to stop and make camp. Instead, we might nurture a will to move ahead regardless of the weather's mood—within reason of course. As with any other type of "obstacle," we benefit tremendously by learning to project our consciousness through it. We might find that by ignoring the rain, it becomes less of a distressing factor.

As a final precaution, we must remain a little more alert to the condition of our feet. When wet they soften and become more susceptible to blistering. And if they become cold then we lose some of our awareness of the blister potential down there.

RAINY WEATHER CAMPING SKILLS

Desert plants sustain themselves by absorbing the nightly dew. As the air cools to what is called the dew point, water vapor in the air becomes saturated. It then condenses onto cooler surfaces, forming tiny droplets. On plants, for example. And incidentally, hoarfrost is frozen dew in the form of a white crystalline coating. Verglas is frozen dew in the form of hard, clear ice.

During the night, as our bodies give off moisture, we are essentially creating our own weather within the micro-environment inside the tent. The local humidity rises until the air becomes saturated. As the tent radiates heat into the night, it cools. Dew, or condensation, might then form on the inside of the tent walls and ceiling. This is called "sweating."

By keeping the tent fly's doorway open we provide for increased ventilation; and consequently we help prevent the moisture content of the air inside the tent from reaching the saturation level. Accordingly, in the morning our tent, clothing and sleeping bags will be far drier than had the door been closed. Nevertheless, most tent flies are not designed to be used with their doorways open except during fine weather. (By this we can guess that their designers had not lived in them for extended periods.) The inappropriately designed tent-fly doorway is slanted up and toward the center of the tent. Any water running down the wall and over the doorway is likely to drip into it. And rain will probably enter the tent's open entrance.

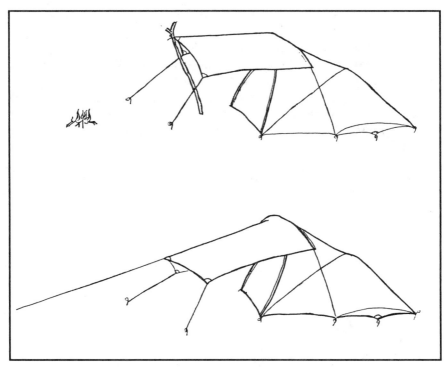

The home-made awning

THE AWNING

One solution is to place a protective awning over the fly's doorway. The awning is best sewn in place, as described on page 201. Otherwise, you can drape a tarp over the tent's entryway to act as an awning.

The awning is another of my modifications. During our first PCT hike we came to realize its need. I designed and sewed one onto our tent fly, and we used it during our second PCT hike. It proved such a resounding success that not once during the summer did we need to close the fly or tent door! (However we almost always kept the mosquito netting door closed.)

The awning's most salient feature is how it facilitates tent life during extended periods of rain. After two or three persistently rainy days, the moisture might begin pervading the hiker's sleeping bag and virtually every item of clothing. Ventilation is of paramount importance.

RADIANT HEAT

But by striking a small campfire several feet in front of the awning, the hiker can sit beneath the awning and dry the sleeping bag and clothing. And the radiant heat of the fire will carry into the tent's open doorway to dry its interior. Of course, **the evening must be windless and the campfire must be built at a safe distance and kept small, so that the tent doesn't catch fire.** Also, the campfire must be extinguished before the hiker retires for the evening. Being trapped inside a rapidly burning tent would be a catastrophe beyond words.

STEALTH CAMPING
Aloof and attuned

And the night shall be filled
with music,
and the cares that infest the day,
shall fold their tents like the Arabs,
and as silently, steal away.
—William Wordsworth.

Clay lies still, but blood's a rover;
Breath's a ware that will not keep.
Up, lad; when the journey's over
There'll be time enough to sleep.
—A. E. Housman, 1859-1936

AVOIDING DESIGNATED CAMPSITES

Imagine that one midsummer's night, every camper in the Sierra Nevada shined a flashlight into the sky, and that a passing satellite photographed the scene with a powerful lens. Rather than showing evenly distributed pinpricks of light, the picture would show small circles of lights, and long strings of clusters. The circles would delineate the lakes. And the linear clusters would depict the trail-side creeks. Otherwise, the photo would show a vast blackness. This blackness would indicate that despite the crowded campsites, the overwhelming majority of the area is normally vacant.

The hikers who learn how to camp away from water sources are at a colossal advantage. For them, that expansive area of blackness on the hypothetical satellite photo becomes a tremendous potential for virtually unlimited camping. Because these hikers camp not in accordance with the usual methods, which are degrading the ecology, I call them stealth campers.

STEALTH CAMPING DEFINED

Stealth derives from the word steal: in the sense of moving, happening or elapsing inconspicuously. Used thus, the word does not have a negative connotation. Stealth camping has to do with backpacking unobtrusively; of making a hidden camp and maintaining a low profile, and of distancing ourselves from the hoards in the late evening. Because it is not common practice, the concept provides us with an entire chapter full of advantages.

In the sense of moving and behaving (and camping) deliberately so as to avoid observation, most wild animals live by stealth. No doubt our distant forbearers camped quietly to avoid danger, and they must have moved covertly in order to locate and approach their prey. The stealth backpacking ethic is indeed more aligned with their ways. Sometimes we are subjected to danger, mainly when near roads. And we try to approach game—not with weapons, but with cameras and appreciative eyes. Grouping together, trammeling the earth, making noise, and broadcasting litter are but a few of the unfortunate ramifications of modern civilization. But they are inappropriate in the wilds.

THE REQUIREMENTS

The first requirement of stealth camping is in learning to sleep away from water sources. One might imagine that I am suggesting carrying the evening's water supply into the distant hills. This is not the case. Instead, I recommend using the evening's water where it is found, and then relocating to a distant and uninhabited region to make a waterless and improvised camp.

The second requirement of stealth camping is the ability to spend the night on sloped ground. This is easily accomplished by sleeping with the feet uphill: an attitude that markedly improves circulation. Also, rain doesn't pool beneath a tent pitched on a gentle slope.

The remaining principles can be addressed by striving to occupy the least personal space, as regarding all five of our senses.

THE ADVANTAGES

By not using conventional campsites, stealth campers encourage environmental restoration. They avoid aggravations from boisterous campers as well as those from marauding bears and pillaging rodents. Their daily mileages are also increased as they hike beyond the conventional campsites. And stealth campers enjoy the ineffable benefits of sleeping on virgin, untrammeled ground.

THE METHODS

After cooking and eating dinner not too near a creek or lake, and after washing up, we stealth campers continue along the trail into the late afternoon or evening. When the time is right we leave the trail and mosey into the forest in search of small, natural clearings, *well out of sight*. Our tents are small, and unobtrusive in their pastel or earth-tone colors. We refrain from building campfires and making excessive noise. Therefore, the chances of an intrusion by man or beast are vastly diminished.

THE PECULIARITIES OF ESTABLISHED CAMPSITES

Camping near water is an unfortunate and almost universal rite practiced by unenlightened outdoor enthusiasts for generations. Preferring to congregate in indiscrete, waterfront tent cities, these people demonstrate oblivion to the ecological damage they are promulgating.

In the process of preparing their tent sites and making them more "comfortable," assiduous campers have most likely scraped away the beneficial layers duff and forest litter. The result is a pervasive dirt-ash mixture that clings to your ground sheet, and a dust that might pervade your nostrils, food, tent, and gear. The ground is not only dirt and ashes; some of it is desiccated stock manure. And horses, mules, donkeys and llamas might have compacted that "soil" as though it had been driven over by a steam roller. The grounds are hard and uncompliant, and require the use of foam mattresses for sleeping. In this compacted and sterilized condition, the vicinity's regeneration is enormously repressed. Furthermore, because of the site's heavy use, the resident rodents maraud the camper's stores nightly. Bits of rubbish might liter the sites, particularly in the ugly and deeply-scarred campfire rings of blackened rocks. There might be small wads of TP crammed in nooks and crannies between nearby rocks and beneath fallen trees. And there is sure to be feces (teeming with coliforms) buried everywhere in the proximity.

The water sources near these established campsites are usually polluted, to greater or lesser degrees. Traditionally, equestrians allow their stock to drink of them freely, and turn a blind eye when their animals urinate and defecate in those same waters, as long as their stock are downstream of camp. Furthermore, the creek and lake beds are likely to harbor sunken scraps of food: well preserved remnants of dish washing.

ENVIRONMENTAL RESTORATION

In congested wildernesses or national park backcountries, the main impact is at the camping sites. Stealth campers have virtually no impact on these sites because they don't use them. In an era of backpacker overpopulation, stealth camping provides at least some alternative to the permit system.

WHERE THE MIND REACHES, THE BODY FOLLOWS

Most distance hikers segment their journeys into daily objectives. But in deciding ahead of time where we wish to camp each evening, we shackle our minds to the objective. Thus, when we arrive at the chosen campsite, most likely we will want to stay there regardless of the time of day. When we reach that creek in the early afternoon, for example, and when we make camp there, we forfeit several miles of the day's otherwise satisfactory progress—for no reasons other than psychological ones. Established campsites act like snares. For the weekend hiker, quitting the day's hiking early to camp at them might be personally desirable (even though ecologically detrimental). But for the distance hiker, the practice can be extremely limiting.

We would do better by pressing on into each late afternoon and early evening, and then by rewarding ourselves with a layover day approximately once a week, in the proximity of a resupply station. The intent is not to set records, but merely to minimize the overall effort of a two and a half thousand mile hike. As such, we need to remain alert to the mental snares that would impede our progress. By keeping our minds off the anchors, and concentrating instead on the sails, we will press ahead to better advantage.

THE CAMPLESS DINNER, AND DINNERLESS CAMP

With little more than a psychological adjustment, we can expedite our journeys considerably. If, in the late afternoon we arrive at the last creek for several miles, indeed, we might stop and relax. Naturally we are tired from the day's exertions—exhausted, it might seem. More than likely, though, much of the fatigue is simply the result of depleted reserves. We might need a hearty meal more than we need a prolonged rest. So almost as though we were making camp, we cook and eat dinner. After washing dishware and bodies we use the Hiker's Friend (see page 99) to filter a quantity of water into our bottles. Then, instead of pitching the tent we re-shoulder our backpacks and press on. If the meal was one of those specified in the food chapter, or an equivalent, then it will most likely provide the energy needed to hike buoyantly a few more hours. And enjoying the nutritional reviving, rather than dragging into the evening camp, we might almost wish for a few more daylight hours. Much farther on, we leave the trail and walk a distance into the forest or desert, and establish a dry camp. With the dinner chores already behind us, the tasks of making camp are greatly simplified. And after turning in, we might enjoy a dessert.

This technique is extremely effective, and with certain variations it can extend the day's mileage considerably. Perhaps the method's greatest benefit, though, is how it can enable the distance backpacker to hike efficiently between distant water sources. The matter is elucidated in the Potable Water chapter, beginning on page 93.

STRIKING NO CAMPFIRES

The campfire has enormous ecological ramifications. True, nature uses lightening-caused fires to maintain her ecology. Although this type of maintenance has proven successful for millennia, it is no longer good enough for humankind. Several decades ago, forest fires were declared egregious, and we instructed our forest service protectorates to declare open war on them. As a result, we have turned our coniferous forests into immense tinder boxes. Of course, policies are beginning to change. Nevertheless, we hikers suffer certain dangers that our campfires might start colossal forest fires. I do not exaggerate; PCT hikers have indeed initiated devastating forest fires. Witness the Clover Meadow fire, started by a PCT hiker reputedly burning toilet paper. As a result of this, and similar mishaps, some locals in the affected areas harbor the false impression that most PCT hikers are inept. Let's examine how these accidents occur.

WET DUFF TAKEN AS DIRT

The surface layer of a typical forest floor is called litter. It comprises recognizable needles, leaves, cones, sticks, and other natural and flammable materials. Beneath the litter is a layer of decomposed and compressed litter called duff. In some areas the campfire builder will have to dig to a surprising depth through the accumulated duff before striking dirt. Nevertheless, even though duff is flammable, ignorant campers commonly mistake it for dirt, and build fires on it. Even if not mistaken, they might misconstrue it as non-flammable, particularly when it is wet or moist. They overlook the probability that the campfire will dry it. And worse, they often extinguish their smoldering campfires using moist duff.

CAMPFIRE DISADVANTAGES

In places where firewood is scarce, we would do well to consider that someone in need (for example during an extended period of rainy weather, or possibly in an emergency) might have better use for the nearby and accessible firewood. And conversely, if you find yourself in an emergency, you might refrain from camping in an established site where the firewood has likely been pillaged to the twig.

The stealth camper uses no campfires, unless genuinely necessary. For one reason, the virgin tent sites usually feature thick and very flammable underlayers of litter and duff. During our two through-hikes of the PCT Jenny and I made only four campfires, and those were to dry clothing.

Some of the disadvantages of campfires are:

☞ Firelight and billowing campfire smoke and its permeating odor draw attention to the camp from far and abroad.

☞ The campfire isolates us from our surroundings, especially at night.

☞ Gathering wood expends time and energy. So does building the campfire, extinguishing it, and attempting to restore the area approximately to its natural appearance.

☞ A campfire scorches the land much deeper than a forest fire, and its open wound might endure for decades.

Because of the numbers of backpackers enjoying campfires each and every summer evening, and practically everywhere throughout upland America, building campfires for mere ambience has become an ecologically unsound practice.

ALTERING THE NATURAL SETTINGS

Another code of stealth camping is in not altering the natural setting while establishing the impromptu camp. There is little harm in hand preening twigs, pine cones, and sharp-pointed cone scales that might puncture the tent's floor. But we must refrain from brushing away the forest litter. Also we would refrain from breaking away green limbs and yanking out saplings that might occupy our prospective site. Instead, we would search elsewhere for a place naturally free of such obstructions.

ADVANTAGES OF A SMALL TENT
If our tents are small, then so will be our terrestrial requirements. It is surprising, the number of impromptu sites that will barely accommodate only a small tent. During rain or snow fall we might want to squeeze our tent into the limited area beneath the sheltering branches of a tree (as long as the threat of a lightning strike is minimal). And in the alpine regions, rarely we might want to camp perched on a rocky and exposed aerie that will accommodate only a small tent.

AVOIDING PREDICAMENTS
Many campers imagine themselves more secure in groups. This might be a delusion, particularly in a group that happened to contain the very occasional miscreant element in society that has somehow found its way into the backcountry. While camping in an established campground, near people you don't know, you might do well to remain mindful of your belongings.

But the better part of vigilance is in keeping clear of the rogue's principalities. At impromptu camps deep in the woods, hidden far from roads and even from the trail, nature will secrete us away in perfect safety; and we can rest assured that our nights will pass quietly and uneventfully.

People-related problems have been extremely rare along the PCT. However, we err by assuming we can camp near roads in perfect safety. Occurrences of hassles (and worse) along the Appalachian Trail are more commonplace because roads there are more ubiquitous. But whatever trail we are hiking, common sense dictates that we refrain from camping near a road, and especially a 4WD road. By "near," I mean within sight, earshot, and haphazard pistol-plinking and beer-bottle hurling range.

There might be a few times during the summer afoot when we are tempted to camp close to a road, albeit covertly in the brush. Having once narrowly averted assassination by a flying beer bottle, I can report that motorists are prone to tossing objects out of car and truck windows, whether aware of our presence or not. If that possibility isn't enough to dissuade us, the traffic's noise might be.

Camping within sight of a road is an open invitation for trouble to come tapping at our frail doors in the blackness of night.

TENT COLOR
As stealth campers, we strive to maintain low profiles. Who knows, we might be avoiding possibly unfavorable encounters with backcountry rangers. No doubt they will not be entirely pleased with my stealth camping

ethic, despite its environmental soundness. But jesting aside, usually the tasks of maintaining our eminent domain are not difficult, owing to the expanse of uninhabited regions we are traversing. However, there might be times when we are tempted to make camp near the outreaches of civilization, particularly near resupply stations. At these times we would do well to attract as little attention to our camps as possible. This is difficult if our tents are brightly colored and designed to attract attention. The suitable tent would be pastel-colored or earth-tone; something that blends in more with the environment. Cammo does not; it merely stigmatizes its owners as potentially hostile.

NOISE MAKING

Another method of attracting perhaps unwanted attention is by talking loudly and clanging pots and pans inattentively while cooking and washing up. Remember that while enjoying our experience, ours is not the privilege of degrading someone else's. Also, we might see and hear far more wildlife at closer range if we travel and camp quietly. And for most hikers, encountering wildlife is one of the more important facets of the wilderness experience.

Often we will hear people long before we see them, especially if they happen to be camped near a lake. Flat water reflects sound, and because the air over it is often cooler and therefore more dense than the surrounding air, the sounds seem amplified. Many people talk loud at home in order to assert themselves above blaring commercials. They talk loud in the city, competing with the congested traffic and noisy offices.. And unthinkingly they might bring their habits into the wilds. Some even fail to restrain their uproarious children. So if distance-hiking in pairs or groups, we would do well to set an example by using the minimum vocal levels needed to maintain our conversations.

CAMPING IN THE QUIET

Another reason not to camp next to a stream is this: we might want to listen for sounds in the distance, for example those of approaching people or bears. This was important in the frontier days, and I suspect that in certain situations it might once again become so. But more importantly, the noise of running water drowns out most of the surrounding noise. And in so doing, it essentially barricades the camp from the natural world at large.

OBVIATING THE BEAR PROBLEM

Stealth camping obviates 95% of the black bear problem. Bears concentrate mainly in the more fruitful areas: normally the human congested ones. So to elude the bears, we need only avoid sleeping at, or near, established campsites.

THWARTING PILLAGING RODENTS

At established campsites, typically the chipmunks, mice and voles have learned that backpackers possess food they will not defend while sleeping. As such, these nocturnal rodents are typically accomplished at raiding backpacks and gnawing into food bags. Also they might purloin socks and small stowbags, presumably to use as bedding. However, their pillaging does not affect stealth campers, who refrain from sojourning in their domains.

DEVELOPING THE SKILLS FROM DAY ONE

When embarking on a journey of the PCT, we might as well begin practicing stealth camping the first evening beyond Campo. By looking for campsites well hidden from the trail we will easily thwart the sometimes overzealous officers of the police and border patrol, who have their hands full trying to apprehend the illegal aliens crossing nocturnally from Mexico. And while on the subject, I recommend not loitering in the vicinity of the Mexican border to 50 miles north. The local residents are understandably suspicious, and might become distraught if they see hikers milling about for no apparent reason. More importantly, though, we will want to begin developing the stealth camping skills early on, for when we reach the mountains we might be regularly camping on small patches of bare ground amid massive snowfields.

SLEEPING ON A SLOPE

Trying to sleep on a gentle slope can be disconcerting to the person unaccustomed to it. Yet stealth camping territory is only rarely level. Few people can tolerate sleeping on ground sloped to one side. And never would we sleep with the feet downhill, because during the night as our leg muscles relax, the vessels dilate, allowing gravity to pool the blood in our lower extremities. This situation drastically curtails circulation, which in turn diminishes the restorative effects of an otherwise good night's rest.

However, by employing the proper technique, camping on non-level ground affords tremendous advantages to distance hikers who aim the feet of their tents directly uphill. That way they will not roll inadvertently to one side. And as they sleep with their feet elevated above their heads, gravity will slowly draw the day's over-fluids from the feet, ankles and legs. This is indeed recommended therapy for stiff and swollen extremities.

Distance hikers don't balk at gradually sloping tent sites, they search for them. And in so doing, worlds of camping possibilities open before them.

And how will you know if the terrain was too steep? By awaking the following morning to discover that you have slid out of the tent.

Traditionally, campers select level sites. These are acceptable if the skies bode well, but they are a gamble in rainy weather. Beneath inauspicious skies the novice errs when pitching the tent on flat and level ground.

If rain falls hard, this person might soon be camped in a deepening pond, despite the presence of an entrenched moat. Indeed, camping on level ground during a heavy rainstorm might test the tent floor's waterproof integrity. But after considerable use, most floors are breached by numerous, if tiny, holes. Many are the stories of distraught individuals packing up in the middle of the night and heading back for their cars. Obviously, though, this is not an option for the distance hiker.

Partly for the same reasons, stealth campers refrain from digging hip and shoulder holes beneath their beds.

So another premium advantage of camping on a slope is that during rainy weather the ground water will likely run off, rather than pool beneath the tent. If rain is falling hard, in the exigency of the moment you might scrape an arrow shaped gutter, a few inches deep, pointing uphill, and centered above the foot of your tent (the foot of which will of course be aimed uphill). The trench would channel the flowing ground water around the tent. Just make sure to eradicate all signs of your excavation before moving on. The necessity of arrow trenching a tent site is extremely rare. I, for example, have done it only twice.

WHICH WAY IS DOWN?

Even at his or her most acute, no person has the ability to determine which way is downhill when the ground slopes but infinitesimally. And for the distance hiker, this shortcoming might be amplified markedly. This is because the fatigue at day's end will invariably effect the hiker's equilibrium. Even on a fair slope, you might pitch the tent in what seems the correct orientation, only to spend the ensuing night trying to prevent yourself from rolling disconcertingly to one side. The solution is twofold. First, walk around your potential tent site's perimeter and examine it from all directions. While you apprise the ground from one vantage it might appear sloped toward you. But when you view it from its far side, again it might appear tilted toward you. Nevertheless, viewing it from all sides is the first method of determining which way is *probably* down. Consequently, you might do well to enact this walk-around routine at each prospective tent site. The second method is to spread your tent's groundsheet, and lay down on it with your feet pointed at what azimuth seems uphill. If it passes the comfort test, you would then pitch the tent appropriately.

If the ground everywhere is hardly sloped, choose a site on a slight rise: an island awaiting its sea. But even thus, any rain water streaming down the walls of your tent might course under the tent.

THE PROTECTED CAMP

In boisterous weather, look for a small tent site protected by foliage, trees, or rocks. If on a ridge against which a tempest is striking head on, and if there is very little danger of lightning, consider pitching your tent, not on the back side of the ridge, but a short distance back from its windward edge. As strong wind strikes a ridge head-on it curls high into the sky and over the top like a giant, standing wave of surf. Inside this "rotor," back from the edge of the bluff, you might find the wind greatly diminished.

ALPINE CAMPING

As a matter of preference, Jenny and I surmount the snowbound mountain passes of the Sierra during the day, then descend to the seemingly tropical settings of the intervening valleys. Then the late afternoon finds us climbing toward the next pass. As we hike generally north we will be climbing the sunnier, southern exposures, which are less snowbound. We continue across increasingly pervasive snowfields until reaching what appears to be the final patch of bare ground en route to the pass. And there we camp. Indeed, the air will be cold, thin and exhilarating in the shadows of those craggy peaks, and the views will extend away to forever. This we find most exhilarating. And we will look far down into the tree-carpeted valleys and think of the bears haranguing the ill-fated campers occupying their officially designated sites.

THE BENEFITS OF SLEEPING ON THE GROUND

Among the innumerable benefits of the backpacking lifestyle are those realized by the hiker's spine from sleeping on the ground each night. Particularly, different ground each night. Most city folks experience difficulty sleeping on the earth simply because their well-entrenched bed-sleeping postures aren't applicable. So as a compromise they lug along their so-called comfortable mattresses: inflatable or thick foam. I maintain, though, that fatigue is the distance-hiker's best mattress. And it is weightless.

RISING EARLY

The conclusion of each successful encampment is the dawn of the new day. The birds bestir themselves at the first *hint* of daylight, and like them, when distance hiking we would do well to awaken, and to rise at dawn. If we are eating nutritional foods, and sleeping feet uphill on virgin earth, then in all probability we will awaken refreshed and full of expectancy in the new day's adventures. The early morning is my favorite time of day, and I find it incredible that most backpackers sleep or lounge through it. In pilot training we learn to take off from the beginning of the runway. "The runway behind, does you no good" is a flight instructor's aphorism. And so it is with the backpacker's day.

HYGIENE

Backcountry practices for the promotion of good health
and the prevention of disease

WASHING DISHES

Washing dishes with soap and water is a carry over from home; and that is a good place to leave this practice when venturing into the back-country.

If our camp dishes are greasy or oily, water by itself will clean them hardly at all, particularly if the water is cold. And unless that water has been treated, it can transmit Giardia. Even drying the dishes, however thoroughly, does not eliminate any clinging Giardia cysts.

Scouring dishes with a nylon scrubber is unhygienic. The pad collects and multiplies bacteria, which contaminates the dishware, and also the water sources when being rinsed out. Consider the pot scrubby as a ticket to visit the nearest doctor.

Soap will cut some of the grease, but it will not sterilize the dishes against Giardia or the harmful bacteria that tends to accrue. The soap residue left on our dishes might give us diarrhea (and soap left in our camp-laundered clothing can irritate our skin). In the backcountry, dish-washing soap is out of its territory.

In the wilds, the best way to clean a dish and cookpot is, first, to pour treated water into them immediately after use. Then after scraping and stirring thoroughly with a spoon, drink the resulting "gruel" if desired. Next, wipe the dish free of any residues using natural materials, without adding more water. Use a handful of weeds, bracken ferns, leaves, or pine needles. Scour any persistent spots using a stick, which is less likely to scratch the dishware. After use, these materials can be heartily dispersed, leaving hardly an indication. If far from the nearest trail, we might even borrow an attached evergreen bough with which to scrub a pot. Finish the job by wiping the dishes with half a bandanna made of cotton.

USE MINIMAL COOKWARE

For best results, we would equip ourselves with the minimum of cookware. This reduces weight, pack volume, and the continual fussing about while washing up. One person would carry one kettle and its lid, one cup and its tight-fitting lid, one small knife, and one spoon. A second person would require another cup with a lid, and a spoon.

STERILIZING KITCHENWARE

It's important to note that all backcountry kitchenware must be "sterilized" once in awhile. Otherwise, bacteria can grow on them to epidemic proportions. The dysentery that this bacteria is capable of inducing is far more serious than giardiasis. Historically, it has killed millions of people. Pouring boiling water into the pot and bowls is the camper's easiest method of discouraging this bacterial growth. When we pour our evening's boiling beverage into the drinking cup, we are repressing its indigenous culture. And while cooking and stirring a meal, we are generally disinfecting both the cook pot and spoon. If not consumed straight from the cook pot, we would do well to eat our cooked meals from our drinking cups. That way, the next boiling brew will disinfect the cup. Categorically, we would avoid the risky practice of eating from a food dish not regularly exposed to boiling water in the course of the meals. To do otherwise might necessitate a most unpleasant side trip for medical attention.

INCINERATING TRASH

When finding bits of trash along the trail, consider picking them up. Otherwise, the next person coming along might think them yours. And remember that no conscientious hiker litters the way with messages for straggling members of the party.

Plastic in any of its forms is best carried out of the woods. If incinerated, its fumes can be toxic. Breathing them might make you ill.

On a windless day, paper, cardboard, and cellulose (a wood product) can be burned at a rest stop. Here's how: first, select a place on bare dirt or sand; not on humus (duff) —which to the novice might appear to be dirt. And not near a tree root (a smoulder could work its way far underground, consuming the sap-rich root as it goes, until eventually reaching the tree). Build a micro fire using match-stick sized twigs. Into this, feed the paper and cardboard, small bits at a time. Occasionally add more kindling. As the ritual is winding down, sweep the unburned shards of wood into the little fire. When the flame self-extinguishes for want of fuel, don't just bury the ashes. Instead, begin stirring them deeper into the earth. The more they are stirred, the more the ashes are ground into powder. And the admixture of dirt cools the particles and distances them, rendering them incapable of rekindling. Sufficient stirring will erase the little fire-site altogether.

THE PRIMITIVE PRIVY

If stooping creates havoc with your swollen knees, try sitting on the edge of a log or rock, or even on the edge of your backpack. First, though, dig a cat hole using an ice axe, or using sticks or stones. But before that, collect a few handfuls of snow, stones or evergreen boughs to use as toilet paper. If you insist on using toilet paper, use the absolute minimum. The animals might dig it up, and buried or not it will probably remain intact for a long time. And while on the subject, contrary to popular belief the pathogens and coliforms in buried fecal matter remain virulent for years.

Burying a tampon is a virtual guarantee that some animal will exhume it. Instead, double bag it and carry it out. The use of a natural (and reusable) sea sponge might be a more sensible alternative.

BODY ODOR

We all know that B.O. is caused by bacteria that thrives on perspiration and its associated extracts, and that it is a normal byproduct of hard work. Oddly, we hardly notice our own, but to city folks we hikers might emanate an effluvium that brands us as positively gross. Consider this before visiting each way post, be it a resupply station, a store, or especially a restaurant. After we have been on the trail awhile, B.O. pervades our hiking clothing as well. Therefore, the conscientious hiker might carry a set of town clothes. These would include a fresh, lightweight shirt, and at least a pair of shorts. And before donning them, he or she would bathe, and maybe break out the small lump of underarm deodorant, carried in a tiny resealable bag, and used sparingly.

THE TUB

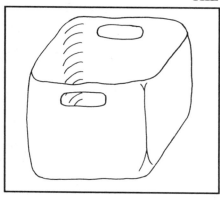

The tub

The tub is a versatile implement for the distance-hiker. Jenny invented the one we use. She simply cut the top off a two and a half gallon collapsible water jug (Reliance, six-liter capacity). We have found all manner of uses for it. These include collecting water from a water source, carrying water miles to camp and storing it there, settling sediment, containing water while pump filtering, pouring water into the Hiker's Friend water filter bag, laundering clothes in, and pouring water onto ourselves when bathing. The tub is reasonably lightweight, and because it folds nearly flat it appropriates but little space in the backpack.

BATHING IN THE WILDS

Swimming or dipping in backcountry creeks and lakes is becoming an increasingly controversial issue. Most hikers take pleasure in the occasional practice. But in our efforts at practicing **zero** impact backpacking, we might consider any adverse ecological consequences of these acts. Particularly as the residues washed from our bodies are *far* more copious than many of us imagine. The following alternative is almost as convenient and refreshing.

Bathing can be a simple matter of collecting water in the tub, moving well back from the water source, and pouring and gasping. Use a small amount of soap if desired; but far more importantly, scrub mightily with the hand towel. Collect more water, back off, and rinse yourself several times. Use the hand towel to dry yourself, wringing it out occasionally. Shampooing the hair is done in much the same manner.

A shortage of water, or a blustery day is hardly an obstacle to bathing. You can sponge-bathe while wearing your clothing by reaching under it and scrubbing your body with a damp hand-towel. Also, you can sponge-bathe while inside the tent, again using a damp hand towel. I perform this ritual nearly every evening.

ORAL HYGIENE

Some dentists suspect that tooth paste complicates various gum problems. Tooth paste is an abrasive, and it is loaded with chemicals (so-called natural ingredients), most having nothing to do with oral hygiene. And many hikers feel that brushing without these agents makes better sense in the woods.

The hiker who eats lots of candy to stoke the metabolical fires is giving tooth decay carte blanche. Candy adheres to the teeth and harbors bacteria that feed on the candy and produce acid as a byproduct. The acid slowly destroys the tooth enamel.

As such, you might carry your tooth brush in your shirt pocket, and habitually brush your teeth after eating. Think of dry- or saliva-brushing your teeth as a pleasant pastime. If you brush while you hike, though, breathe through your nose. Brushing creates a fine mist: something you wouldn't want to inhale while breathing hard. And remember that rinsing the toothbrush in untreated water might greatly increase your chances of contracting giardiasis. At some of the resupply stations you would do well to soak your toothbrush in a small amount of hydrogen peroxide, to disinfect it. And consider flossing between the teeth daily.

RESTAURANT ETIQUETTE

Well meaning hikers have been known to behave antisocially in restaurants, when failing to keep in mind that they are not in camp. So we might remind ourselves to keep our shoes on, use the forks and knives, to refrain from licking the plates clean, and from pulling out our toothbrushes until we have left the premises.

PHOTOGRAPHY
Camera, film, contrast, and the art of seeing

*A man must carry knowledge with him
if he would bring home knowledge.*
—Samuel Johnson

In a popular distance hiking narrative written in 1985, the author describes how he carried 12 pounds of SLR camera gear the entire summer. In the *Handbook*, I describe my photo outfit, which weighs 6.2 ounces (excluding film, which weighs 1 ounce per roll).

Typically, hikers accept the weight of heavy cameras and lenses, yet even lavishly over-equipped they are prone to bringing home disappointing pictures. Why? They often overlook one simple principle: it is the mind's eye, not the camera's any stupendous qualities, that must first capture the image. A load of heavy and expensive camera gear is of little benefit to the hiker that lacks the expertise and patience to use the equipment to best advantage.

My advice to the non-professional-photographer distance-hiker is this: For best results consider using a *quality* point-and-shoot, rangefinder autofocus camera with a self-timer and a built-in flash. These models are reasonably light in weight, and in 95% of the cases they will markedly improve the quality of the owner's photographic portfolio. And for most of us this is the ideal compromise.

THE CAMERAS

I relegated my well-worn SLR to the miscellaneous equipment box long ago. For years I have used the Olympus Infinity, and with satisfactory results. This camera is weatherproof, meaning that it doesn't require a protective bag. It weighs 10 ounces including lanyard, a roll of 36 exposure film, and a lithium battery. It features a self timer, allowing me to set the camera on a rock, and then to back off and hike into the photograph. Its autofocus feature insures crispness in the greater majority of the images, particularly the ones shot in haste. It has a sliding cover that conveniently protects the lens when not in use. And it features a built-in flash that allows me to shoot close at hand in conditions of minimal light. I carried the Infinity on both PCT hikes. One fresh battery easily lasted a summer. Please note that I am not advertising the camera, but am merely using it as an example to elucidate the desirable features.

Presently, I use the Olympus Stylus. At 7.2 ounces, including lanyard, a roll of 36 exposure film, and a battery, this cut the weight of my photo outfit by a whopping 28%. However, the camera is not weatherproof;

meaning that it requires a home-made bag for stowage. And being lighter, its battery is not as long lasting, requiring that a spare be included in a resupply parcel. But the Stylus has certain redeeming features. Its lens is sharper, and its fill-in flash can be **force**-activated. The latter feature can be extremely important when shooting close up in situations of high contrast.

Ardent camera buffs usually consider the point-and-shoot models too limiting. And they need little advice as to which cameras they prefer. But for the novice, I maintain that a quality rangefinder will bring home comparable photos without adding significantly to the pack weight.

THE FILM

The film's ISO (formerly ASA) rating identifies its sensitivity to light. The higher the ISO, the more sensitive the emulsion, but the more grainy and less color saturated will be the final transparency or print. Whether you use slide transparency or print film is a matter of preference. Most photographers striving for quality use slide film. Color separations for books, etc, are best made from transparencies.

ISO 400 film is designed for use in low-light situations. However, being far more light, heat and time sensitive, it is less durable in the field. Also, its results are usually far less color saturated.

I usually buy film and pre-paid processing mailers in quantity from firms advertising in the national photo magazines. I shop around, calling their 800 numbers for quotes, asking how soon they will ship, and inquiring as to what are their (often compensating) shipping and handling charges.

During our 1991 through-hike we shot some 1500 slide transparencies, using Fujichrome 100. We included pre-paid processing mailers in the resupply parcels; then from each resupply station we mailed the exposed film to the processing plant. As a return address we specified our home address. This method was expedient and convenient, but it precluded feedback as to how the camera and film were performing. Nevertheless we had tested them extensively before the hike, and were reasonably confident. As a precautionary measure, one might use the address of a relative or close friend as the return address, and ask them to examine the photos and alert you to any problems.

THE BULB BRUSH

Grit can enter the camera during film changing, and can scratch the acetate or the emulsion horizontally as the film is advanced. The disconcerting result is what appears to be one or more power lines traversing each scene. To reduce the problem, when changing film use a small blower brush to thoroughly clean the camera's interior.

QUALITY PHOTOGRAPHY

While gazing upon a scene to be photographed, our eyes constantly adjust focus as we look from one part of a scene to another. Our pupils constrict and dilate to the varying intensities of light, from those objects in direct sunlight to those in shade. And most importantly, our brain interprets the image, and automatically compensates for harsh contrast. The effect is a pleasing rendition, perceived via an unimaginably complex battery of faculties.

Even the most technologically advanced camera and lens are severely limited when registering the same image. And unfortunately, our brains are generally incapable of softening the resulting photographs. Therefore, quality photography consists of carefully selecting the scene so as to minimize the effects that the camera is incapable of compensating for.

SHADOWS: THE PHOTOGRAPHER'S NEMESIS

High-contrast is the harsh difference in light intensities between objects in direct sunlight and those in deep shade. Cameras and film are generally incapable of dealing with it. And the hiker-photographer who ignores this problem is almost guaranteed to bring home a load of substandard photographs.

Looking through the viewfinder, examine the scene carefully for shadows. Think of them as patches of photo blackness. They do not appear black to your eyes because your faculties are working to smooth the contrast. A photo taken mid-day in the forest, where shadows from the trees fall across a figure, is likely to prove a disappointment. The same would hold true of the photo of people wearing shading brim hats in direct sunlight. The forest scene is best photographed early or late in the day, or with the subject fully illuminated in a patch of sunlight, or during cloudy weather when shadows are largely absent. Portraits and close-ups are best taken using a *manually-activated* fill-in flash.

A FINAL NOTE

When photographing the magnificent forests of the PCT, consider yourself recording the scenes for posterity. At the present rate of logging decimation, those forests might be categorically doomed within a few decades. To site but one example, the non-recycled portion of America's Sunday newspapers consumes some 500,000 trees, on ten thousand acres, each and every Sunday. Many outdoor enthusiasts suffer delusions that the national park and wilderness designations will protect the enclosed timber forever. But an increasingly vehement demand for timber products (for the Pacific yew to begin with) might breach those legal barriers as though they never existed.

SEWING
The machine can pay for itself in its first season of use

*Are most people inept at sewing
because of ignorance or apathy?
I don't know and I don't care.*
—Apologies to William Safire.

If you have no intention of sewing any of your own gear, read this paragraph then skip to the end of the chapter. A reasonable facsimile of the Jardine tent awning might enhance your journeying considerably, but currently it is not available commercially. The final paragraph of the chapter describes how you can contrive one to suit your tent.

Those who would avail themselves of the ensuing opportunity to expand their horizons: proceed. To begin, consider driving your TV to the pawn shop and exchanging it for a sewing machine. The high-tech garments you can easily sew will pay for the machine the first season of use, even if you purchase a new one. And after you attain even a modicum of proficiency you might look askant at the time wasted worshipping the tube.

Many older sewing machines are more robust and powerful than those of our plastic genre. Furthermore, the machine required to sew the following projects need not feature the usual confusion of bells and whistles. It needs only the capability of sewing three stitches: the straight, the zigzag, and the reverse stitch. The straight stitch joins fabrics that do not stretch appreciably. The zigzag joins stretch fabrics, for the stitch itself is elastic. And the reversing mechanism finishes each row of stitching; by sewing backward a short distance it prevents raveling (fraying).

Ask the salesperson to show you how to wind, load, and tension the threads, and how to operate the machine in question. Practice on scraps similar to the materials you will be sewing. Adjust the upper and lower tensions so that the thread pattern is reasonably identical on both sides of the fabrics. If you can't get it right, turn your attention to a different machine. When you succeed in sewing two pieces of material together with a balanced stitch, you become capable of making an entire line of backcountry wear, including Gore-Tex parkas, fleece jackets, wicking garments, windproof pants, sleeping bags, mittens, hats, and so on.

I have arranged the following projects with the novice in mind. They range from extremely simple to barely simple. The beginning ones use less material, and are less time consuming. Remember that sewing is analogous to distance hiking; proceed ahead while focusing only on the job (the terrain) immediately at hand. And take one step at a time.

MATERIALS

Those illustrious garments in the backpacking stores and catalogues began as sheets of high-tech fabrics. In most cases these fabrics are available also to the individual. Consider the various types:

Waterproof fabrics are commonly abbreviated "WP". You can test a sample by pressing it to your mouth and trying to draw air through it. If air passes through the fabric, slow or fast, then for the purposes of this discussion the fabric is not waterproof. Currently, there are two types of WP fabrics: breathable, "B", and nonbreathable "NB". Contrary to what you might expect, air cannot be sucked through WP-B fabrics in any noticeable quantity. This indicates that these fabrics are only barely breathable. However, they do admit water vapor, to a greater or lesser extent depending on various factors. One factor is the difference in ambient temperature from one side of the fabric to the other. WP-B fabrics include Gore-Tex and a host of others in its genre. WP-NB fabrics are coated with plastic, and are not normally the best choice for clothing.

Companies are introducing a wealth of patterns and materials in response to the increasing demand, as hikers everywhere are rediscovering the benefits of sewing their own gear. The patterns and fabrics listed below are not absolute recommendations; there are many equals.

HOW TO BEGIN

Visit your local fabric and sewing shops. Many sell fabrics of nylon, WP-B, WP-NB, wicking fabrics and fleece. While there, you might buy a few spools of thread. The color choices are three: those matching your chosen fabrics; trendy contrasts; or generic tones. The thread of choice is a 100% long-fiber polyester. Avoid buying thread with a cotton content.

Also while there, peruse the highly recommended book *Sewing Activewear*, by Singer; available also from Cy DeCosse Inc. 5900 Green Oak Drive, Minnetonka, Minnesota 55343. This is not a book of patterns, but of ideas and techniques.

Also at the fabric store, ask the salesperson whether they sell patterns for the project(s) that interest you. And finally, sift through their scrap bin if they have one.

Back home, request a fact-filled catalogue from The Rain Shed Outdoor Fabrics, 707 NW 11th, Corvallis, OR 97330; (503) 753-8900. Also request one from Outdoor Wilderness (Is there an indoor one?) Fabrics, 2511 Latha Drive, Nampa, ID 83651; (208) 466-1602. Both of these excellent firms sell most of what you might need in terms of patterns, fabric, and hardware. The sequins, you probably don't need.

SKULLCAP

Let's begin by making a simple cap. Using an inexpensive scrap, perhaps of sweatshirt fleece, sew together a pair of head-sized, dome-shaped pieces, leaving the bottom open. Don the resulting hat. If it's too large, try again. Make the hat long, so that it folds up over the forehead for wearing by day, and down over the face for wearing at night. Once sized correctly, the resulting prototype can act either as a hiking and sleeping hat, or as a pattern upon a piece of high-tech wicking fabric.

My distance-hiking hat is a bomber hat I made of an outer shell of Gore-Tex, and a liner of wicking fabric. It features a chin strap with a toggle.

MITTENS

The second project in the series is a pair of mittens guaranteed to serve you well through the High Sierra. Once again, because your first mitten will be a sizing prototype you would make it from scrap. To make the pattern, lay your hand on a piece of paper in the mitt position (fingers loosely together, thumb at a 45° angle), and trace around it. Cut out the silhouette somewhat larger than your hand, and lay the resulting pattern on a scrap of material. Trace round the pattern, then cut the material on the line. Make a second half-mit, identical to the first. Sew the two pieces together, except where the hand goes in of course, then turn the mitt right-side out. If the mitt fits, all is well. If not, re-size the pattern accordingly. Once you get it right, SAVE THE PATTERN. I re-use mine nearly every year. Finally, lay the pattern on a piece of fleece, then cut out and sew together the finished products.

DITTY BAG

Our third project is a small bag. This could contain your daily accoutrements: tooth brush, knife, compass, sealed emergency matches, film, money (if any), and the page of poetry you might be memorizing.

The ditty bag features a drawstring closure with a barrel-lock toggle, size small. The usual material is ripstop nylon, 1.9 oz. coated. But the bag need not be waterproof and you are therefore free to select the material with more imagination. My current ditty bag is made of a see-through mesh. The starting piece would measure 7" X 20". After cutting it to size, sear the edges lightly with a flame to prevent raveling.

Fold the material in half, end to end, and wrong sides out. Sew the edges together along both sides. Using a hot piece of wire, such as an ice pick or coat hanger, melt a drawstring hole in one side of the fabric, midway between the side stitches and 1½" from the top edge. Then fold back the top edge to form a 1¼"-wide drawstring casing. Stitch it down round its circumference, then turn the bag right-side out. Attach a safety pin to the end of a nylon drawstring and feed it into the burned hole, round the bag inside the casing, and back out the hole. Voilà!

Complicating matters only slightly, we can sew the ditty bag's bottom into a rectangular shape. Turn the bag inside out and lay it flat, the seams centered. The bottom should form a pair of concurrent triangles. Midway from the base to the apex of each triangle, separately, sew the fabric together—perpendicular to the original lengthwise line of stitching. Trim the excess.

WATERPROOF CLOTHING BAG

Next on the list of functional items is another Jardine design: a waterproof bag used to protect the clothing. Begin with a piece of ¾ to 2 oz. waterproof-nonbreathable coated nylon, measuring 36" X 15". Fold it in half, side to side and wrong-side (coated side) out. This gives a 36" X 7½" rectangle. Sew the long edge together using a felled seam, known for its strength, light weight, and its seam-sealing retention. (This is not a flat felled seam, which is slightly heavier, and which might encapsulate water.) To sew a felled seam, place the edges together and sew along their length, ¼" from the edge (forming the "seam allowance"). Peel apart the layers opposite the seam allowance, and lay them flat on the table. Crease down the seam allowance to one side or the other, and stitch it down. As you sew, apply tension to the original seam.

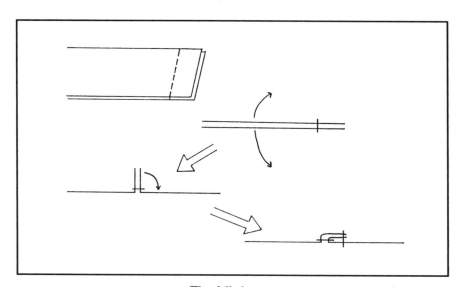

The felled seam

To continue with making the clothing bag, lay the tube-bag flat, seam centered, and stitch the bag's bottom together, again using the felled seam. Then roll it 90° and make the rectangular bottom, as described previously.

Turn the bag right-side out, lay it flat, and draw two parallel lines around its circumference: one 12½" from the opening, and the other 13½". Fold the bag in on itself, and crease it along the 12½" line so that the raw-edged opening is inside the bag. Sew round the bag twice, along the 13½" line. Run the machine back and forth across the side seam several times. You've now made the drawstring casing. Slit the side-seam at the casing, and insert the drawstring. The resulting bag features a long collar. Its use is explained, below.

Using one of the two sealing compounds I recommend on page 50, seal the bag's every seam on both sides. When dry, test the seam sealing by inflating the bag like a balloon.

To use the bag, insert the contents, squeeze out some of the air, then twist the collar by holding it with one hand while twirling the bag with the other. Don't overdo it. Cinch the drawstring a ways, tuck the twisted collar beneath the casing, and cinch home the drawstring. To prevent ripping the casing, *always* cinch by pulling on the drawstring with one hand while pushing on the toggle with the other.

I made my most recent clothing bag, which weighs a mere 1.7 ounces, of a 1 oz, 2 ply Gore-Tex. It survived our recent PCT hike in fine condition, and is fit for another extended foray.

SATISFACTION

Once again, sewing your own bags will insure both their custom fit and their waterproof integrity. Think of the satisfaction and pride, and of the money saved! And remember George Bernard Shaw's epigram for amateur seamsters: "Success covers a multitude of blunders."

SLEEPING BAG STUFF-SACK

We could make this one similar to the clothing bag. The material should be a little heaver. I recommend using a 1.9± oz. urethane coated nylon. My down-filled sleeping bag, rated at 20°F, fits nicely into a stuff-sack with dimensions of 8¼" X 20", as measured with the sack lying flat on the table. To make it, I began with a piece of material measuring 37½" X 17". The collar is 11½" long, and the drawstring casing is 1½" wide. Across the bottom of the stuff-sack I sewed a length of webbing at each side, to aid in extracting the sleeping bag.

When a stuff-sack is crammed with a sleeping bag, the taut seams are prone to leakage. The felled seam, combined with one of my recommended sealants, obviates this problem.

PACK COVER

I recommend you sew your own pack cover, using a ¾ oz. coated nylon, nondescript of color. What follows is again a Jardine design. After filling your pack to capacity, use an inverted plastic bag, a pair of scissors, and some masking tape to make a general pattern. Using this for sizing, sew together a nylon bag, open at the bottom. Place this over your pack. The bottom should extend roughly 6" beyond the bottom of the pack. Imagine that the cover has a small hole where a pack strap exits at the top, and one where it enters near the bottom. Altogether, the cover would have four imaginary holes, two for each strap. Between a top and a bottom imaginary hole, slit the fabric in a straight line, then withdraw the strap. Ditto the other side and the other strap. Have someone shoulder the pack while you inspect that the cover fits correctly. Don't be afraid to cut here and repair there. Re-stitching and seam sealing will make the necessary amends.

When the fit is correct, sew a storm flap onto one side of each slit, and fit it with a length of hook and loop (such as Velcro™). The storm flaps open to withdraw the straps, then close securely.

Already our custom design is superior to most commercial ones. But we will not cease yet, as we need to provide ready access to the pack's contents. If your pack is top loading, then you need an opening running two-thirds the way around the pack cover's perimeter, and down several inches from the top. Thus, you can open the lid and fold it back. To secure the lid closed, you could use hook and loop tape, with or without a lightweight zipper. If your pack loads instead from the front or sides, design your access accordingly. Having finished that, sew a casing around the bottom perimeter and install a thin drawstring, which would tuck up inside during use.

Finally, consider that the cover needs to accommodate the backpack as it shrinks alarmingly while you hike from one resupply to the distant next, consuming your stores. Simply sew on a few lengths of hook and loop in the appropriate places, and use them to cinch the cover snug around the pack. This will prevent it from flapping in the gale.

LYCRA PANTS AND SHORTS

To sew Lycra, use a zigzag stitch adjusted to a short length and width, a metal pressure foot, and a small needle (Universal, size 65/9). Use the same polyester thread as when making the previous items. Avoid stretching or pulling the material through the feeder. Use a ¼" seam allowance, and if desired trim it afterward to no less than ⅛".

Insure that the material will stretch at least as much as that specified on the pattern. The leg cuff does not need to wrap underfoot, nor does it require a self-fabric cuff. Keep the elastic waistband to a minimum, as it absorbs and retains sweat.

I use the Kwik-Sew Pattern 1567, which delineates both long pants and mid-thigh shorts.

SHIRTS AND PANTS OF A WICKING MATERIAL

Wicking materials are best stitched using a size 70/10 Universal needle. Adjust the zigzag stitch to a short length and medium width. If your machine can sew a shell-edged stitch or its equivalent, all the better; this lends a professional touch.

All wicking materials, even of the same name, are not equal. They come in different weights and stretch factors. Once again, make sure that the material you have selected will stretch at least as much as that shown on the pattern in question.

I recommend the Kwik-Sew Pattern 1295 for making pants (such as sweat pants) and shirts. The pants pattern is sized smaller than one would expect. Simplify the design by omitting the fly.

INSULATING JACKET

When sewing non-stretch fleece, use a straight stitch. To sew stretch fleece, use a zigzag stitch with a short length and width. A shell-edge stitch, with a small stitch length and a medium to small width, works even better.

I use the SewEasy pattern 163, with these changes:

✓ Omit the waistband. Make the jacket *longer*, and apply a Lycra binding.

✓ Omit the sleeve cuffs. Make the sleeves longer, and apply a Lycra binding.

✓ Reduce bulk in the collar by using a wicking fabric for the collar facing.

✓ Make the pockets thus: Slit the jacket where you deem the pocket openings will be the most comfortable. Affix 6" or 7" zippers (cut to length). Turn the material over and sew a single piece of wicking fabric (the backing) around its perimeter. This forms the pocket.

✓ I use a 29" zipper; Jenny, a 27". I prefer a single-acting zipper, which in many cases is easier to start.

MOSQUITO/WIND JACKET

This can be made from any number of lightweight fabrics. Years ago I made mine of Versatech. This is not as breathable, but it refuses to wear out. The jacket's color is of the utmost importance, and should be as light as possible.

I use the Kwik-Sew pattern 1367. You can modify the pockets to resemble those of the above fleece jacket. The zippers can be lightweight.

MOSQUITO/WIND PANTS

There are many patterns on the market suitable for this project; for example, the Green Pepper pattern No. 128. Install an elastic waistband with a drawstring, and elastic in the leg cuffs. The pant-leg zippers are unnecessary. The emphasis, as with all your initial projects, should be on simplicity.

MOSQUITO NETTING GLOVES AND HEAD-NET

The ideal head net is nothing more than a fitted sheet of netting draped loosely about the head, and with front and rear flaps that could be tucked beneath the mosquito jacket. Its weight is minimal, its use only occasional, and its value might be inestimable.

Make the netting gloves oversized and without thumbs. They would extend to mid-forearm and be fitted with thin elastic.

THE JARDINE TENT AWNING

Few lightweight tents on the market are capable of providing a suitable environment during protracted rain. The current genre ventilate poorly at best, and the occupant who opens the fly's door to admit fresh air might also admit the rain. Old timers used tents of less flammable materials and with open, sheltered doorways. Thus, they could build a fire in front of the entryways. The fire lent immeasurable assurance and comfort, and the radiant heat dried any soggy belongings. With a few minor modifications, and a great deal of caution, we can enjoy the same benefits.

I sewed a simple awning over the doorway of our tent. See the illustration on page 175, and the related material. The awning shelters our packs at night, and allows us to sleep before an open doorway, even during the heaviest of rain. In *extremely* rare instances, after a long, wet day of trudging we might strike a small fire at a distance in front of the awning, which we would then sit beneath while drying our clothing.

The awning permits us to enjoy life in the woods regardless of the weather's vagaries. When not needed, it folds back. Its guy lines are sized to attach to the aft-end tent pegs.

The fabric used for the awning can be gossamer, but its flammability is a genuine consideration. Most tent fabrics are treated for flame resistance, which is not to say that they are fireproof. Be forewarned, though, that untreated nylon catches fire easily. Most micro-porous fabrics are even more flammable. Purchase your awning material only from an outlet that can assure you that it has been treated for fire resistance. And if you build a fire before it, keep it distant and small.

To my tent fly I sewed the awning along its 58" back edge. It extends 41" from the back to the front edge. The front edge is 68" wide, and features three guy line attachment loops. The loops are reinforced, each with a patch of semi-circular material with a 2" radius. The patch in the center is a half-circle, while those on each corner are quarter-round.

The shape of your tent fly, and its doorway placement, will dictate the appropriate design of its awning. My tent is symmetrical about its long axis. To insure proper fit, I made the awning from two pieces: a left and a right. After pitching the tent and fitting its fly, I taped each piece in place onto the fly, over the doorway and a few inches behind the tent's fore-and-aft apex. Holding the pieces forward and slightly downward, I found that they overlapped at their front edges. I marked where they crossed the centerline, then removed them to the sewing machine. After fell-stitching them together I sewed the resultant awning to the fly.

Those unwilling to sew an awning onto their tent fly can simply drape an awning sheet over the tent's doorway. This arrangement is more prone to leaking at the juncture, and to being dislodged by the wind. And it adds somewhat to the time required to pitch the tent. Nevertheless, it is far better than nothing.

KNIFE SHARPENING

THE SHAVE TEST

Spit on the back of your forearm.

Now use your pocket knife to *gently* try to shave a small patch of hair.

Most backcountry enthusiasts think they know how to sharpen a knife; yet few are those whose knives can pass the shave test. If you scraped at hairs to no avail, consider the advantages of unlearning what you know about knife sharpening, and instead of learning the following method to hone a blade to a razor edge.

THE CARBORUNDUM STONE

The only sharpening tool required is a small, inexpensive carborundum-stone. I recommend that you do not apply oil, water or saliva to it, because these will congeal the grinding dust to form a pernicious gum that will only act as a buffer between the blade and the grinding surface. If your whetstone's pores are clogged and shiny, clean the stone with WD-40.

THE CORRECT GRINDING ANGLE

For an idea of the correct grinding angle, fold a sheet of paper diagonally, left edge aligned with bottom edge. That gives a 45° angle. Now fold it once again for a 22½° angle, which is *about* the angle the blade should scrape across the stone.

THE METHOD

Grasp the stone from beneath, keeping the tips of your fingers clear of (below) the sharpening surface, in case the blade runs amok. Draw the blade across the whetstone, edge first, as though you were shaving the stone. Near the end of the stroke lift the knife's handle gradually so as to keep the blade's curved edge in contact with the stone. This sweeping action grinds the full length of the blade in one continuous stroke. Continue honing one side of the blade until a burr begins to form. In rubbing your finger lightly, *perpendicularly* across the blade, you might feel the burr. If not, resume honing. If you succeed in forming a burr, then you are on your way to producing an exceedingly sharp knife. Continue honing until the burr extends the blade's entire length.

Now turn the blade over and begin honing its opposite side. Stroke lightly, and grind the blade's entire length. Pay close attention that your fingers are clear. Obviously, the former burr will be the first material removed. Hone the blade until a second burr emerges. Again, the burr will appear in one section of the blade first. Continue honing until it forms along the full length.

BUILDING THE RAZOR'S EDGE

The blade should now feature the properly ground angles. Next we will fine tune the edge. Turn the blade over and grind six gentle strokes, carefully honing its full length. Turn the blade over once again, and grind six strokes on its opposite side. Try to maintain a constant angle with every stroke. Repeat the above sequences with 5 strokes on both sides, then with 4, 3, 2, and finally with 1. With each cycle, lessen the pressure; the edge of the blade becomes more fragile the thinner it is honed.

With the process now complete, it's time to test the edge. Gently, try to shave a small patch of hair from the back of your spit-wetted forearm. (Note: those who lack the skill to shave with an open blade would do well to omit this test. The razor-sharpened knife could now inflict serious damage.) If the hairs do not easily drop away, leaving bald skin, then go back and repeat the entire honing procedure. And be assured that once you have ground the proper angles, the knife will be much easier to sharpen in the future.

HIKING PACE
Gear it to the cardiovascular, and add miles to your day

When I was on the Yukon trail
The boys would warn, when things were bleakest,
The weakest link's the one to fail—
Said I: "By Gosh! I won't be weakest."
So I would strain with might and main,
Striving to prove I was the stronger,
Till sourdough Sam would snap: "Goldurn!
Go easy, son; you'll last the longer."
—R. Service, Take It Easy

In any type of running competition, the longer the race, the slower the pace. It seems that each day our bodies are capable of producing only a certain amount of work. We can expend most of our energy in a few minutes, as do sprinters, or we can apportion it over many hours. If athletics teaches us anything, it is the trade-off between speed (or physical exertion) and endurance.

Put differently, the harder a person labors, the less will be the *overall* mileage gained. Running a marathon is a considerable achievement, but with a little training, a walker can cover the same distance day after day. The top runners can manage little more than 20 miles a day when training for competition, but the average backpacker, carrying a heavy load over rugged terrain, and gaining and loosing thousands of feet elevation, can hike at least 20 miles a day. And the reasonably fit and motivated backpacker can cover 30 or more miles a day. In 1972, John Lees of Brighton, England, walked 2,876 miles from Los Angeles to New York in just 53 days. Of course, he walked reasonably graded terrain while not carrying a pack. Still, his 54 miles a day average was an enlightening achievement.

During our PCT trek of 1987 we encountered a fellow who claimed to be running the trail. Receiving extensive assistance from a number of load carriers and resupply people, he and his running friend carried no packs, although they wore a few garments wrapped around their waists. They were the epitome of fitness and organization. And from what we saw, during each day of their "running" they covered a respectable mileage. However, they seemed to require one or more days of recuperation between nearly each day afoot. Because of the required recuperation time between runs, perhaps, these runners were actually among the season's slowest distance-travelers.

This taught that walking is a much more efficient means of traveling the PCT than running. But what is the optimum hiking speed that maximizes the day's, and the week's mileage? This depends a great deal on the terrain.

More accurately, though, for each individual there is an optimum cardiovascular rate that maximizes the distance achieved.

To the inexperienced, hiking beyond this rate might seem impressive. But overexerting drastically curtails long-term mileage. And this is particularly true once the body's reserves are depleted, several weeks or months into the hike.

The optimum hiking pace, then, is a function of our pulses. To maximize distance gained, we need to maintain a pace that, in turn, maintains our heartbeats at a certain BPM (beats per minute).

POWERHIKING

The conditioning begins at home, not with training hikes, but with contemplative exercises in deep breathing and body awareness. These teach us to concentrate on the beating of our hearts; to become aware of our cardiac rhythms. Then, by practicing this newly developed cardio-awareness on the trail, we can readily find and maintain our optimum pace. The technique is to gear the hiking pace to the working pulse rate, while being careful not to over-rev the heart rate. In aeronautical jargon, we must hike on the backside of the power curve.

There is one ideal cardiac BPM that will gain us the best mileage. If we are careful to maintain this rate by attuning ourselves to our heart rates, and by learning to sense over-exertion and over-heating, then we will hike the farthest for the least amount of energy. When our heart rates begin to increase, we slow down; when they begin to decrease, we speed up. This is the real powerhiking.

We have all encountered machismo backpackers hiking near the upper limits of human speed and endurance. Typically, they rocket past, and that is the last we see of them—until we pass by their camps later in the afternoons. And curiously, these are the same tents we might have passed that morning. And in all likelihood that will be the last we see of them. I am not advocating competition. On the contrary, I am merely suggesting the results of hiking inefficiently.

CONTINUITY

Many backpackers tramp in heavy-labored bursts, as though trying desperately to reach the next shelter before the onset of some colossal storm. The procedure might enjoy certain merits along the AT, where hikers sleep mainly in permanent structures, and where persistent rain showers are often commonplace. But here in the western states the gang buster's pace is ordinarily counter-productive.

There are times, though, when the circumstances might behoove us to hike a slightly elevated pulse rates. Consider the following examples:

Let's imagine we hike 10 miles on flat and level ground at 3 mph. Except for periods of rest, we would cover the distance in 3.33 hrs. Now let's say we hike slower uphill for 5 miles, and reaching the top we then hike faster 5 miles down the other side. Will we still travel the 10 miles in 3.33 hours? For an answer to the question, examine the following table. In each case, a certain speed is subtracted from the 3 mph going uphill, and then added back twofold during the descent.

steepness of the hill	Speed while hiking 5 miles uphill	Speed while hiking 5 miles downhill	Time required to hike the 10 miles
flat	3 mph	3 mph	3.3 hours
moderate	2 mph	4 mph	3.8 hours
steep	1 mph	5 mph	6.0 hours
craggy	0.5 mph	5.5 mph	10.9 hours

So we see that hiking downhill at a fast clip does not recoup the time expended while hiking slowly uphill. This is because while hiking uphill we are hiking slower for a longer period of time. And the two effects multiply against one another, to our disadvantage. This demonstrates the benefits of hiking uphill with a slightly elevated pulse, of maintaining a steady pace, and of not attempting to make amends for lost time by hiking aggressively downhill.

ITINERARIES

Choose one of the four standard plans

I know of no more encouraging fact than the
unquestionable ability of man to elevate his
life by a conscious endeavor.
--Thoreau

THE FOUR ITINERARIES

The four standard through-hiking itineraries were computer engineered by yours truly. They are arranged according to their durations, which decrease in half-month intervals; the first one represents a 5½ month through-hike, and the last one a 4 month hike.

The best feature of these itineraries is that, as much as possible, they place the hikers in the right places at the right times. This insures the optimum (as opposed to the perfect) weather and trail conditions all along the way. Secondly, the itineraries take into account the varying difficulties of terrain throughout the full distance of the Mexico-to-Canada PCT. For each duration category, the computer used the foregoing information to suggest the appropriate resupply stations, based on the number of hiking days between them. It then calculated the average daily hiking mileages between those resupplies, so you will know about how far to hike each day in order to reach you next resupply on schedule. And the computer figured the number of days of food and supplies you will need to include in each of those resupply parcels.

The information in this chapter represents something of a breakthrough in PCT through-hiking. No longer do trekkers need to pore over unfamiliar place names while planning their food drops. No longer do they need to guess how much food and supplies to put in each resupply parcel. The itineraries spell out the requirements in black and white.

If you want to hike the trail in five months, for example, select the corresponding itinerary, load the detailed number of resupply parcels with the specified number of days of food, arrange to have the parcels mailed to the appropriate stations, and hit the trail, confident that your planning was expertly done. And how will you know you are most likely to reach Canada

in five months? The itineraries suggest the appropriate departure dates from
each resupply station.

MAKING THE SELECTION

As a prospective through-hiker, your first task is to select the itinerary
that is likely to serve you the best. The computer could not do that, but it
could, and did, provide plenty of latitude among the four levels. Begin by
examining the itineraries and noting the daily mileages between resupply
stations. Obviously, the lesser duration itineraries require higher daily
mileages. The following table summarizes the figures.

ITINERARY SUMMARIES mpd = miles (hiked) per day.				
Journey's Duration	Daily Mileage **During the Initial 2 weeks**	Infrequent Maximum Mileage	Start and Finish Dates	Number of resupplies
5½ months	15 mpd	22 mpd	Apr 26 Oct 10	29
5 months	17 mpd	25 mpd	Apr 27 Sep 27	27
4½ months	19 mpd	28 mpd	May 5 Sep 17	24
4 months	21 mpd	30 mpd	May 10 Sep 10	17

In each case, the first two weeks of the trek represent the journey's
warm-up period. During this time the daily mileages are relatively minimal,
encouraging the hiker to adjust to the rigors of trail life. The "infrequent
maximum mileage" represents the occasional higher mileages attained during
the course of the journey. Note that because of considerable variations in
terrain, the average mileage would be much lower than this figure.

The computer assumes that all hikers travel at equivalent speeds.
Consequently, **those hikers who travel more miles per day, do so merely by
hiking more hours per day.** But daily mileages are only a part of the picture.
As the above table illustrates, the lesser duration itineraries necessitate far
fewer side-trips to resupply stations.

HIGHER MILEAGE HIKING

For the same number of total miles, the shorter the journey's duration, the less overall energy it requires. Even though they hike at virtually the same speed, the 5½ month hikers expend far more effort as do those in the 4 month category. Because they spend proportionally more days and nights on the trail, they must haul a far greater quantity of supplies over the same distance, even though on a daily basis their packs may be somewhat lighter. And what's more, the higher-month hikers detour **much** farther off-route to visit many more resupply stations. To gain a better understanding of the correlations, refer to The Pyramid of Hiking Style, beginning on page 31. In summary:

FOR THE EASIEST HIKE

✓ Carry the lightest equipment and the least amount of it.

✓ Spend the fewest nights en route to the next resupply station by hiking as many hours each day as practical.

✓ Spend the most time making way toward the distant objective, by using the least number of off-trail resupply stations.

✓ And take the weekly layover days in the proximity of the supply stations.

LAYOVER DAYS

By far the best distance-hiking tactic is to tramp with a purpose between resupply stations, and then to rest, or layover near (but please not at) the stations. **Built into the itineraries is one layover day for each six days of hiking.** This explains why the days and the dates don't match. For every six days of hiking, the calendar advances seven days, as it accommodates the weekly layover. Which days you select as layovers, and where, are your choices.

AVOIDING EARLY-WINTER STORMS

Those adhering to the lesser-month itineraries will reach Canada sooner. Consequently, they have greater chances of finishing before the early-winter storms of the far north. Those through-hikers in the 5½ month category, and who are planning to adhere to the PCT where safe and practicable—take note: In order to hike the entire tri-state distance in one season you must not dally. Generally, your count-down clocks begin ticking from Kennedy Meadows. From there you need to redouble your hiking efforts. The way is long, and the early-winter snowstorms of the North Cascades loom over the far horizon. The 5½ month itinerary reaches Canada October 10. **This is quite late in the backpacking season.** In the *"average"* year, storms begin hitting northern Washington in mid October. But in some years they arrive much earlier. However, their durations are usually only two or three days, after which time the sun may reappear for several days until the onset of the next storm. And typically, the first few snow falls remain powdery and fairly easy to traipse through. The water sources begin freezing in late season, though, requiring the hiker to carry more stove fuel. Indeed, the late-season days are brisk and short, but they usually offer hiking experiences nonetheless rewarding to those who persist. Even so, anything the 5½ and 5 month hikers can do to pull ahead of schedule once departing Kennedy Meadows will increase their chances of success.

Those who find themselves falling vastly behind schedule might consider terminating their journeys, and resuming them the following season. Or they might consider flip-flopping to the Canadian Border and hiking south. The dubious advantages of the latter technique are discussed on page 251.

THE 6-MONTH SCHEDULE

Those hikers wishing to use a 6 month itinerary (not included in *The Handbook* because it is not *technically* feasible during a year of average snowfall) would begin 2 weeks earlier than the 5½ month one. However, they would still plan on departing Kennedy Meadows June 13, and from there they would use the 5½ month itinerary. CAUTION: The 6 month hikers should not plan to follow the PCT over the San Jacinto mountains unless they are experienced at winter mountain travel. Those early season hikers unsure of their skills might plan on hiking instead according to the details given on page 145.

LAYOVER TIME SPENT HIKING

Consider yourself as effectively beginning a "layover" when leaving the trail to visit a resupply station. If you plan on backtracking to the trail, rather than on short-cutting a segment of it, then while hiking out to the station you are not progressing toward Canada. So technically, if you spend a half day walking or hitchhiking out, and an equal time returning to the trail, you have just expended a layover day. This is a major reason why the lesser-month itineraries are more efficient. Hikers following them bypass stations distant from the trail, and therefore they avoid the associated off-trail exercise, which in some cases is prodigious.

ASSERTIVE PLANNING

When selecting your itinerary, consider that your body will most likely toughen to the rigors of hiking, over the course of several months. This is particularly true for those hikers that follow the principles included in the training, nutrition, and food chapters of the *Handbook*. As you persist with the journey, you may find yourself hiking many more miles per day than you had first imagined. So be careful when choosing a lesser itinerary, against the tendency to later find yourself psychologically locked into it. And when on the trail, use the tables as guidelines, but travel in accordance with your abilities and motivation.

If these discussions on maximizing the daily and weekly mileages seem tedious and contrary to the standard backpacking methods of taking things easy and enjoying life, remember that we are considering the requirements of through-hiking more than two and a half thousand miles in one season. The border-to-border, single-season trek can be an extremely rewarding experience, but it is not for everyone. Those fond of lounging would be wise to segment their hikes into two or more sections.

STATION DEPARTURE DATES

The dates listed in the itineraries are station departure dates. They are not intended to be adhered to strictly. Instead, they are merely guidelines, or useful references. In the field, should you find yourself falling behind schedule, then your chosen itinerary might suggest the need to adjust your daily and weekly mileages accordingly. And instead, if you find yourself pulling ahead, then you may be assured that you are cruising, and traveling in good stead.

MOUNTAIN SNOWPACK

The treks' beginning dates are irrespective of the mountain snowpack. This reflects the impossibility of anticipating nature's vagaries. Anyway, such prognosticating is largely unnecessary if the hiker remains flexible. If, for example, the previous season was one of extreme snow accumulation, then the slower hikers (who begin earlier) must plan, not on beginning later and compromising their chances of reaching Canada before the onset of winter, but on starting on time and leaving the trail where necessary to hike around the higher mountains. However, the itineraries are shaped to avoid most of the snow, even in years of fairly heavy snowpack.

THE ANNUAL CONCLAVE

The itinerary dates indicate when best to begin the hike. Of necessity, the slower hikers would begin earlier than the faster ones. This means that while hiking through southern California, most of those ahead of you will be traveling fewer miles per day than you, and most of those behind are likely to be traveling more miles per day. This is good news, for it greatly increases your chances of meeting other distance-hikers somewhere along the way. And in fact, that somewhere is Kennedy Meadows. All itineraries are designed to converge there June 11. So plan on spending a few days at the Kennedy Meadows PCT through-hiker's annual conclave. This is as yet an unofficial event, but considering its potential the author hopes that something grand will someday become of it.

While moiling about K-Meadows, resting from your trek through Southern California, you might meet other distance hikers adhering to the same itinerary that you are, and with whom you might wish to join forces for the push through the High Sierra.

And because the majority of hikers would be arriving around the same time, the proprietor of the Kennedy Meadows store could plan to stock their shelves accordingly. Nevertheless, you would do best to include extra morsels in your resupply parcels, in case the demand exceeds the store's supplies, which is often the case.

THE DEPARTURE FROM KENNEDY MEADOWS

The departure date from Kennedy Meadows is not mere happen-stance. It is the fulcrum about which hinges the entire through-hike. And it is based on the AVERAGE early season snowpack in the Sierra Nevada. Furthermore, the itineraries are bounded at their beginnings by southern California's early-season mountain snowpack, and more importantly, at their terminations by the early winter snowstorms that typically begin beleaguering northern Washington in early or mid October (sometimes sooner, sometimes later). In designing the four itineraries, then, I used the computer to fit each one optimally within these constraints.

All itineraries specify departing Kennedy Meadows on June 13. This "mass" exodus would have a number of decided advantages. Banding **loosely** together on the JMT-PCT, hikers would benefit from one another's route-finding expertise and footsteps in the snow. This in itself would increase almost everyone's chances of success. And should someone encounter difficulties, the others could render assistance.

THE SNOWPACK AT COTTONWOOD PASS

The chapter on snowpack teaches that the snowpack at Cottonwood Pass (the first high pass along the way) is entirely representative of the depth and consistency of the snowpack throughout the higher regions of the ensuing 195 miles to Tuolumne Meadows. If you are following one of the *Handbook's* itineraries, and if you find yourself wallowing or postholing laboriously at Cottonwood Pass, then the season is later than normal. That being the case, your best maneuver would not be to fight the snow, but to allow it to coalesce by descending to Horseshoe Meadows and hitchhiking down to Lone Pine for a week's layover.

MILEAGES EXPLAINED

The itineraries specify the **trail** miles between resupply stations. These are the distances **from** where the hiker joins the PCT coming from one resupply station, **to** where he or she leaves it en route to the next station. And they leave no PCT gaps untrod. The distances from the PCT to the resupply stations, on the other hand, are given in the following chapter. These distances are listed separately because in a number of instances they are hitchhiking miles rather than hiking ones. For those reluctant to hitchhike, note that the lesser-month itineraries necessitate the least amount of it. The 4 month itinerary requires none.

INDULGING IN ACCOMMODATIONS

Think about carrying contingency funds for a motel room. The civilized interlude can have an almost magical effect at rejuvenating the wayfarer's sinking spirits, particularly during inclement weather. Nevertheless, motels are not a necessity. As a matter of principle, many hikers categorically avoid them.

THE DATA

The spreadsheet itineraries list the resupply stations, and the dates of departure from the stations. They also provide the intervening **trail** miles, the computer-calculated number of days of food required, and the AVERAGE daily mileage (mpd) between stations.

Note that the days of food required are given in tenths rather than in quarters to enable the hiker to better apportion goods such as snack items.

THE 5½ MONTH ITINERARY

5½ MONTH ITINERARY Copyright (c) 1992 Ray Jardine		
MEXICAN BORDER		April 26
43 miles	2.8 days food	15.2 mpd
MT LAGUNA		April 29
71 miles	4.7 days food	15.2 mpd
WARNER SPRINGS		May 5
70 miles	4.6 days food	15.2 mpd
IDYLLWILD		May 10
97 miles	5.8 days food	16.7 mpd
BIG BEAR CITY		May 17
90 miles	4.9 days food	18.2 mpd
WRIGHTWOOD		May 23
89 miles	4.9 days food	18.2 mpd
AGUA DULCE		May 28
99 miles (a)	5.4 days food	18.5 mpd
MOJAVE		June 4
142 miles (b)	7.5 days food	19.0 mpd
KENNEDY MEADOWS		June 13
85 miles (c)	5.6 days food	15.2 mpd

5½ MONTH ITINERARY Copyright (c) 1992 Ray Jardine		
INDEPENDENCE via Kearsarge Pass		June 19
89 miles (d)	5.9 days food	15.2 mpd
VERMILION VALLEY RESORT		June 28
67 miles	4.4 days food	15.2 mpd
TUOLUMNE MEADOWS		July 1
151 miles	8.2 days food	18.5 mpd
ECHO LAKE RESORT		July 11
103 miles	5.0 days food	20.7 mpd
SIERRA CITY		July 16
96 miles	4.7 days food	20.5 mpd
BELDEN TOWN		July 22
88 miles	4.3 days food	20.5 mpd
OLD STATION		July 27
53 miles	2.4 days food	21.7 mpd
BURNEY FALLS C.S.		July 30
84 miles	4.2 days food	20.2 mpd
CASTELLA		Aug 4

5½ MONTH ITINERARY Copyright (c) 1992 Ray Jardine		
154 miles	7.5 days food	20.5 mpd
SEIAD VALLEY		Aug 12
88 miles	4.2 days food	21.1 mpd
HYATT LAKE		Aug 17
79 miles	3.5 days food	22.5 mpd
CRATER LAKE		Aug 21
87 miles (e)	3.9 days food	22.5 mpd
CASCADE SUMMIT		Aug 26
46 miles	2.3 days food	20.1 mpd
ELK LAKE RESORT		Aug 29
94 miles	4.7 days food	20.1 mpd
OLALLIE LAKE GUARD STATION		Sep 3
54 miles	2.6 days food	20.5 mpd
TIMBERLINE LODGE		Sep 6
50 miles	2.5 days food	20.4 mpd
CASCADE LOCKS		Sep 9
148 miles (f)	7.6 days food	19.5 mpd
WHITE PASS		Sep 18

5½ MONTH ITINERARY Copyright (c) 1992 Ray Jardine		
99 miles	4.7 days food	21.0 mpd
SNOQUALMIE PASS		Sep 24
75 miles	4.5 days food	16.6 mpd
SKYKOMISH (via Stevens Pass)		Sep 29
98 miles	5.6 days food	17.5 mpd
STEHEKIN		Oct 5
81 miles	4.4 days food	18.4 mpd
CANADIAN BORDER		Oct 10
	143 days food total	

5½ MONTH ITINERARY NOTES

(a) This mileage is subject to change as the PCT is completed through the Tehachapi mountains.

(b) Consider hitching to the P.O. at Onyx.

(c) + 9 miles to Onion Valley. Those planning to climb Mt. Whitney might resupply in Lone Pine instead of Independence.

(d) + 9 miles from Onion Valley.

(e) Use only if planning to hike along the highway to the lake's rim.

(f) Those falling behind schedule might consider resupplying at Carson.

THE 5 MONTH ITINERARY

5 MONTH ITINERARY Copyright (c) 1992 Ray Jardine		
MEXICAN BORDER		April 27
43 miles	2.5 days food	17.1 mpd
MT LAGUNA		Apr 30
71 miles	4.2 days food	17.1 mpd
WARNER SPRINGS		May 5
70 miles	4.1 days food	17.1 mpd
IDYLLWILD		May 10
97 miles	5.7 days food	17.1 mpd
BIG BEAR CITY		May 16
90 miles	4.8 days food	18.8 mpd
WRIGHTWOOD		May 22
89 miles	5.2 days food	17.1 mpd
AGUA DULCE		May 28
99 miles (a)	5.8 days food	17.1 mpd
MOJAVE		June 4
142 miles (b)	7.6 days food	18.8 mpd
KENNEDY MEADOWS		June 13
85 miles (c)	5.0 days food	17.1 mpd

5 MONTH ITINERARY Copyright (c) 1992 Ray Jardine		
INDEPENDENCE via Kearsarge Pass		June 19
120 miles (d)	7.0 days food	17.1 mpd
RED'S MEADOW		June 27
36 miles (e)	2.1 days picnic food	17.1 mpd
TUOLUMNE MEADOWS		June 30
151 miles	7.2 days food	20.9 mpd
ECHO LAKE RESORT		July 8
103 miles	4.4 days food	23.3 mpd
SIERRA CITY		July 13
96 miles	4.2 days food	23.1 mpd
BELDEN TOWN		July 18
88 miles	3.8 days food	23.1
OLD STATION		July 22
53 miles	2.2 days food	24.5 mpd
BURNEY FALLS C.S.		July 25
84 miles	3.7 days food	22.7 mpd
CASTELLA		July 29

5 MONTH ITINERARY Copyright (c) 1992 Ray Jardine		
154 miles	6.7 days food	23.1 mpd
SEIAD VALLEY		Aug 6
88 miles	3.7 days food	23.8 mpd
HYATT LAKE		Aug 10
79 miles	3.1 days food	25.3 mpd
CRATER LAKE		Aug 14
87 miles (f)	3.4 days food	25.3 mpd
CASCADE SUMMIT		Aug 18
140 miles	6.2 days food	22.6 mpd
OLALLIE LAKE GUARD STATION		Aug 25
104 miles	4.5 days food	23.1 mpd
CASCADE LOCKS		Aug 30
148 miles	6.8 days food	21.9 mpd
WHITE PASS		Sep 7
99 miles	4.2 days food	23.6 mpd
SNOQUALMIE PASS		Sep 12
75 miles	4.0 days food	18.6 mpd

5 MONTH ITINERARY Copyright (c) 1992 Ray Jardine		
SKYKOMISH (via Stevens Pass)		Sep 17
98 miles	5.0 days food	19.7 mpd
STEHEKIN		Sep 23
81 miles	3.9 days food	20.7 mpd
CANADIAN BORDER		Sep 27
	131 days food total	

5 MONTH ITINERARY NOTES

(a) This mileage is subject to change as the PCT is completed through the Tehachapi mountains.

(b) Consider hitching to Onyx.

(c) + 9 miles to Onion Valley. Those planning to climb Mt. Whitney might resupply in Lone Pine instead of Independence.

(d) + 9 miles from Onion Valley.

(e) Parcels not accepted.

(f) Use only if planning to hike along the highway to the lake's rim.

THE 4½ MONTH ITINERARY

4½ MONTH ITINERARY Copyright (c) 1992 Ray Jardine		
MEXICAN BORDER		May 5
43 miles	2.3 days food	19.0 mpd
MT LAGUNA		May 8
71 miles	3.7 days food	19.0 mpd
WARNER SPRINGS		May 12
167 miles	8.8 days food	19.0 mpd
BIG BEAR CITY		May 22
179 miles	7.9 days food	22.8 mpd
AGUA DULCE		June 1
99 miles (a)	4.3 days food	23.2 mpd
MOJAVE		June 5
142 miles	6.0 days food	23.8 mpd
KENNEDY MEADOWS		June 13
85 miles (b)	4.5 days food	19.0 mpd
INDEPENDENCE via Kearsarge Pass		June 18
156 miles (c)	8.2 days food	19.0 mpd
TUOLUMNE MEADOWS		June 27

4½ MONTH ITINERARY	Copyright (c) 1992 Ray Jardine	
151 miles	6.5 days food	23.2 mpd
ECHO LAKE RESORT		July 5
103 miles	4.0 days food	25.8 mpd
SIERRA CITY		July 10
96 miles	3.7 days food	25.7 mpd
BELDEN TOWN		July 14
88 miles	3.4 days food	25.7
OLD STATION		July 17
53 miles	1.9 days food	27.2 mpd
BURNEY FALLS C.S.		July 20
84 miles	3.3 days food	25.3 mpd
CASTELLA		July 24
154 miles	6.0 days food	25.7 mpd
SEIAD VALLEY		July 31
88 miles	3.3 days food	26.4 mpd
HYATT LAKE		Aug 4
79 miles	2.8 days food	28.1 mpd
CRATER LAKE		Aug 7

4½ MONTH ITINERARY		
Copyright (c) 1992 Ray Jardine		
87 miles (d)	3.1 days food	28.1 mpd
CASCADE SUMMIT		Aug 11
140 miles	5.6 days food	25.1 mpd
OLALLIE LAKE GUARD STATION		Aug 17
54 miles	2.1 days food	25.7 mpd
TIMBERLINE LODGE		Aug 20
50 miles	2.0 days food	25.5 mpd
CASCADE LOCKS		Aug 22
148 miles	6.1 days food	24.3 mpd
WHITE PASS		Aug 29
99 miles	3.8 days food	26.2 mpd
SNOQUALMIE PASS		Sep 3
173 miles	8.4 days food	20.7 mpd
STEHEKIN		Sep 13
81 miles	3.5 days food	23.0 mpd
CANADIAN BORDER		Sep 17
	115 days food total	

4½ MONTH ITINERARY NOTES

(a) This mileage is subject to change as the PCT is completed through the Tehachapi mountains.

(b) + 9 miles to Onion Valley. Those planning to climb Mt. Whitney might resupply in Lone Pine instead of Independence.

(c) + 9 miles from Onion Valley.

(d) Use only if planning to hike along the highway to the lake's rim.

THE 4 MONTH ITINERARY

4 MONTH ITINERARY Copyright (c) 1992 Ray Jardine		
MEXICAN BORDER		May 10
43 miles	2 days food	21.5 mpd
MT LAGUNA		May 12
71 miles	3 days food	23.7 mpd
WARNER SPRINGS		May 16
167 miles	8 days food	20.7 mpd
BIG BEAR CITY		May 25
179 miles	7 days food	24.5 mpd
AGUA DULCE		June 2
241 miles (a)	9 days food	28.2 mpd
KENNEDY MEADOWS		June 13
241 miles	12 days food	20.1 mpd
TUOLUMNE MEADOWS		June 27
151 miles	6 days food	25.2 mpd

RESUPPLY

4 MONTH ITINERARY Copyright (c) 1992 Ray Jardine		
ECHO LAKE RESORT		July 4
199 miles	7 days food	28.6 mpd
BELDEN TOWN		July 12
88 miles	3 days food	28.6
OLD STATION		July 15
53 miles	2 days food	30.3 mpd
BURNEY FALLS C.S.		July 18
238 miles	9 days food	28.0 mpd
SEIAD VALLEY		July 28
88 miles	3 days food	29.5 mpd
HYATT LAKE		Aug 1
166 miles	6 days food	30.1 mpd
CASCADE SUMMIT		Aug 8
194 miles	7 days food	28.0 mpd
TIMBERLINE LODGE		Aug 16
50 miles	2 days food	25.2 mpd
CASCADE LOCKS		Aug 18
148 miles	6 days food	26.9 mpd
WHITE PASS		Aug 25

4 MONTH ITINERARY Copyright (c) 1992 Ray Jardine		
99 miles	3 days food	28.4 mpd
SNOQUALMIE PASS		Aug 29
254 miles	11 days food	23.0 mpd
CANADIAN BORDER		Sep 10
	106 days food total	

4 MONTH ITINERARY NOTES

(a) This mileage is subject to change as the PCT is completed through the Tehachapi mountains.

COMMENTS

1) The trail is slated for construction through the Tejon Ranch, skirting the Mojave Desert. This new section will obviate the historic, easily hiked and usually well-watered, but often sweltering stroll along the L.A. Aqueduct. For more information, request the latest guide books supplement from Wilderness Press (2440 Bancroft Way, Berkeley, CA 94704). Until this section opens to hikers in its entirety, the intervening distance is approximate.

2) The water sources along the PCT flow generally in accordance with the abundance or paucity of the previous season's rain and snowfall. During periods of extreme drought, such as the one California sustained between 1988 and 1990, the through-hiker may wish to rely on the maximum-distance-between-water-sources techniques specified in the Potable Water chapter, beginning on page 93. Using these techniques, only in rare instances should hitch-hiking out for water prove necessary.

If, while planning the through-hike, the season seems as though it will be exceptionally dry, refer to the information on page 98 regarding water in San Felipe creek at Scissors Crossing. Ditto for those hikers beginning their hikes later in the season.

RESUPPLY STATIONS

I journeyed fur, I journeyed fas';
I glad I foun' de place at las'!
–Joel Chandler Harris
Nights with Uncle Remus

The resupply stations represented in this chapter are linked with the computer-generated itineraries. In fact, the computer recommended the stations and helped associate them into coherent groups.

These stations are of three general types. The post offices (P.O's) offer the usual sending and receiving services. Parcel Accepts (P.A.'s) are private concerns that generously receive and hold resupply parcels for hikers, sometimes at a charge, but that do not normally handle return packages. Outfits designated as Tourist Supplies Only (T.S.O.'s) sell minimal supplies, often *very* minimal; but they do not handle resupply or return parcels.

Those stations marked "U.P.S." normally accept parcels sent via the United Parcel Service. At most of these, your parcel is more likely to arrive with expediency if shipped by that service. This is because U.P.S. delivers the parcels directly to the resort's premises, while the postal service delivers only to the nearest post office, leaving the management to transport them from there. Most of those stations not marked "U.P.S." do not receive parcels from this company.

Virtually without exception the folks operating the post offices, stores and resorts along the way are friendly, and sympathetic toward the hikers' plights. To them we owe a great deal; for without their help our through-hikes would hardly be possible. Show your appreciation by arriving at their stations clean and properly dressed, by being considerate in every regard, and by thanking them for their help. At the same time, it would be a mistake to expect these folks to cater to us; often they are busy. And remember: your smile is likely to be felt by those hikers who follow.

PCT TRAIL REGISTERS

At most of the resupply stations listed in this chapter, the postmasters or store proprietors keep an official PCT register. If you wish to log in and to write your comments, and we recommend that you do, ask for the register when you collect your parcels.

PERSONAL TRAIL REGISTER

Also, you might keep a personal trail register. This can be a small notebook, or simply a sheet of paper, used to record the names and addresses of fellow distance-hikers you meet along the way. Then once home at journey's end, consider sending each of them a post card.

When someone does you a favor, hand them your personal register and ask them for their particulars so that you can send them a post card to express once again your appreciation. This is particularly important with people living near the trail or the resupply stations. This simple gesture often leaves very positive and lasting feelings.

THE BARRIER

And finally, we all know that most resupply stations are located at inconvenient distances from the PCT. But do we also realize that this is to our advantage? These distances and paucity of accesses provide a barrier of sorts between the nearly-pristine wilderness and the neighboring cities. The remoteness tends to exclude those who broadcast their litter and loud music wherever they go, and who often regard the backwoods as a grandiose unimprovement, and think nothing of degrading it. The PCT represents an attempt to provide the backpacker with as great a wilderness experience as possible. So while hiking from it, down toward a resupply station, we can only count our blessings with every step of the intervening way.

STATION DATA

The majority of post offices are closed during national holidays. Those during the trekking season include Memorial Day (the last Monday of May); Independence Day (July 4th); Labor Day (the first Monday of September); and Columbus Day (October 12).

Obviously, the data herein is subject to interminable change. In particular, the out-of-the-way stores might be well stocked or not, depending on when the proprietor last traveled to town for supplies. The station hours are also subject to revision. If in doubt, call or write with an SASE the ones you plan on using, before sending your parcels. And any changes you discover, please pass them along to AdventureLore Press so that they can be incorporated in a future edition of the *Handbook*.

FROM THE MEXICAN BORDER:

MT. LAGUNA (Mile 43, 0.6 mile off route) Leave the trail at the northern boundary of Burnt Rancheria Campground. Proceed west through the campground, then veer north-northwest and ascend a dirt road (very quietly) past a few cabins. Descend their access road to the paved highway. Turn right, cross the highway and reach the Laguna Mountain Lodge, housing a well-stocked store and the Post Office.

Post Office MT. LAGUNA, CA 91948 (619) 473-8341						
SUN	MON	TUE	WED	THU	FRI	SAT
	8-12 1-5	8-12 1-5	8-12 1-5	8-12 1-5	8-12 1-5	8-12

WARNER SPRINGS (Mile 114, 1.3 miles off route) Upon reaching Highway 79 collect water at the fire station if needed, then continue following the PCT. Leave the trail at the next highway crossing—at Agua Caliente Creek—to determine whether or not water is available there. Hike east along the highway to the P.O. If Agua Caliente Creek was dry, fill your bottles at the gas station, which might sell snacks. The "town" lacks amenities and camping facilities.

Post Office WARNER SPRINGS, CA 92086 (619) 782-3166						
SUN	MON	TUE	WED	THU	FRI	SAT
	8:30- 4:00	8:30- 4:00	8:30- 4:00	8:30- 4:00	8:30- 4:00	10:00- 1:30
Comments: "Due to space limitations, we can hold parcels for a maximum of 30 days from date of receipt."						

IDYLLWILD (Mile 184; a 4.5 mile, 2,300 foot descent from Saddle Junction at the PCT) It is a rare border-to-border hiker who manages to follow the PCT along the Desert Divide and across the flanks of Mt. San Jacinto before the late May thaw. Most bomb off the Desert Divide after encountering snowpack, which in some years can be treacherous, and in some other years is merely laborious. Some hikers do not even attempt the Divide; instead they walk along Highway 74 (the Pines-to-Palms Highway). Idyllwild features a P.O, a mountain shop with sporadic hours, plenty of camping, showers, laundry, and of course restaurants and supermarkets. It is a suitable place to rest and recuperate from the first few weeks of the hike.

Post Office IDYLLWILD, CA 92349						
SUN	MON	TUE	WED	THU	FRI	SAT
	8-12 1-5	8-12 1-5	8-12 1-5	8-12 1-5	8-12 1-5	8-12
Note: Saturdays—parcel pick-up only. If the front counter door is closed, try knocking.						

BIG BEAR CITY (Mile 281, 3.0 miles off route) Leave the trail at Van Dusen Canyon Road. Proceed down-canyon along the dirt road, turn left onto Highway 38, hike ½ mile northeast, then turn right onto Greenway and walk south ½ mile to Country Club Blvd. From there turn right and walk west 1 block to the P.O. (1 block southeast stand several amenities.) The vicinity lacks camping facilities.

Post Office BIG BEAR CITY, CA 92314 (714) 585-2322						
˙SUN	MON	TUE	WED	THU	FRI	SAT
	9:00- 4:30	9:00- 4:30	9:00- 4:30	9:00- 4:30	9:00- 4:30	1:00- 2:00

WRIGHTWOOD (Mile 371, 4.4 miles off route) Leave the PCT at the Acorn Canyon Trail and descend 2,500 vertical feet into town. The town features a P.O, well stocked stores, and the usual amenities. Inquire locally about camping.

Post Office WRIGHTWOOD, CA 92397						
SUN	MON	TUE	WED	THU	FRI	SAT
	8:45-5:00	8:45-5:00	8:45-5:00	8:45-5:00	8:45-5:00	9:00 - 11:00
Notes: Saturdays—parcel pick-up only.						

AGUA DULCE (Mile 460, on route) This burgeoning community features a usually well-stocked mini-grocery and a few restaurants; but it lacks camping. The P.O is located across the street from the General Store in the Hallmark store.

Post Office AGUA DULCE, CA 91350						
SUN	MON	TUE	WED	THU	FRI	SAT
	9:00-5:30	9:00-5:30	9:00-5:30	9:00-5:30	9:00-5:30	9:00-4:00

MOJAVE (Mile 559, 10 miles off route) Leave the new section of trail (the guide book's Section E) at Tehachapi Willow Springs Road—7 miles short of Highway 58. Turn right and walk southeast for 0.3 mile to Oak Creek Road. This is a lightly traveled two-lane road that usually affords easy hitchhiking into Mojave. Note: Highway 58 is a high-speed, divided, limited-access highway, and is not conducive to hitchhiking. Mojave is a highway town; it features a P.O. and the typical amenities. Inquire at the trailer park (east of McDonalds) regarding showers, laundry, and spartan camping.

Post Office MOJAVE, CA 93501						
SUN	MON	TUE	WED	THU	FRI	SAT
	8-12 1-5	8-12 1-5	8-12 1-5	8-12 1-5	8-12 1-5	8-12

ONYX (Mile 652. Leave the trail at Walker Pass, and hitchhike 18 miles west along Highway 178.) Onyx features groceries and a P.O.

Post Office ONYX, CA 93255						
SUN	MON	TUE	WED	THU	FRI	SAT
	9:30-1 2-4	9:30-1 2-4	9:30-1 2-4	9:30-1 2-4	9:30-1 2-4	7:30- 10:30
Note: Saturdays—parcel pick-up only.						

KENNEDY MEADOWS (Mile 701, 0.7 mile off route, Parcel Accept, U.P.S.) At Sherman Pass Road, leave the trail near the bridge, turn right and hike southeast along the road to the general store. Understandably, its supplies fluctuate markedly. A busy campground lies a few miles north.

KENNEDY MEADOWS GENERAL STORE P.O. BOX 367 INYOKERN, CA 93527						
SUN	MON	TUE	WED	THU	FRI	SAT
9-5	9-5	9-5	9-5	9-5	9-5	9-5
Notes: These hours are effective generally from April 25 to October 31. After May 20th, the store is normally open until 8 pm on Fri and Sat. The proprietor charges a (reasonable) handling fee for each parcel.						

INDEPENDENCE (Mile 786, off route) Reached by hiking over Kearsarge Pass on the trail of the same name, 9 miles to Onion Valley, then by hitchhiking down the mountain. Located on busy Highway 395, the town has three cafés, five motels, two mini-markets, and a grocery & mercantile.

Post Office INDEPENDENCE, CA 93526						
SUN	MON	TUE	WED	THU	FRI	SAT
	8:30-5:00	8:30-5:00	8:30-5:00	8:30-5:00	8:30-5:00	

VERMILION VALLEY RESORT (Mile 875, 1½ miles of walking and a 4½ mile boat ride (twice daily) from the PCT, Parcel Accept) The resort features a café and a small store, and is near a campground. Write to them for information regarding their package handling services.

VERMILION VALLEY RESORT C/O RANCHERIA GARAGE HUNTINGTON LAKE ROAD LAKESHORE, CA 93634			Or P.O. Box 258 Lakeshore, CA 93634 (209) 855-6558			
SUN	MON	TUE	WED	THU	FRI	SAT
7:00 a 7:00 p	7:00 a 7:00 p	7:00 a 7:00 p	7:00 a 7:00 p	7:00 a 7:00 p	7:00 a 7:00 p	7:00 a 7:00 p

RED'S MEADOW RESORT (Mile 906, 0.3 mile off route, TOURIST SUPPLIES ONLY) Leave the PCT at the abandoned stage coach road. In season, the resort's store is well stocked and a cafe is adjacent. However, the resort doesn't open until early or mid June (and sometimes later), depending on the snow conditions. Its staff does not handle hiker's resupply parcels. A campground is nearby, as are the naturally heated (and free) showers. One can ride the shuttle to the ski resort, then hitchhike or walk the remaining 5 miles down the hill to the town of Mammoth Lakes, (93546). Failing that, hikers can buy a few picnic supplies and canned goods at the Red's Meadows Resort, and tough it to Tuolumne Meadows.

TUOLUMNE MEADOWS P.O. (Mile 942, 0.3 miles off route) (pronounced TWAL-uh-me) Leave the trail at Highway 120 in Tuolumne Meadows. To reach the tent-cabins, restaurant and showers, turn right, cross the bridge, and follow a roadside trail 1 mile. Otherwise, from the trail turn left and hike southwest along Highway 120 to the well-stocked store, grill, and P.O. The Mountain Shop, presently located in the gas station a short distance west, sells backpacking gear.

Post Office TUOLUMNE MEADOWS STATION YOSEMITE NATIONAL PARK, CA 95389 (209) 372-0263						
SUN	MON	TUE	WED	THU	FRI	SAT
	9-5	9-5	9-5	9-5	9-5	9-12

Notes: Opens approximately June 15, depending on the snowpack. Until then, the parcels are held in Yosemite Valley, accessible by hitchhiking.

ECHO LAKE RESORT (Mile 1094, on route; Parcel Accept, U.P.S.) The typically friendly staff at the well stocked store and grill make exemplary milk shakes. Camping within the vicinity of Echo Lake is prohibited.

Post Office ECHO LAKE RESORT, CA 95721 (916) 659-7207						
SUN	MON	TUE	WED	THU	FRI	SAT
	8-12 1-5	8-12 1-5	8-12 1-5	8-12 1-5	8-12 1-5	8-12

Note: Request permission before sending your parcel. Otherwise consider using Twin Bridges, 95735.

SIERRA CITY (Mile 1196, 1½ miles southwest along Highway 49) The store is usually well stocked. The town has a P.O, but lacks camping facilities other than at the distant Wild Plum Campground, which is within range of the PCT.

Post Office SIERRA CITY, CA 96125						
SUN	MON	TUE	WED	THU	FRI	SAT
	8:30- 4:30	8:30- 4:30	8:30- 4:30	8:30- 4:30	8:30- 4:30	
Comments: "Due to a lack of space, we prefer that parcels arrive no earlier than 15 days ahead of their owners."						

BELDEN TOWN (Mile 1292, on route) Features a P.O, camping, public showers, laundry and a store well stocked with picnic items.

Post Office BELDEN, CA 95915						
SUN	MON	TUE	WED	THU	FRI	SAT
	8:30- 5:00	8:30- 5:00	8:30- 5:00	8:30- 5:00	8:30- 5:00	8:30- 12:00
Comments: "We have enjoyed talking with the PCT hikers that have come through here."						

OLD STATION (Mile 1380, 0.1 mile off route) The area in the vicinity of the P.O features a store and a resort.

Post Office OLD STATION, CA 96071						
SUN	MON	TUE	WED	THU	FRI	SAT
	8:30- 4:30	8:30- 4:30	8:30- 4:30	8:30- 4:30	8:30- 4:30	

CAMPER'S SERVICES in McARTHUR-BURNEY FALLS STATE PARK (Mile 1433, 0.1 miles off route; Parcel Accept, U.P.S.) Within earshot of Burney Falls, leave the trail and turn right, cross the bridge over Burney Creek, and saunter to the grill and well-stocked store. Coin-op showers are nearby. Due to its accessibility and amenities, this is an excellent place to indulge in a layover day.

BURNEY FALLS CAMPER SERVICES						
McARTHUR BURNEY FALLS STATE PARK						
ROUTE 1; BOX 1240						
BURNEY, CA 96013 (916) 335-4214						
SUN	MON	TUE	WED	THU	FRI	SAT
8-8	8-8	8-8	8-8	8-8	8-8	8-8
Comments: "We are open mid-May through early October, everyday including holidays. It is beautiful and restful here. We are avid hikers ourselves, and enjoy helping PCT'ers in any way we can. If we don't stock something you need, please recommend it to us."						

CASTELLA (Mile 1517, 2.5 miles below the PCT, initially along the Bobs Hat Trail) The campground features a site designated for PCT hikers. Farther along is the market, which is normally well stocked. The adjacent bar might sell meals. Farther along still is the laundromat.

Post Office						
CASTELLA, CA 96017						
SUN	MON	TUE	WED	THU	FRI	SAT
	8:30-5:00	8:30-5:00	8:30-5:00	8:30-5:00	8:30-5:00	8:30-10:30

SEIAD VALLEY (Mile 1671, on route) (SIGH-add) Camping, coin-op showers and laundry are available at Hawk's Roost, adjacent the building housing the P.O, a well-stocked store, and a café. Take the chef up on his PCT Pancake challenge, if you dare.

Post Office SEIAD VALLEY, CA 96086						
SUN	MON	TUE	WED	THU	FRI	SAT
	8:30-5:00	8:30-5:00	8:30-5:00	8:30-5:00	8:30-5:00	12:00-2:00

HYATT LAKE RESORT (Mile 1759, 0.7 miles off route; Parcel Accept, U.P.S.) At Hyatt Lake Road, leave the trail by turning left, then shortly veer right and continue along the paved road leading into the campground. Proceed to the lakeshore, turn left and continue to the resort. The resort features a laundry and shower facility, a campground, and a restaurant. It provides a relaxing, out-of-the-way ambiance, ideal for a layover day.

HYATT LAKE RESORT (P.O. BOX 3120) 7979 Hyatt Prairie Road ASHLAND, OR 97520 (503) 482-3331 (Note: Please try to ship your parcels via UPS)						
SUN	MON	TUE	WED	THU	FRI	SAT
6:00a 9:00p	6:00a 9:00p	6:00a 9:00p	6:00a 9:00p	6:00a 9:00p	6:00a 9:00p	6:00a 9:00p
Comments: "We are open 7 days a week from April 25th through October 31st. We look forward to having the hikers stop in and we try to make their visits pleasant."						

CRATER LAKE NATIONAL PARK (Mile 1838, 4.5 miles off route, although most hikers go that way anyway, en route to see the stupendous lake.) Before climbing to the rim, shop at the campground store, if desired. It is a level one-mile detour. The rim store carries only snack items, but has a cafeteria. The Crater Lake detour rates practically zilch as a trail hiking experience. If you've seen the lake before, or plan to return later, consider following the well-routed PCT, which makes for excellent hiking, appropriately far removed from the motorized multitudes.

Post Office CRATER LAKE NATIONAL PARK, OR 97604						
SUN	MON	TUE	WED	THU	FRI	SAT
	10-4	10-4	10-4	10-4	10-4	10-2

CASCADE SUMMIT (Mile 1925, 1.4 miles off route) 1.6 miles short of Highway 58, leave the trail at the 4WD road signed "Pengra Pass," and which here is an unofficial trailhead. Turn sharply right, descend the road to the railroad tracks, cross them and descend to the paved road. Turn right and hike along the road 1.1 miles to the Shelter Cove Resort. The moderately-stocked store houses a deli and the impromptu P.O. The establishment lacks laundry facilities, but offers coin-op showers and two free campsites for PCT hikers.

Post Office CASCADE SUMMIT, OR 97425 (503) 433-2548						
SUN	MON	TUE	WED	THU	FRI	SAT
	8-12	8-12	8-12	8-12	8-12	8-12
Comments: "Hikers are most welcome, and can receive their parcels anytime the store is open."						

ELK LAKE RESORT (Mile 1971, 1.3 miles off route; Parcel Accept, U.P.S.) The resort has a fair store, a grill, and pay showers. There is a campground nearby.

| ELK LAKE RESORT
Century Drive
(P. O. BOX 789)
BEND, OR 97709						
SUN	MON	TUE	WED	THU	FRI	SAT
	8-12 1-5	8-12 1-5	8-12 1-5	8-12 1-5	8-12 1-5	8-12
Comments: "We are open Memorial Day through late September. Please send your parcels via U.P.S."						

OLALLIE LAKE GUARD STATION (Mile 2065, 0.2 miles off route; Parcel Accept) The nearby Olallie Lake Store is usually well supplied with picnic items. Camping abounds in the not-too-immediate proximity.

| OLALLIE LAKE RANGER STATION
C/O CLACKAMAS RANGER DISTRICT
61431 EAST HIGHWAY 224
ESTACADA, OR 97023						
SUN	MON	TUE	WED	THU	FRI	SAT
8-5	8-5	8-5	8-5	8-5	8-5	8-5
Notes: Normally open from mid-June to mid-September. If the ranger is absent when you arrive, (a genuine possibility) try asking for your parcel at the nearby store.						

TIMBERLINE LODGE (Mile 2119, 0.1 miles off route; Parcel Accept) Walk across the paved street from the lodge and enter the WY'EAST ANNEX. The store, which sells no food but which handles resupply parcels for a fee, is on the lower floor of the annex. The cafeteria is on the upper level. The area lacks camping.

TIMBERLINE SKI AREA WY'EAST STORE TIMBERLINE LODGE, OR 97028 (503) 266-7979							
SUN	MON	TUE	WED	THU	FRI	SAT
8-5	8-5	8-5	8-5	8-5	8-5	8-5
Notes: Currently charges $1.50 per package per week, or $4.00 per package per month.						

CASCADE LOCKS (Mile 2169, 0.4 miles off route) Nearly to the Bridge of the Gods turn right and walk along Wa Na Pa street to the P.O. The town features the typical amenities, including a well stocked grocery and a laundromat. The Marina offers coin-op showers, and camping on the adjacent lawns.

Post Office CASCADE LOCKS, OR 97014							
SUN	MON	TUE	WED	THU	FRI	SAT
	8:30-1 2-5	8:30-1 2-5	8:30-1 2-5	8:30-1 2-5	8:30-1 2-5	

If you plan on short-cutting to Carson via Stevenson, (both full service towns) instead of using Cascade Locks as a resupply station, consider using the post office at Carson, WA 98610. However, please be advised that this short-cut involves hiking along minimum shoulder roads that in some places are potentially dangerous.

WHITE PASS (Mile 2317, 0.7 miles off route) At Highway 12 near White Pass, leave the trail by turning left, and hike uphill along the highway to the well-stocked Kracker Barrel Grocery and P.O. The establishment offers laundry and an *alfresco* public shower. Camping is nearby.

Post Office WHITE PASS RURAL BRANCH (AT THE KRACKER BARREL STORE) NACHES, WA 98937						
SUN	MON	TUE	WED	THU	FRI	SAT
8-6	8-6	8-6	8-6	8-6	8-6	8-6

SNOQUALMIE PASS (Mile 2416, 0.3 miles off route) Near Interstate 90 at Snoqualmie Pass, leave the trail by turning right, and walk the frontage road into the village. The P.O is located in the well-stocked Time Wise Grocery and Deli. Be sure to order one of their "Colossal '906' Super Burgers." The local hotel has the usual sybaritic amenities, but because its rooms are expensive most hikers choose to stay at the moderately-priced Wardholm-West Bed and Breakfast: (206) 434-6540. One can also reach a NFS campground by hiking one mile northwest.

Post Office (AT THE TIME WISE GROCERY & DELI) SNOQUALMIE PASS, WA 98068						
SUN	MON	TUE	WED	THU	FRI	SAT
	7-5	7-5	7-5	7-5	7-5	7-5
Comments: "We make exceptions for PCT hikers, allowing them to pick up their parcels anytime between 7:00 am and 11:00 pm, 7 days a week. We at Snoqualmie Pass appreciate the endeavors of the PCT hikers, and would like to help make their journey as pleasant as possible."						

SKYKOMISH (Mile 2491, a 14 mile hitchhike (usually easy) west from Stevens Pass) The town features a P.O, accommodations, an adequately stocked general store, and 3 restaurants. However, it lacks laundry facilities.

Post Office SKYKOMISH, WA 98288						
SUN	MON	TUE	WED	THU	FRI	SAT
	8-12 1-5	8-12 1-5	8-12 1-5	8-12 1-5	8-12 1-5	8-12

STEHEKIN (Mile 2589, a 10 mile shuttle bus ride or hitchhike) The store might be poorly stocked, and the camping is austere and normally over-crowded. Shower stalls and a laundromat are located at the public restroom building.

Post Office STEHEKIN, WA 98852						
SUN	MON	TUE	WED	THU	FRI	SAT
	8:00-4:30	8:00-4:30	8:00-4:30	8:00-4:30	8:00-4:30	11-1:00
Comments: "We are open 2 hours on Saturdays. Which two depends on the ferry's arrival time. Have a nice season!"						

MANNING PARK LODGE (Mile 2680, T.S.O.) Be sure to stop at the Visitor Center and sign the trail register. If it is closed, you might leave a note asking the receptionist to write your name and the date in the PCT register. Farther west, the Lodge sells showers and saunas, and features a restaurant. The Greyhound Bus makes daily stops in front of the Lodge's office.

TOURIST FOOD

In many cases, considerable supplies are for sale at or near the resupply stations. Typically every summer, hikers send home quantities of their repetitious backpacking food, and for variety they supplement it with picnic-oriented goods purchased along the way. At the least, the stores usually sell canned beans, chili, fruit, etc. After opening the cans and emptying their contents into plastic, lidded bowls, the hiker can dispose of the cans in the store's garbage bins. This practice keeps the metal out of the mountains.

FILLING THE PARCELS

Begin the task by collecting and recycling discarded boxes from various shops near your home. Or purchase them, for example from the U-Haul company. Select sturdy boxes; and once home, tape any suspect edges secure, and double-tape the bottoms. Keep in mind that resupply parcels are subject to rough handling en route to their destinations. And "Special Handling" is unlikely to improve the way your parcels are treated.

Arrange the boxes in a line and tape a temporary label onto each, specifying its destination. According to your chosen itinerary, fill each box with its specified number of days of supplies. These supplies will normally include food, film, the appropriate section of the guide book (severed through the glued binding, and taped) additional maps if any, flashlight batteries, first aid items, and any replacement or additional articles of clothing. If the parcel weighs more than 50 pounds, for example if it contains supplies for two or more hikers, consider repacking it into two smaller boxes.

MAILING THE PARCELS

Most hikers enlist the services of a relative or close friend, who "volunteers" to mail their resupply parcels. This is a lackluster job: driving interminably to the P.O, lugging ponderous boxes inside, and standing in line with them. But the arrangement has decided advantages to you. Using this method you might leave the boxes open, so that your helper could add things to it prior to sending. For example they might add fresh potatoes, home-baked goodies, and whatever exigent items you might request by telephone.

And finally, leave a list of mailing dates with whomever you've arranged to send your parcels. And once on the journey, telephone them occasionally to relate the news of your progress, and more importantly, to encourage them and to show your appreciation.

Twice I have used professional mail forwarding services. The first one proved an abysmal failure; I had to return to it, collect my parcels, and mail them en masse to a friend who agreed to handle them. The second service, in a different state and year, was a resounding success. So if you use a mail forwarding service, plan for contingencies.

SAMPLE SHIPPING LABEL

FROM:

TO: (YOUR NAME) C/O GENERAL DELIVERY (STATION ADDRESS)   Expected pick-up date:_____
PLEASE HOLD FOR PACIFIC CREST TRAIL HIKER

Your expected arrival date helps the station masters organize the parcels. And in the unlikely event of a possibly missing hiker, it could provide useful information.

Don't forget to include a return address on all packages. And if, during the course of the summer, you change your mind about continuing the trek, be sure to notify the stations, asking them to return your parcels "return postage guaranteed."

Have your parcels mailed two to four weeks before your scheduled arrival—depending on how far you live from the trail.

THE RETURN PARCEL

At those resupply stations featuring post offices, you might wish to send unneeded items home. To facilitate the procedure, include a shipping label and a small roll of boxing tape in the corresponding parcel. Once at the station in question, recycle your resupply box by cutting it down to size. Fill it with the items to be returned, tape it closed, tape the new shipping label into place, and mail the parcel home.

THE RUNNING RESUPPLY

Consider also using a running resupply parcel: a small box sent ahead, rather than home. This could contain items maybe needed later, but not presently. These might include a spare pair of shoes and fresh insoles, a spare water filter element, an extra camera battery, a miniature whetstone, boxing tape, a spare spoon, and an extra sweater. Send the box two or three weeks ahead, to increase its chances of arriving before you do. And as a precaution, write a set of forwarding instructions beneath the mailing address, in case the parcel arrives too late.

CARRYING VALUABLES

During the summer's journey, carry your valuables, including money, journal and film, in a small, unobtrusive bag. And carry that bag with you whenever you leave your pack to patronize a store or restaurant. Entering a restaurant, ask if you may bring your pack with you; and if so, ask that you might be seated near the door as a matter of convenience. Otherwise, ask to be seated by a window, and place your backpack outside that window where you can watch it.

KEEP A JOURNAL!

Those who do not keep journals are prone to forget many interesting details of their journeys. As Oscar Wilde quipped:
I never travel without my diary.
One should always have something sensational to read on the train.

DISTANCE HIKER ANARCHISM

And finally, keep in mind our need to be particularly considerate of those that live near the trail. Not everyone is awed by our distance-hiking endeavors; especially in the instances where rude hikers might have preceded us. It is our job, then, to help reverse any stigmas by being clean, free of b.o, appropriately dressed, and friendly.

Furthermore, in town we would err by creating scenes or situations that might provoke the locals to disgust. If we arrive en masse, we might appear to some as a pack of scoundrels drifting through. It is possible that each additional hiker in the group doubles the group's impact. Declaring a hiatus in public view, and spreading gear massively and haphazardly about creates a scene that some folks might find distressing. Laundromats are particularly vulnerable to distance-hiker anarchism. So be considerate, and practice minimum impact resupplying.

HIKING STANDARDS

Suo marte: by one's own exertions.

RECKONING WITH THE TRAIL'S CIRCUITY

Currently, the PCT is almost 2,700 miles in length. However, the straight-line distance from the Mexican border, south of Campo, to the Canadian Border at Monument 78, is only 995 miles. Consequently, journeying the trail's length is like hiking the straight-line distance, turning around and hiking back, and then turning and hiking over half of it again. So to allude to the PCT's circuity is to speak understatements. The trail takes roundabout courses having little to do with leading in the intended direction. And often it climbs or descends for no apparent reason. Summarily, the trail might not conform to our expectations that it should resemble an efficient, modern expressway. Nevertheless, no river formed by nature runs straight. Likewise, trails must follow contours, not only of hills and mountains, but of mountain ranges. And valid reasoning often underlies much of the trail's meandering. For example, in many places it circumvents private property. But sometimes the trail routing simply defies logic, and that seems to be its own form of logic.

Consider the cases where the trail "parallels" a nearby road, at some distance from it but weaving into and out of every gully. In the process of hiking it you might travel twice the intervening distance. In such an instance, the trail might be misbehaving no more than usual. Instead, it is the road that mocks. Which belongs in the wilds, the straight road bearing high-speed missiles of metal and glass, litter fairly swirling in their wakes? Or the rambling trail?

Consider also that the trail is a fixed object, lying inanimately upon the earth. Circuity and the protracted grade mean nothing to it. Despite its illimitable patience, though, still it leads us to our objectives.

During our first PCT through-hike, Jenny and I were striving to hike from Mexico to Canada. With that objective in mind, I often found the trail's wandering frustrating. As such, we revelled in taking every short-cut we could discover or contrive. Once we reached the Canadian border, though, I began to realize that those frustrations had been borne, not of the trail's inefficient lay-out, but of my own insecurities. Essentially, we had lacked confidence in our capacity to walk two and a half thousand miles. So every extra mile imposed on us had only heightened those anxieties. During our second PCT through-hike we felt a little more confident. Accordingly, we strove to hike as much of the trail as was safe and practicable. And with that goal in mind, the trail's circuity seemed generally inconsequential.

HIKING STYLE
Expressing individuality while distance-hiking

Aspiring PCT hikers might be wise to decide upon their degree of trail-adherence before setting off. This is because the journey's continuity is for many hikers a fragile tendril, particularly as their nutritional reserves become depleted. And once the continuity is broken, (however the individual had defined it) the hiker's will to continue might begin to crumble.

Today's PCT is a *nearly* continuous trail—imperfect though it is. Blindly seeing magic in this Congressionally designated National Scenic Trail, hikers in ever-crescive numbers are committing themselves with a will to adhering to the trail, where safe and practicable. And this trend is likely to gain even wider prevalence in the ensuing years.

However, the hiker who departs Campo intent on following every inch of the trail might be suffering various delusions. Hiking the entire trail is extremely impractical. So in order to succeed in their quests, hikers might do best by remaining flexible. Recall the hypothetical avalanche ripping apart the stalwart timbers and leaving the pliant aspen and willows in place.

Certain sections of the trail might require circumventing, perhaps because of lightning, or during early season because of the occasional avalanche hazard. Again in early season, torrents might breach the route, requiring hikers to leave the trail and wander up or downriver in search of wind-felled trees spanning the creeks. In the high mountains, snowpack might preclude hiking some or much of the official trail. While hiking on snow, you might be above the trail, or you might not be; there might be no way to know. Also, there are currently two or three short places where no trail exists, and where instead one must hike cross-country, map and compass in hand. This is easily done, but it illustrates the impracticality of trying to follow the official trail the entire distance. Furthermore, the trail is a dynamic entity; virtually all sections are subject to occasional rerouting, minor or major.

Some hikers are intent on walking the entire distance, and once again, they are intent also on following as much PCT as safe and practicable. They will go to considerable lengths to remain on the trail. True enough, in many places they will be performing the regimen for its own sake. And granted, at times the adherence might detract from the esthetics. However, they will be seeing a great deal of interesting country that the other hikers might miss.

Some through-hikers want to walk the entire distance from the Mexican to the Canadian borders, while at the same time they care not whether they walk the PCT, various alternate trails, cross country, or roads. They might arrange their resupplies and scheduling to coincide with a hike of the PCT, and they might hope to hike much of the main trail. But by design they are not willing to shackle themselves to the tyranny of the trail. For them, the summer's journeys are more extemporaneous. They might allow themselves the independence to go where they feel like going at the moment. Or perhaps they enjoy the challenges of finding and planning more expedient alternate routes, daily and hourly.

And some hikers strike a compromise. They might prefer to walk the entire distance, and to follow most of the trail, but also they might have no objection in leaving the trail at times, and indulging in various short-cuts. For example after leaving the trail to visit a resupply station, they might prefer not to backtrack, but to hike ahead, and to rejoin the trail farther on.

The summer's essence is to decide the issues for yourself. Shape your journey however you deem it will be the most rewarding. And consider shaping it to resemble how you might wish to look back upon it, years later.

KICKING A BOULDER

Most, but certainly not all, of those who reach their goals consider hitchhiking for forward gain to be incongruous with the essence of the primal backpacking experience. They might hitchhike out for supplies and so forth, but they are generally careful to return to the place they left off hiking. For example, in his excellent book *The Longest Walk*, (Paragon House: 1989) George Meegan narrates his seven year continuous trek along the lengths of the American Continents. One passage describes his hiking standards:

If I left the route because I needed to seek water, or wanted to visit an ancient temple, or simply wished to post a letter, I would conscientiously mark my farthest point of advance, note my exact distance, run my errand, eventually return to the "mark," and start clocking my distance again. Setting my mark might involve circling a conspicuous tree two or three times, scoring the dirt in the shape of an arrow, or kicking a boulder. This was crucial; if I didn't take these precautions, the entire line of my steps would be irreparably broken and the journey compromised—and my peace of mind destroyed forever.

HITCHHIKING

Of the scores of PCT hikers who have abandoned their quests in early or mid summer, hitchhiking has been a predominant factor. Perhaps hitchhiking degrades a person's resolve to continue, by breaking the journey's continuity. Or conversely, perhaps a degraded resolve merely leads to hitchhiking. Some distance-backpackers might consider hitchhiking as a convenient method of dealing with an undesirable section of trail. However, there is a chance that the act teaches them to rely on it as a means of solving the problems at hand.

THE TELLING OUT-BACK REGISTERS

There is absolutely nothing morally wrong with hitchhiking around a particular stretch. But those who indulge in the practice might consider the benefits of not trying to conceal the acts. Hikers coming along behind will know whether they signed only the occasional station registers and not the out-back ones. And the hiker's grape vine is remarkably effective.

[Some people] regard truth as their most valuable possession,
and therefore are most economical in its use.
–Mark Twain

THE FLIP FLOP

One current trend in distance hiking is in using the flip-flop technique. PCT hikers might walk from Mexico to Walker Pass, for example, then hitchhike or ride the Greyhound bus to Castella, in far northern California. From there they might hike to south to Walker Pass, then ride back to Castella, and continue hiking north. This is the theme, and the variations are almost unlimited. And the approach has worked for some people particularly during years of little snowpack

I see two disadvantages in the practice.

First, it breaks the journey's continuity, which to me is the very essence of the summer's pilgrimage.

And second, to site the most common example, thinking that hitchhiking around the Sierra Nevada will enable a person to avoid the snow is a misconception of the highest rank. In early season during a normal year, the snowpack will be abundant generally all the way to the Canadian border. To hitchhike around the Sierran snowpack will only place a person in the snow farther to the north. Succinctly, if you need to hitchhike around snow, you are there too early in the season. By adhering to one of the *Handbook's* itineraries, you are more likely to avoid most of the snow.

Those hikers in the 5½-month category who find themselves falling behind schedule might imagine that they would benefit from flip-flopping to Canada and then hiking south. Possibly; but considering the resulting break in the journey's continuity, they might do better by compensating in other ways: namely by keeping a close eye to the itinerary from Kennedy Meadows, and by maintaining, or preferably exceeding, the associated daily mileages. Of course, the itineraries do not guarantee a snow-free trail, but then neither does the flip-flop technique.

PERMITS

Documents granting authorization (!)
to travel through wildernesses and National Parks.

> *This land is your land, this land is my land,*
> *From California to the New York island,*
> *From the redwood forest to the Gulf Stream waters,*
> *This land was made for you and me.*
> —Woody Guthrie

AMERICA, LAND OF THE FREE AND THE BRAVE

Some hikers see the permit system as reminiscent of twentieth-century communism, where in countries behind the iron curtain travelers were required to carry papers of identification and authorization, and to present them on demand of the polizei. These hikers might see no cogent reason why their particulars should be included in the giant NFS/NPS database. Some refrain from recording their particulars on the permit applications because they fear that should a forest fire eventuate, or vandalism occur, they might find themselves wrongly accused.

And a minority of these hikers might worry also that once the bureaucrats begin charging money for permits, and when they begin otherwise tightening the controls, and when certain back-country users begin rebelling, then the database of names and addresses are likely to be scrutinized more carefully.

And besides, many of these hikers imagine better methods of regulating the backcountry. They might favor closing the access roads, for example, and extending the trails from the erstwhile trailheads miles down to the major roads.

Some other hikers prefer to follow the procedures of least resistance. They see outright refusal in carrying permits as too blatant. They imagine that a certain amount of compliance is beneficial in satisfying the voracious System and the minions who run it. Yet perhaps they interpret compliance in many colors, shades, and depths of field. For example, they might fill out the paperwork using pseudonyms and fictional addresses.

And finally, the remaining hikers exhibit absolute obedience to authority. Seeing the permit system as part of the Great American Way, they apply for, and fill out the forms correctly.

PERMIT FOR ENTRY INTO CANADA

Crossing an international boundary is a different matter altogether. During the preparatory stages, all through-hikers who are not Canadian citizens should write to:

> Canadian Immigration Centre
> Huntington, B.C.
> Canada V0X 1M0

Hikers would request the form for entering Canada on the Pacific Crest Trail. Those planning to through-hike the trail according to one of the *Handbook's* itineraries might fill out the form, and place it in their resupply parcel going to Belden Town. Once they reach Belden Town, they might carry the form with them until two months prior to their estimated arrival in Canada. They would then mail it, using General Delivery, Snoqualmie Pass, WA 98068 as their return address. And they might ask the immigration center to write on the outside of the envelope: "Please Hold For PCT Hiker."

REACHING CAMPO

And what to do, once there

· To reach Campo from San Diego, ride the trolley 15 miles to El Cajon (ELL-cah-HONE), and then ride the Southeast Rural Transit van to Campo.

THE DETAILS

Those arriving at the San Diego airport would take a city bus to downtown San Diego, and disembark at the Civic Center.

Those arriving downtown San Diego via Amtrak train or Greyhound bus would walk from their respective stations to the Civic-Center trolley station.

Buy your trolley ticket at one of the vending machines, and board the "Center City Trolley" to El Cajon. Retain your ticket because it also counts as partial fare for the bus ride to Campo. Disembark from the trolley at its last stop: the El Cajon Transit Center.

The Southeast Rural Transit bus (#894) travels to Campo only once a day, and not on Sundays. It departs the El Cajon Transit Center currently at 3:04 p.m. By showing your trolley ticket you will receive credit for it. The bus arrives Campo at about 5:00 p.m.

The sundry fares and schedules are subject to change.

For information regarding the trolley and city bus, telephone (619) 233-3004.

For information about the Southeast Rural Bus, telephone (619) 478-5875. You might ask the dispatcher whether they require a reservation. If they do, mention that you will be carrying a backpack. Also, you might ask if they know whether the creek at Scissors Crossing (San Felipe [fa-LEE-pay] Creek) is flowing. This key source of water for PCT hikers is on another bus route; and the drivers frequently act as dispatch officers. (Refer to the associated logistics in the chapter Potable Water, page 93).

If arriving at Campo on the five o'clock bus, and if you have not brought enough water with you, then your first task would be to procure · enough for the night's camp, and for the following day's 15 mile hike to Hauser Creek. Ask for water at the store, or at the U.S. Border Patrol Station. Finding personnel at the Patrol Station is a hit-or-miss proposition, except at the changing of the guard, which occurs daily at 7:00 am, 3:00 pm, and 11:00 pm.

For our purposes, the territory between Highway 94 and the Mexican Border is "sensitive." It is a place where nighttime games are played that we do not wish to participate in.

After obtaining water, consider hiking to the border, perhaps taking a few inaugural photographs, and then hiking back to the Campo store. This is a pleasant stroll in the evening (or early morning). If when returning to Campo the day has grown late, consider making a low-profile and impromptu camp behind the store, by the creek. Avoid leaving your camp, or any of your gear, unattended.

As precautionary measures, PCT hikers might practice stealth camping each night between Campo and Boulder Oaks.

THE HAT CREEK RIM

The wayfarer,
Perceiving the pathway to truth
Was struck with astonishment.
It was thickly grown with weeds.
"Ha," he said,
"I see that none has passed here in a long time.
Later he saw that each weed was a singular knife.
"Well," he mumbled at last,
"Doubtless there are other roads."
—Stephen Crane

Historically, the Hat Creek Rim has been one of the more problematic sections of the PCT. In the past, the authors of the PCT guide book did not comment favorably on this section of trail, mainly as a reaction to complaints that a few hikers had become ill from drinking cattle-polluted water found along the Rim. Also, at the time the descriptions were written, the trail was in exceptionally poor condition.

The northern section of the Rim appears to have been logged fairly recently. In the process of forest succession, the area is currently habitat to numerous species of sun-loving weeds, notorious for adhering to the hiker's footwear, socks and pant legs. Complicating matters, in 1987 a fire devastated many acres of terrain. Trail crews reconstructed the Rim trail in 1990, although only lightly, and are scheduled to continue with maintenance annually.

Formerly, the Hat Creek Rim was the PCT's longest waterless section. Many felt that the 44 miles between reliable water sources was a prohibitive distance. So in 1991, trail crews began rerouting the PCT through lower climes, alongside the way-post of Old Station, and then back up to the Rim. This realignment bypassed 13½ miles of excellent hiking mainly through shady stands of conifers, from road 30N12 to Highway 44. And it increased the overall distance. But it also reduced the maximum distance between water sources to about 30 miles.

Highway 89 might seem to offer a more direct and well watered alternate route leading to the Burney Falls environs. But in the interests of personal safety, the *Handbook* recommends against hiking along this usually busy highway. Narrow shoulders, oversized motor homes sometimes piloted by inexperienced drivers, vehicles passing others at ultra-high speeds, passengers lobbing objects from windows, and the very occasional renegades yanking their steering wheels menacingly in the hiker's direction are among the greater perils. Locals have complained that they've seen hikers walking the pavement obliviously, and up to five abreast. In any event, highway-shoulder hiking imposes our backpacking values upon the general public, in a place where those values are largely inappropriate.

In 1987 Jenny and I hiked along Highway 89. The experience was one we do not plan to repeat. In 1991 we hiked the Rim trail. There, we enjoyed the solitude, the scenery, and the views. By chance perhaps we encountered no rattlesnakes. And by design we suffered no thirst. The stickers pervaded our shoes and socks massively, though, and these proved torturous until we protected our footwear by applying duct tape. We would have gladly worn gaiters (as recommended in the guide book) had we included them in a previous resupply.

Trail crews are expected to widen the trailway leading along the Rim. If they do not, and if the season has been uncommonly wet, then hikers might find themselves wading through fields of weeds. This would not be difficult, but it might slightly increase the chances of encountering a rattlesnake. Therefore, purely as a precaution, hikers might consider equipping themselves with leg protection. At home, they might make leg tubes of double-layer 1000 denier Cordura. Or if nothing else they could contrive leg chaps of cardboard, held together with tape and string.

ALTERNATE ROUTES

In all likelihood the authors of the invaluable guide books wrote their material primarily for day-hikers and weekend-hikers. According to one of the authors, people who hike only shorts sections of the trail account for about 95% of the books' sales. So we can probably assume that the profusion of alternate routes so described were designed for them.

I have hiked a number of the guide's recommended alternates, and many of my own invention. Some of these proved exceptionally rewarding. And I have also hiked most of the official route. But in terms of border-to-border through-hiking, in no instance have I found the main trail inferior or disadvantageous to an alternate route.

The *Handbook* does not recommend doggedly following the PCT every step of the way. On the contrary. The summer belongs to the hiker, not to the trail. Those bent on following the trail might consider that in the face of a lightning storm, for example, they might err by following the route up an exposed crest. And we would all be drowned who unthinkingly ford every early season creek when and where the Congressionally designated trail crosses them.

Nevertheless, tri-state hikers might consider the Rim trail as merely another of the PCT's innumerable challenges. The difficulties that might be encountered there are no greater than in many other places along the way. Rattlesnakes are a part of the natural ecology from the Mexican to the Canadian borders. There are probably no more snakes along the Rim than in many places along the PCT. The stickers of the Rim (actually they usually occur most prolifically from the Rim's northern terminus, onward) are no genuine obstruction. The lack of potable water along the Rim is nothing but a minor inconvenience: one encountered in many other sections along the way.

In our quests to become ourselves, each of us must strike the most befitting compromises. In years past, through-hikers traditionally avoided the Rim trail. But I maintain that if our intent is to experience the natural world, then we delude ourselves by striving to avoid the parts that are described as being *too* natural.

So carry your water from the Cave Campground, avoid drinking the stock-polluted water found along the Rim, and enjoy your journey.

STOCK

At least as far as the Pacific Crest Trail is concerned, I am prepared to invoke the wisdom of Thomas Jefferson:

> *"Walking is the best possible exercise.*
> *Habituate yourself to walk very far.*
> *The Europeans value themselves on having subdued the horse*
> *to the uses of man;*
> *but I doubt whether we have not lost more than we have gained*
> *by the use of this animal."*

The Pacific Crest Trail by William R. Gray
Special Publication, 1975 by National Geographic.

The presence of pack and saddle stock is perhaps the most controversial of all PCT use-issues. Many backpackers and hikers, if not the vast majority, feel that massive domestic animals, including horses, mules, donkeys, llamas, yacks, and elephants, do not belong in the backcountry, or at least on the Pacific Crest National Scenic Trail. On the other side of the fence, many, if not most, equestrians view the presence of hikers as somewhat of an inconvenience, and might be just as happy if we were absent from the trails. Even so, when hikers and equestrians meet, the encounters are usually amicable. And this is the favorable situation. Animosities benefit no one.

The PCT was intended primarily to accommodate pack and saddle stock. Many were the stockmen who acted as planners, supporters, and trail builders. Undoubtedly these people felt that if the trail were suitable for stock, then it would also be suitable for backpackers. This arrangement is a pragmatic compromise, but it might be analogous to smokers assuming that an enclosed room is suitable for occupancy by both smokers and non-smokers.

Nevertheless, the majority of PCT is currently in use by both concerns. So it seems incumbent upon both to accept the presence of the other, and not to become obsessed with the differences, to the detriment of the overall wilderness experience.

THE RIGHT-OF-WAY

The current doctrine that stock enjoys the right-of-way over hikers might seem unreasonably slanted in favor of the horseman. But this convention is not without its reasons. The pack animal is less maneuverable than the hiker. And in most places in the mountains, the land incurs the least damage when the heavily loaded, steel clad hooves remain on the trail. Alas, a horse leaving the trail to circumvent a hiker will invariably wreak far more ecological damage than would a hiker leaving the trail to circumvent a horse. This is evident in innumerable channels hoof-plowed around early season, wind-felled trees.

HIKER SAFETY

When encountering equestrians, we hikers should always maintain obliging dispositions. But at the same time we need to regard pack animals as potentially dangerous. When these massive animals approach closely, for our own safety we should stand well clear.

The average mule or horse is innately afraid of backpackers. Thus, we should never try to pet the animals, lest they over-react by biting or stepping on us. And beware: these animals are well known for kicking pedestrians. When a horse strikes out, the thrust is usually blindly to the side. But a mule can take deadly aim; its blow is likely to connect, and the resulting injuries can be maiming.

If a horse should suddenly bolt, and if you are down slope of it, it could fall on you, or buck its rider or panniers onto you, or knock rocks onto you. It could kick out and catapult you down the slope, or it could bolt, and cause you to lose balance, such that you could fall down the slope. So remember that the highest position is by far the safer one. When giving way to equestrians, leave the trail by climbing the slope, not by descending it.

CONSIDERATIONS

I think it would be folly to recommend banning stock from the backcountry. Unconscionable hikers mete out their share of ecological damage also. Nevertheless, some sort of compromise might beneficially take place. Separate trails might make a lot of sense, and perhaps we should consider this as an option for the future. Meanwhile, I think it is important that we recognize the relevant issues.

Like motorbikes and ORVs, horses, mules and llamas are objects of conveyance, used to transport people and luggage. Unlike wild animals, domestic stock follow the trail, which in many places was routed to accommodate them, but which in most places was not constructed to withstand the abuse. Each pack horse weighs between 1,000 and 1,200 pounds, and most carry loads weighing 150 to 200 pounds. Thus, each of the animal's hooves applies considerable crushing and lacerating pressure.

Horses and mules were not built for mountain travel. Rugged terrain would break up their hooves, which therefore require steel shoes. The calks, or protuberances on the shoes, inflict even greater damage. At camp and rest stops, these animals often paw and dig. And when tied to trees they pack the root systems. And unfortunately, picket-lines (ropes tied between trees) don't help much.

Some people consider it out of keeping with the wilderness ethic that long strings of pack animals transport into the back country hundreds of pounds of baggage, and that in some cases they transport out of the back country wild animals killed largely for sport. And many people are uneasy at the sight of the handguns and rifles often carried openly by packers, and rarely by other hikers.

Each pack animal disperses between 15 and 25 pounds of manure a day. Equestrians argue that this is merely fertilizer. By whatever euphemism, feces are not readily biodegradable. If not ground into powder by the passing of hooves and boots, they can endure for years; and so can the pathogens teeming within them. As propelled by the rains and melting snow, fecal and urinary coliforms in significant quantities enter the water systems. Some of these microbial contaminants are from wild animals, and some are from the occasional human that fails to bury his or her stools, or who buries them at a less than suitable distance from the water source. But the vast majority of contaminants are from pack and saddle stock, while grazing livestock also contribute.

To many, it seems contradictory that the administration allows domestic stock to broadcast their excreta *ad libitum*, while at the same time they require emphatically that people bury their stools far from trails, campsites and water sources. The pathologist might see this as an illogical and discriminatory double-standard, citing that many of the same pathogens are present in the intestines and urinary tracts of both human and beast.

Here's what Karl Diederich, who through-hiked the PCT in 1991, had to say:

> *If with a declaration and a wave of my hand, I could change any one thing about the PCT, banning pack and saddle stock would be it. I used to estimate that one pack animal did as much damage as ten to twenty people, depending on the trail conditions. In watching large hiker and stock groups pass by during this summer, I specifically looked at the trail damage they did in passing. I am forced to revise my estimate upward to one stock beast causing as much damage as one hundred back-packers. But trail damage is only their first offense. Their urine causes the trail to reek long after the manure is pounded into dust. Being designed for horse travel, the trail was in many places overly graded; and it detours away from scenic areas that would be too heavily damaged with stock access. Trailside trees were cut out, and this exacerbates the brush problem. Foot bridges were obviously placed exclusively with stock in mind. In many places*

the trail detours away from areas where it couldn't be constructed to stock standards, but where a perfectly acceptable foot trail could have been built. This translates to greater costs in building the trail to stock specifications, and also in repairing the stock damage.

THE WILDERNESS BUSHIDO
The earth's capacity to absorb and to forgive is not infinite.

GEARING DOWN
The descent back to civilization

Here I am, safely returned over those peaks
from a journey far more beautiful and strange
than anything I had hoped for or imagined.
How is it that this safe return brings such regret?
—Peter Matthiessen

One always begins to forgive a place
as soon as it's left behind.
—Charles Dickens

Reculer pour mieux sauter
(Draw back in order to make a better jump)

THE PASSING OF THE GATE

An ancient maxim teaches that the longest and hardest part of a journey is the passing of the gate. But it has been my experience that the passing back through that gate, on returning home to civilization, can be an even more challenging assignment.

Granted, quitting the hike prematurely can be a summer-rending experience; but so can quitting the hike on schedule at Manning Provincial Park. Nearly all distance hikers experience the end-of-the-hike syndrome, to greater or lesser degrees, and whether or not they achieve their goals. This is because, psychologically, both success and "failure" culminate the glorious summer afoot.

For the adventurer, a goal is a journal of not-yet written pages. And indeed, goals are some of the more important driving forces in our lives. But when a hard-won goal is ultimately achieved, it is likely to leave us feeling nearly as devastated as had we not achieved it. Standing at Monument 78, we are like mountaineers: having climbed a great peak and reached its summit, we have nowhere higher to climb. The fun and games are over, for a time. And the descent back into what we might view as the banalities of ordinary living can be precipitous and fraught with obstacles.

The solution, at least in part, is to realign our goal philosophies into direction philosophies. A goal has a sudden end; while a direction is ongoing. Living life in certain directions, we might or might not accomplish our goals along the way, but more importantly we move ahead with purpose. And a direction need not be singular; like a tree trunk that branches, it can take any of many different configurations. Each one can be designed to probe the wild places, to experience more of nature, and to stretch ourselves.

When we move ahead with direction, rather than toward a volatile goal, we might agree with a fellow through-hiker who wrote in a far-north trail register:

> *Finishing the PCT*
> *will be like waking up*
> *from a very nice dream.*

If you have quit the hike ahead of time, remember that the trail will be there, if and when you choose to return to it. Keep in mind also that your "failure" was only temporary. In fact, it was no failure at all, but possibly a most valuable learning experience. We all know that there is no such thing as a perfect winning streak. A checkmate teaches us the most valuable lesson of all; perhaps that we might not have achieved the requisite proficiencies. In the aftermath we might realize in what areas our skills need improving. As did those who reached their goals, you hiked, camped, and enjoyed a time among the wilds. And then you returned home. But so did everyone else; so who is to say who succeeded and who failed?

For those through-hikers who reached Monument 78: welcome to the PCT alumni, a widely dispersed, but elite group of trail-tested PCT affectionados.

PRESERVATION

To all who have journeyed through the magnificent regions flanking the PCT, no doubt you have gained a first-hand awareness of the need for ardent preservation. When we think of conservational efforts, we look ahead to the future. This corridor through the timeless but vulnerable succession of ecosystems, how shall we attempt to leave it for those who will follow in our footsteps?

Aldo Leopold wrote, "We abuse land because we regard it as a commodity belonging to us. When we see land as a community to which we belong, we might begin to use it with love and respect."

Alas, the PCT hiker sees innumerable examples of how our prevailing culture has been treating the land as a commodity, taking from it and giving nothing in return. And we all know of the dire need to reverse this trend.

The fragile ecology doesn't recognize the legal rights of massive bulldozers excavating virgin territory for new roads, of squads of chain-saw-wielding commandos harvesting timber, hoards of unconscionable campers, or cavalries of packers trammeling the wilderness for their amusement. But let us not deceive ourselves. The timber industry, to site but one example, functions exclusively on the principles of supply and demand. The egregious clearcuts are the result of the market for wood. Chain-link fencing the wilderness, and locking behind bars what we might perceive as avaricious loggers would do nothing to save our forests. What would? Reducing the domestic demand for wood, and banning its foreign sale.

THE TRAIL NEEDS OUR HELP, FOR WE NEED THE TRAIL

After our hikes, it might behoove us to consider returning, sooner or later, and making token recompense. In light of the ineffable experiences we might have gleaned during the summer's trekking, we might consider laboring one or several days to maintain the track. And we who have traveled it know better than anyone where the maintenance needs lie.

HANDS OFF HIKING

It is but another misconception that trail maintenance must be performed only by the government or its assigned contractors. Indeed, the PCT is federally funded and operated, so to speak. But this is something of a mixed blessing. The arrangement has provided us with a convenient and well-graded tread most of the way. But one of the shortcomings of the arrangement is that PCT hiking tends to be a "hands off" experience. Hikers ambulate hands in pockets, as it were. For example, if they encounter something amiss, however minor, they hike on, deferring the work to the trail crews. But in many cases the maintenance funds are lacking, however they might have been misappropriated.

That some of us come into the woods bloated with expectations is but another spin-off of our culture. When we encounter a problem, our reaction might be to complain about it, rather than to roll up our sleeves and remedy the situation. On the Appalachian Trail thousands of private citizens donate their time and effort working on the trail every summer. And this spirit of comradery is one good reason that the AT community is more tightly-knit.

So we see that the nation's long trails are not commodities belonging to the hiker, but communities to which all hikers belong. The wild places they pass through are not waste lands, nor do they represent only miles to be gained. Instead, they are marvelous ecologies to be revelled in, and to be loved and respected. Their survival depends on our caring and fighting for them, as our survival depends on them.

STICK SLINGING

Those setting out on the long hike can work on the trail as they go. For example, they might groom the trail using a procedure I call *stick slinging*. It is a pastime "played" with a chest-high stick. As you hike along, use the stick to sling other sticks, branches and pine cones from the trail.

With a little practice in flicking the wrist, branches can be slung considerable distances. And this is a good form of amusement.

Also, you might adopt a rock-a-day policy, by removing one untoward rock from the trail each day.

When you come to a confusing juncture, and when finally you deduce the proper way, feel free to mark the way for those who follow. One method is to place a couple of sticks across the incorrect junction.

And during the course of your journey, you might jot down notes pertaining to any trail problems.

TRAIL "IMPROVEMENTS"

The PCT was designed to provide as pristine a wilderness experience as possible. So those who work on the trail would do well to avoid trying to civilize it. One exception is that sometimes pipes installed at the more fragile springs make sense, in that they might help protect the spring from being trammeled. Otherwise, the wilderness experience must not be tamed into resembling what we had hoped to leave behind. For example, we don't need a five-foot wide, well groomed trail leading across bridges at every creek and embellished with huts every 10 miles. Instead, we might do better maintaining the trail in a "minimal" condition. As Ruben Rajala wrote in *THE AMERICAN HIKER*: *The focus should be on maintaining basic passage, rather than creating a manicured trail corridor. A more natural look is desired. Smaller blow-downs that can be easily stepped over might be left. Because we are striving for a natural environment, resource protection is the key. The overall goal should be to keep the wilderness experience as natural as possible through trail work that is simple and that blends in. Avoid being obtrusive.*

VANDALISM

Manmade and trailside objects of convenience represent targets for vandalism. These would include water basins or wells, huts, etc. But what are vandals but agents of Mother Nature working thanklessly to destroy intruding articles. Whether or not they realize it, in effect they are helping shove back encroaching civilization, and hastening the ravages of time. For your amusement I recommend reading Edward Abby's *The Monkeywrench Gang*, and Dave Foreman's *Ecodefense*.

CHECK LISTS

Our loads at the conclusion of our PCT trek of 1991

Every extra ounce in the through-hiker's backpack works
two thousand six hundred and sixty fold against.

A (relatively) lightweight pack-load is no accident. It is the result of a great deal of forethought, planning, and trial and error. The Pack Weight chapter (page 35) details the considerations. This Check-lists chapter analyzes the gear that Jenny and I used during our PCT trek of 1991. These items are not intended to represent the ultimate equipment. Far from it. Instead, the lists are merely a snapshot of the current state of the our agglomeration. Their main purpose is to aid readers in the planning stages of their backpacking journeys, and to illustrate the method of detailing their equipment and its weight.

The first two tables itemize the contents of our packs, when at the trek's completion we reached Canada's Manning Provincial Park. Generally, this is the gear we used throughout the entire trek.

The second two tables inventory additional gear we used only for certain sections. These items include boots and a few extra clothes we carried through the Sierra Nevada, and shoes and socks that we wore out.

RAY'S 20 POUND PACK-WEIGHT AT MONUMENT 78	OZ.
Eyeglasses, prescription	1.8
Watch	0.8
Shirt, short sleeves (polyester)	4.4
Pants, wind/mosquito (nylon)	4.8
Shoes (borrowed from Jenny)	23.0
Orthotic	2.3
Insoles, 1 pr	1.8
Backpack (5782 cu in)	71.5
Rain cover, for backpack (coated nylon)	7.1

RAY'S 20 POUND PACK-WEIGHT AT MONUMENT 78	OZ.
Top pouch contents:	
Gospels	0.2
Guide book section (Snoqualmie to Manning)	2.6
Journal pad	0.7
Pen, writing, ball point (2 each)	0.2
Camera (Olympus Infinity) with lanyard, film and battery	10.0
Sunglasses, prescription and bag (homemade: sweatshirt fleece)	1.8
Repellent, mosquito (2 fl oz.) Bottle carried in resealable bag in case of leakage	3.0
Toothbrush	0.4
Windex, in plastic bottle (for cleaning eyeglasses)	0.7
One-half of a bandanna (for cleaning eyeglasses and camera lens)	0.5
Foot-care bag (resealable plastic bag) contents: 8 band-aids, packet of 2nd Skin™, artificial sinew, hydrogen peroxide in plastic vial, Neosporin™ antiseptic.	1.8
Flashlight (Rayovac Roughneck), with two AA batteries.	2.4
Ditty bag, with draw string and clamp	0.3
Knife, with lanyard	0.8
Compass, with lanyard	0.7
Matches, emergency (home double-sealed)	0.2
Duct tape, 5 feet length	0.3
Lighter, small	0.3
Film (Fujichrome ISO 100, 36 exp) 5 rolls in plastic canisters: 1.0 oz. each	5.0

RAY'S 20 POUND PACK-WEIGHT AT MONUMENT 78	oz.
Bag of valuables (resealable plastic), includes paper money, travelers checks, drivers license, blank personal checks, photocopy of passports, (3) coffee (water) pre-filters, list of addresses and telephone numbers, poetry, and Canadian immigration papers.	4.0
Clothing bag (homemade: waterproof, 2 ply Gore-Tex with drawstring and clamp) Contents:	1.7
Hand towel (cotton, 12"x12")	1.7
Bomber hat (homemade: fleece lined, Gore-Tex shelled)	2.1
Mitten shells (homemade: Gore-Tex)	0.7
Jacket (homemade: fleece)	23.8
Jacket, wind/mosquito (homemade: Versatech)	7.8
Pants (homemade: wicking)	6.9
Shorts (homemade: Lycra)	3.0
Socks (wool/synthetic) 3 pairs: 2.3 oz. each	6.9
Parka, rain (Gore-Tex)	15.9
Sleeping bag (home-modified, down-filled)	57.6
Stuff-sack for sleeping bag, (homemade: waterproof, urethane-coated 1.9 oz. nylon) with draw string and clamp	1.9
Tent, in homemade coated-nylon bag	26.7
Fly for tent (home-modified) in bag (homemade)	27.3
Stakes for tent (skewer) 6-count, repair sleeve, and bag- (homemade: nylon)	2.7
Ground sheet (Cut to approximate tent floor size)	6.1
Water bottles (1-liter) 2-count: 3.2 oz. each.	6.4
Umbrella	10.0
TOTAL PACK WEIGHT	323.7

JENNY'S 17 POUND PACK-WEIGHT AT MONUMENT 78	OZ.
Eyeglasses	1.0
Blouse, short sleeve (homemade: polyester)	1.6
Pants (homemade: Lycra)	4.5
Fabric boots	31.3
Socks (wool/synthetic) 1 pair	2.1
Insoles, 3 pair	5.0
Backpack (home-modified, size medium 5390 cu in)	65.7
Padding, pack-straps (homemade: pile)	2.3
Rain cover, pack (heavy duty black-plastic garbage-bag)	3.5
Clothing bag, (homemade: waterproof, 2 ply Gore-Tex) with draw string and clamp. Contents:	2.9
Hat, rain/sun (Gore-Tex)	1.9
Bomber hat (homemade: fleece-lined, WP-B shelled)	2.3
Shirt, long sleeve (homemade: wicking)	5.7
Jacket, wind and mosquito (nylon)	6.0
Parka, rain: Gore-Tex	14.4
Jacket (homemade: fleece)	20.9
Mittens (homemade: fleece)	1.3
Shells for mittens (homemade: Gore-Tex)	0.5
Skirt (homemade: polyester)	3.0
Underwear (nylon/Spandex)	0.7
Pants, wind and mosquito (nylon)	5.7
Pants, (homemade: wicking)	7.0
Socks (heavy, wool/synthetic) 1 pair	4.8

JENNY'S 17 POUND PACK-WEIGHT AT MONUMENT 78	oz.
Socks (wool/synthetic) 2 pairs (1.4 oz. each)	2.8
Socks (wool/synthetic) 3 pairs (2.1 oz. each)	6.3
Bandanna (cotton)	0.9
Foam pad (⅜" closed cell, 3' 5" long, 2' 11" wide at the top and 2' 3" at the bottom)	9.9
Poles for tent in bag (homemade: coated nylon)	16.7
Emergency whistle, with lanyard (not used)	0.4
Parachute cord (15 feet) for clothesline	0.4
First Aid, in resealable bag, includes: Kenelog (for poison oak), poison oak compress, lanolin (for swollen, cracked fingertips), Betadine (an antiseptic), quinine sulfate (for malaria relapse), Neosporin (antiseptic), Amoxicillin (antibiotic), Cortaid (topical lotion), Blistex (lip balm)	1.8
Water bottles (1-liter) 2-count (3.2 oz. each)	6.4
Hiker's Friend Water Filter, includes element, nylon bag, tubing, and stowbag	8.5
Pump for water filter, with tubing and bag-(homemade: nylon; draw string and clamp)	2.8
Stove	18.0
Fuel and container	10.0
Stove kit, includes lighter (small), and outer bag for stove (homemade: nylon & velcro)	0.8
Bag, food (homemade: nylon, yellow) with P-51 can opener and drawstring clamp attached to drawstring; contents:	1.1
Cook pot (aluminum, 2 qt. capacity) with lid	7.2
Spoons (Lexan) 2-count (0.4 oz. each)	0.8
Towel, dish (1/2 bandanna, cotton)	0.5

JENNY'S 17 POUND PACK-WEIGHT AT MONUMENT 78	OZ.
Bowls with lids; for drinking and eating from; 2-count (2.8 oz. each)	5.6
Tub (plastic, folding 6-liter jug, truncated)	2.8
Ditty bag (homemade: nylon) with draw string and clamp. Contents:	0.7
Sewing kit, includes aluminum canister, needles, safety pins, and thread (wrapped around canister)	0.5
Toothbrush	0.4
Aspirin and vitamins, in resealable bag	0.5
Emergency fire-starter packet (home-sealed) contains small lighter and 2 small candles (not used)	0.8
No-fog cloth in resealable plastic bag (for eye-glasses)	0.2
Hair barrettes (2-count) and hair band, elastic	0.3
Dental floss in canister	0.4
Comb	0.1
Lip balm	0.2
Shampoo (home-packaged)	0.3
Packet of deodorant	0.2
Note pad, mini ball-point pen, postage stamps, poetry, clasped with a rubber band	1.8
Dr. Bronner's soap in plastic vial, 1/3 full	1.4
Repellent, insect; pump spray, 3/4 full	1.8
Sunglasses, prescription in bag (homemade: fleece)	1.4
Umbrella	10.1
TOTAL WEIGHT	273.4

ADDITIONAL GEAR WE USED DURING THE 1991 TREK

RAY'S ADDITIONAL GEAR USED DURING THE 1991 TREK	
Straw hat, carried during the first 3 weeks.	5.0
Hat, sun (white) with chin strap	2.2
Shirt, button-down (Homemade: wicking)	8.0
Sweater (polyester) with full-length zipper	15.8
Socks (synthetic, lightweight) many pairs	0.9
Socks, low cut (synthetic) many pairs	0.9
Socks, (wool/synthetic) many pairs	2.3
Socks, heavy (wool/wicking) 3 pairs	4.2
Socks, lightweight (100% wool) Not recommended	1.8
Insoles, several pairs	2.0
Shoes, 2 pairs	12.8
Shoes, 1 pair	10.0
Fabric boots (worn only along some parts of the PCT-JMT)	41.0
Gaiters (home-modified, Gore-Tex) (used little)	5.9
Bag, for parka (homemade: Gore-Tex)	0.5
Deodorant, in plastic vial	0.5
Soap, in resealable bag	1.1
Soap (Dr. Bronner's, peppermint)	2.0
Windex, in plastic vial	1.2
Rope (Perlon, 8mm, 20')	12.2
Water bag, 3 gallon capacity	4.1
Ice Axe with lanyard	19.0

JENNY'S ADDITIONAL GEAR USED DURING THE 1991 TREK	
Hat, sun; with chin strap	2.4
Shirt, sleeveless (polyester)	1.6
Shirt, short sleeve (home-made, wicking)	3.9
Sweater (polyester) with full length zipper	12.1
Pants (sweat-shirt fleece)	6.2
Socks, (wool/synthetic) many pairs	1.4
Socks, low-cut (synthetic) 2 pairs	0.8
Socks, lightweight (100% wool) Not recommended	1.5
Shoes, 1 pair	24.0
Shoes, 1 pair	21.8
Insoles	1.9
Gaiters (home-modified, Gore-Tex) (seldom used)	4.9
Ice Axe with lanyard	18.1

POKING AT THE EMBERS

Two or three angles
Came near to the earth.
They saw a fat church.
Little black streams of people
Came and went in continually.
And the angels were puzzled
To know why the people went thus,
And why they stayed so long within.
                    —Stephen Crane

Nature is but a name for an effect,
                Whose cause is God.
        —William Cowper (1731-1800)

One of backpacking's quintessential benefits is the escape it provides from the distractions of city life. On the trail, we can become more in tune with the spiritual aspects of ourselves and of nature.

And indeed, we find the backcountry a marvelous creation, comprising expansive forests (hear those chain saws buzzing?), lofty, snowpacked mountain ranges, and pristine, trickling brooks teeming with myriad aquatic organisms, Giardia included. Who can deny that in her variety, nature is immense yet infinitesimal; incalculable, and never ending.

NATURE'S COMPLEXITIES: ACCIDENTAL?

With each object in nature, the more we examine its inner complexities, the more they befuddle us. How does the brain of a chipmunk work, and how does it grow from an embryo? Why does the structure of its inter-atoms relate to that of the outer-cosmos? Could the billions of similar unknowables represent an organized plethora of cosmological accidents? Maybe; but even within the framework of 12 billion years since the theoretical Big Bang, the odds seem immeasurably against it.

THE CREATION

I perceive all objects in nature as wrought by a Creator. But more importantly, looking inward I *feel* much of that same evidence of an infinite spirit. I love Nature; else why would I spend so much time bumbling around in it? And therefore I love God, who obviously (it seems to me) created nature. Consequently, I have faith.

THE INFINITY OF NATURE

In fact, nature has strengthened my faith far beyond what she alone is capable of gratifying. Yet because Nature is infinite, it seems to me that so is my soul, along with that of everyone else.

I learned of the Gospel some 30 years ago; and the event brought about a major turning point in my life. In a nutshell the tidings are these: The breach between God and us is unfathomably immense. By piling rocks we cannot reach the stars, and by practicing religion we cannot reach God's eminence. God loves the mountains, trees, and even our stealth campsites; else why would He have created them? And He loves us too. And it was love that prompted Him, some two millennia past, to send Jesus, who provided transit across the colossal gap between God and us.

Faith is the evidence of things unseen. Still, many ignore their spiritual destinies on the basis of "insufficient evidence." But by my reckoning, nature is our compass, pointing the way to the Creator. The Holy Bible is our guide book, providing directions at each of life's confounding junctures. And Jesus provides us passage over the unwadeable gap, and to eventually triumph in our celestial quests.

Speaking of himself, Jesus said:

> *For God so loved the world,*
> *that he gave his only begotten Son,*
> *that whosoever believeth in him should not perish,*
> *but have everlasting life.*
> —John 3:16.

I like to think that Jesus was a hiker. One of his last acts on earth was to sit with a few of his disciple-friends before a campfire. They roasted fresh-caught fish, ate bread, then perhaps sat long into the night talking heavenly subjects while poking at the embers.

SELECTED BIBLIOGRAPHY

THE PACIFIC CREST TRAIL VOLUME 1: CALIFORNIA,
Jeffrey P. Schaffer, Thomas Winnett, Ben Schifrin and Ruby Jenkins.
Wilderness Press: 4th ed, 1989. (The PCT guide book, southern portion.)
This guide and the one that follows make PCT hiking the clearly defined
experience that it is. Almost every PCT hiker finds these well written and
accurate guides indispensable.

THE PACIFIC CREST TRAIL, VOLUME 2: OREGON & WASHING-
TON, Jeffrey P. Schaffer, with Andy Selters. Wilderness Press: 5th ed, 1990.
(The PCT guide book, northern portion.)

THE PACIFIC CREST TRAIL, William R. Gray. Special Publication,
National Geographic: 1975.

A PACIFIC CREST ODYSSEY, Walking the Trail from Mexico to Canada,
David Green. Wilderness Press: 1979. (Currently out of print.) This is *the*
classic PCT through-hiking narrative.

FOR LOVE OF MOVEMENT, Lawrence Budd. Backpacker Magazine,
March 1989, p.41. An excellent and all too brief account of the author's
hikes of the PCT, AT, and CDT in consecutive seasons.

THE LONG WALK, A GAMBLE FOR LIFE, Slavomir Rawicz. Harper &
Brothers: 1956. This is literature's preeminent distance-hiking narrative.

LIGHTWEIGHT CAMPING EQUIPMENT AND HOW TO MAKE IT,
Gerry Cunningham and Margaret Hansson. Charles Scribner's Sons: 1976.

RICHARD HITTLEMAN'S YOGA 28 DAY EXERCISE PLAN, Richard
Hittleman. Bantam Books: 1969.

RATTLESNAKES, Laurence M. Klauber. University of California Press:
abridged ed, 1982.

DAVE FOREMAN'S BOOKS OF THE BIG OUTSIDE, available free
from Ned Ludd Books, P.O. Box 5141; Tucson, AZ 85703. No outdoor
enthusiast should be unfamiliar with this important compendium of books.

INDEX

TO ORDER
A HANDBOOK

Send $16.95 to:

AdventureLore Press
P.O. Box 804
LaPine, OR 97739

ABOUT THE AUTHOR

Ray Jardine holds a degree in Astronautical and Aeronautical Engineering, with a minor in mathematics, from Northrop University. He worked for several years in the field of space flight mechanics. A computer programmer for 30 years, he now works (sporadically he asserts) as a mechanical engineering programming consultant, and as a computer systems and applications specialist.

He has actively pursued outdoor interests most of his life.

A mountaineer, he has climbed most of Colorado's fourteeners, many in winter, and has climbed extensively in the Tetons, and in South America. His highest peak was Peru's Mt. Huascaran, at 22,205 feet.

A wilderness instructor, he taught for the Colorado Alpine Winter Mountaineering School for two seasons, and for Outward Bound for seven. In the process, he backpacked several thousand miles.

A rock climber for 25 years, he established some of the era's toughest climbs, including the world's first 5.12 graded climb (The Crimson Cringe) and the first 5.13 (The Phoenix). He climbed extensively in Great Britain, and across western America. In Yosemite Valley he established 50 new ascents, and made the first unaided ascent of a grade VI climb, on El Capitan. He invented a protection and anchoring device known as the "Friend," which revolutionized the sport.

In 1982, he and his wife Jenny put to sea aboard their ketch SUKA. The pair sailed around the world in $3\frac{1}{2}$ years.

A hang glider pilot, Ray has logged some 400 hours aloft. He has flown to 16,000 feet, cross country 50 miles, and has thermal gained 9,100 feet. He has also flown sailplanes, and holds an Australian Restricted Private Pilot's Licence.

A sea kayaker, he has paddled several thousand miles in areas including offshore California, The Sea of Cortez, French Polynesia and Australia. Embarking from Anacortes, Washington in 1988, he and Jenny paddled their two-person kayak 3,300 miles to the Bering Sea. Later, he developed one of the few workable sailing rigs for kayaks, and used it to advantage on a 650 mile expedition along the inside length of Baja.

In 1987 he and Jenny through-hiked from Mexico to Canada, generally along the PCT, in $4\frac{1}{2}$ months. And in 1991 they hiked the PCT once again, in 3 months and 3 weeks.